T B Burgess

D0812400

02/24
STAND PRICE
$ 5.00

Edited by Eric H. Monkkonen

W A L K I N G

TO WORK

Tramps in America, 1790–1935

University of Nebraska Press: Lincoln and London

"The Strolling Poor: Transiency in Eighteenth-Century Massachusetts," by Douglas Lamar Jones, was first published in the *Journal of Social History* 8 (Spring 1974), 28-54. "Tramping Artisans: Carpenters in Industrial America, 1880-90," by Jules Tygiel, first appeared in *Labor History* 22 (Summer 1981), 348-76. "The 'Traveling Fraternity': Union Cigar Makers and Geographic Mobility, 1900-1919," by Patricia A. Cooper, is taken from *From Hand Craft to Mass Production: Men, Women, and Work Culture in American Cigar Factories, 1900-1919* (Urbana-Champaign: University of Illinois Press, forthcoming), and has previously appeared in the *Journal of Social History* (Fall 1983).

Copyright 1984 by the University of Nebraska Press
All rights reserved
Manufactured in the United States of America

The paper in this book meets the guidelines for permanence and durability of the Committee on Production Guidelines for Book Longevity of the Council on Library Resources

Library of Congress Cataloging in Publication Data
Main entry under title:
Walking to work.
Bibliography: p.
Includes index.
1. Tramps – United States – History. 2. Unemployment – United States – History. 3. United States – Social conditions. I. Monkkonen, Eric H., 1942-
HV4504.W34 1984   305.5'68   83-21807
ISBN 0-8032-3087-7

Eric H. Monkkonen

Introduction

For at least a century, tramps have fascinated us. In the popular press, in literature, in short stories, and in folk tales, we have discussed them, portrayed them, and fantasized about them. Much more than it might at first appear, scholars have counted tramps, walked with them, photographed them, corresponded with them, tried to reform them, and even tried to change the socioeconomic or personal conditions which seem to have produced them. Yet in an important way, this literature is as marginal as its objects of interest. The reason is simple enough. We do not know how to think about tramps. Our inability to integrate them into a coherent view of society or social history mirrors their apparent social condition. The failure of historians to incorporate them as a subject has been masked by the earlier silence on tramps as integral members of society. Thus, even though the gamut of attitudes expressed in this previous literature is enormous, and although some of the extraordinarily sensitive and intelligent insights have been offset by others more execrable, few have been analytical or historical.

Recent developments in the study of social history make the understanding of tramps as a historical and social phenomenon possible. The articles collected in this book represent several different methodological and theoretical streams of recent social historical research. All aim at a whole view of American society, or societies, at including the excluded, and at understanding the complex currents of social change, drawing out the implications for the broad range of American experiences. Alert to and generally critical of earlier literary and reform traditions, the contributors to this book have all approached their examination of tramping with methodological and conceptual apparatuses representing purposes different from those taken by most other authors and commentators on tramping. The work presented here removes the sentimental veil from the world of the industrial tramp and at the same time restores tramps to their rightful place in the social history of the United States.

Almost without exception, previous approaches have sensationalized, sentimentalized, or trivialized tramping, thus obscuring it. The contributors to this book all came to the topic independently while researching other topics—none came in search of sensation. Rather, we stumbled on these tramps as we searched for other materials, other kinds of people, other kinds of questions. In other words, we began not looking for sensations, much less an unusual topic. Therefore the theoretical and methodological approaches represented in this book do not try to glorify or demean the subjects of the investigations. Other research topics piqued our curiosity about the murkily conceptualized mass phenomena of tramping.

The story of tramping is the story of the mass population movement caused by the industrial transformation of the urban United States. In the 110 years since the industrial tramp appeared on the urban scene, social, political and economic changes have occurred with modest but concrete ameliorative consequences. Today, unemployment forces fewer people to tramp, although the recession of 1982–83 reminds us in a way of the plight of the roving unemployed. Nevertheless, employment and welfare have become an accepted national responsibility, even if not always one shouldered with enthusiasm. For the comparatively small number of tramps today, tramping is no longer an expected and rational part of the search for work. That is, they did not grow up in a culture where the tramp for work was expected and predicted. For the capable, it is a trauma, one producing anger and loss of self-esteem. Only for the incapable and the mentally ill has tramping become a way of life in the late twentieth century. That the mentally ill and the incapable should have no alternative than to tramp may be an indictment of our society comparable to that caused by the existence of mass tramps of a century ago, but the homeless people of the late twentieth century do not emblematically represent the same socioeconomic system which their nominal predecessors did.

The disappearance of the industrial tramp occurred in the new world of the social welfare state. Several significant intellectual and political changes have altered the social landscape of tramping.[1] These include social security, unemployment benefits, worker's compensation, various forms of subsidized medical care, and the disappearance of the ideological notion which claimed that to be effective welfare had to be dispensed in the controlled environment of an institution—"indoor relief" as opposed to "outdoor relief." The pitiful deviants who still ride the rails and congregate on skid rows are in fact less the lineal descendants of the industrial tramp than are migrant farm workers.

Migrant farm workers, in the deep sense, represent the margins of a production process still not yet totally rationalized. Functionally, farm workers, like their predecessors, make possible production processes which depend on varying unskilled labor inputs. When natural cycles have been removed from the agricultural industry, there will be no more migrant workers. The continual efforts of agricultural researchers to mechanize the tasks done by migrant workers has exactly this goal: to rationalize the production process and to make all labor inputs nonseasonal. But the functional similarity ends at this point, for tramps of the industrial era never had the regular seasonal employment expectations of today's migrant farm workers. The essence of a tramp's working career was erratic employment, of seasonal work overlaid with hundreds of varying jobs and locales.

There are still tramps. Who can guess how many? Anyone curious enough can walk through the industrial wilderness adjacent to any railroad switching yard or past those points where freight trains slow down on the urban fringe and find the campgrounds of modern tramps. One such visit should dispel and deromanticize any notions about the wonders of the nomadic life of the tramp.[2] For the more timid, reading any of the several recent studies on contemporary tramping or skid row will accomplish nearly the same goal.[3]

Tramping is not now, nor was it ever, a pleasant form of life. Unfortunately, experiencing life on the literal margins of society did not necessarily allow the participant to get any closer to the essence of life itself. Tramps were not creating a Thoreauvean experience by "driving life into a corner." Jack London did manage to make his tramping have such an end, but it would be incorrect to generalize his intellectual experience, for like Thoreau's, his adventures were willed philosophical acts. It is unfair to see tramps as having a privileged perspective on the rest of society, for this mode of thinking finds a value and dignity in tramping in an ultimately patronizing way. To tell those unfairly exploited by a social and economic system that they have benefited is akin to congratulating the victim of a crime for his or her remarkable and expanding experience. If anything, life on the margins is perforce more attuned to the trivialities of the social and economic system, to its wastes and excesses, to its rough edges, ensuring that petty hassles encompass the totality of existence. If in "getting and spending we lay waste our powers," then surely tramps were forced to lay waste their powers.

The steely-eyed view of tramps and tramping contained in the articles in this book derives from a specific attempt to set the topic in the appropriate sociohistorical context. In the burgeoning industrial world of the nineteenth-century United States, the growth in the numbers of tramps directly paralleled the growth of industrial capitalism. The decline of the industrial tramping system by the 1920s coincided with the emergence of corporate capitalism and the modern welfare state. The complexity of tramping and its resistance to thoughtful analysis came from the complexity and depth of the economic change. At the same time that these deeper forces drove tramping, it is important also to recognize that the social systems of tramping resulted from the remarkable adaptive and creative capacities of the workers in the changing industrial world.

Cyclical unemployment and economic crises directly caused the most prominent bursts in tramping. Sometimes these were national phenomena, but often they were local, regional, or industry and firm specific. The most spectacular was the financial panic precipitated in the fall of 1873 by the failure of Jay Cooke and Company, a crisis which reverberated throughout the 1870s and which culminated dramatically and tragically in the strikes of 1877. This depression sent workers by the thousands, perhaps millions, on the road and rail searching for jobs. Again, the depression of 1893 had a similarly devastating impact on occupational security, the ranks of tramps swelling enormously, the extraordinary, bizarre and inspiring march to Washington of the unemployed in Coxey's Army punctuating their circumstances.[4]

Major economic cycles and the larger transformation of the economy formed only a submerged part of the drive behind tramping. In the best of times local and regional change often sent younger workers out to tramp. Single men tramped first; then, if things continued bad, older married men with families moved out. In the major period of the industrial tramp, 1870–1920, few nuclear families tramped as a family unit. In fact, only in the preindustrial period and during the Great Depression had whole families tramped. These changes in the family structure of tramping serve to highlight one of the many differences between tramps prior to World War II and the migrant agricultural workers who grew to such numerical importance during and after the war. It is important to understand that the industrial tramp, the major focus of this book, in fact differed significantly from the wandering poor of the preindustrial era and from migrant farm laborers in today's age of capital intensive agriculture, both of whom also differed from each other.

The ebb and flow of seasonal labor filled and emptied boxcars, cities, and the local jails which boarded tramps. In the winter tramps cut ice, lumbered forests, and shoveled snow and coal. In the spring and fall tramps worked on farms, and the summer found them in the construction trades. These tramps traveled in specifically urban patterns. That is, they used cities as the hubs of their information networks, traveling back from a farm to a city, then moving out to another farm or to a forest or another city. This differentiates them from migrant farm workers today, who can connect both with a different information network and with different traditions in order to follow harvests in a far less "urbancentric" and more direct manner. In between these seasonal excursions, and sometimes instead of them, tramps worked in factories and shops as skilled artisans and as unskilled "hands." Tramps were, in other words, the ordinary working people of the United States on the move between jobs and residences. While desperate, the very commonness of their plight integrated them with the larger working class's cultural systems and traditions.

The ethnic, regional, and occupational complexity of the United States kept the tramp world from ever becoming as organized as that of the tramp in Europe or England. Thus tramping was at one time a part of both the common work experience and the culture of industrial America, even though its enormous variety and fluid change kept it from ever becoming a highly developed and regularized system. Because the American economy changed too quickly, the emerging traditions never really crystallized, thus adding another reason to that long list cordoning off the world of the tramp from historical analysis for so long.

The period loosely spanned by this book, 1790 to the 1930s, covers the decline of commercial capitalism and the subsequent growth of industrial and corporate capitalism. Within this broad economic framework, the period between the Civil War and the early 1920s formed the era of mass tramping. Prior to this era, tramping had had a different character, and by the last decade of this era, tramping had begun a precipitous decline which even the Great Depression did not reverse. The preindustrial tramps of the antebellum era were, in fact, the wandering poor—men, women, children, and whole family units. The transition to industrial tramping became visible in cities earliest, but after the Civil War a whole new form of tramping had taken shape. Early observers concluded that the tramps were war veterans, fired with unquenchable and irresponsible wanderlust acquired during the war. Certainly many were veterans, but more impor-tant, they were single males in the early years of adulthood, smoothing the rough edges and filling the holes of labor demands in the expanding industrial economy. As employment declined or shifted location, young men took to the road, walking, riding the rails when possible, seeking not their fortunes, not adventures, but simply jobs. Their individual stories vary in details, of course, but from the perspective of the larger economic system, they made up the workers magically at the ready for economic enterprise. In many ways the desperate long walk and search for work in the story narrated by Terence Powderly and cited in Michael Davis's article could stand for the experience of thousands of American workers. Some-one had to be the most mobile of an already residentially mobile society as it expanded geographically and demographically, transforming its eco-nomic structure.[5] As employers were able to shirk their responsibility, this burden fell on all workers, and collectively they transferred it to single young men.

The completion of the mature urban industrial system of the United States ended the era of intense industrial tramping. In 1870, a sketch of the mature urban system existed, but the infrastructure, the roads, rails, bridges, sewers, water systems, houses, and buildings, had only begun to be built. Once this structure was built and peopled, once it was rationalized in the Weberian sense, once it was working smoothly and predictably, the need for tramps would disappear. In one sense tramps were not a reserve army at all, but rather a highly mobile infantry. The "vast reserve army of labor" posited by Marx was not necessarily a mobile one. We must therefore be cautious both in conceiving of the tramps as the only component of this army and in viewing their decline as indexing the disappearance of such a reserve.

The large structural reasons underlying the eventual end of industrial tramping have a close analogue to the reasons for the closing of the settlement frontier. Frederick Jackson Turner's subtle insights on the significance of the frontier's closing can easily be extended to the closing of the era of the industrial tramp. The closing of the tramp's frontier followed the closing of the territorial frontier by thirty years or so. Both filled out the shape of the settlement patterns of the continental United States. By 1920 the urban networks, the actual urban hierarchy, the rail connections, the industrial, extractive, and agricultural locations of the twentieth century economy had been established. The exceptions to this generalization have occurred mainly in the recently emerging urban sunbelt, and these exceptions are instructive, for the newspapers of the winter of 1982–83 were filled with images reminiscent of those of the labor press 100 years earlier. They carried "stay away" messages, stories of the out-of-work job seekers living on the margins of society once again, and stories of poisoning garbage in order to discourage scavengers.[6]

By the second decade of the twentieth century, tramps had helped to build a dispersed economic and social system in which their brothers' and sisters' children, if not their own, would find a modicum of residential and occupational stability. It is no wonder that during the Great Depression of the thirties, the plight of tramps shocked many, for by then the earlier period of industrial tramping had faded. The widespread sympathy concerning the tramps' plight, and the eventual legislation which at least attempted to deal with their needs, illustrate dramatically the distance traveled from the 1870s, when some newspapers had actually proposed exterminating the tramps. Even the willingness of southwestern cities in the 1980s to consider fairly radical means of keeping the indigent poor away comes from an understandable desire to keep away the welfare burden posed by the poor.[7]

The annual number of tramps lodged in police stations indirectly graphs the massive rise and fall of tramping in the era between the Civil War and the 1920s. Prior to the Civil War, only a few cities had established the formal organizations which we now recognize as the police. Consequently, what tramps there were stayed in many different places— poorhouses, jails, various charitable houses, and in the open. But with the emergence in most cities of the formally organized police, tramps began by the hundreds of thousands to stay in station houses, most often in special lodging rooms, but sometimes just on the floor. The graph of these station house lodgings shows a quick rise after the Civil War, followed by major peaks in the 1870s and the 1890s, and then a clear decline. Police lodging data can only be used to give hints as to the numbers of people actually tramping or even staying in police stations, but the federal censuses of 1880 and 1890 (two years with relatively few tramps compared to the depressions of the 1870s and 1890s) provide supplemental information. Thus, adjusting for missing reports, we can estimate with some accuracy that in 1880 631,637 and in 1890 615,131 persons stayed in police stations. Using these and other data, I estimated elsewhere that between 10 and 20 percent of the U.S. population in the late nineteenth century came from families with a member who had tramped in search of work.[8]

Although depressions had large and definitive impacts on the numbers of tramps, their activity was by no means limited to times of crisis only. Millions of people left their homes in search of work during "good" times as well as bad. The various working class cultures of this era incorporated tramping as a rational response to underemployment as well as unemployment, thus making the mass tramping of the depressions a change only in quantity, not in kind. When business failed and unemployment struck, workers knew exactly how to respond. For example, when the news of the Jay Cooke failure reached Duluth, Minnesota, the terminus for his Great Northern Railroad, work ceased and 3,700 of the city's 5,000 people left within a month.[9] What proportion of those leaving had to become lodgers in police stations cannot be estimated. A search of the Minneapolis newspapers turned up not one reference to this dramatic exodus, suggesting how quickly and invisibly these people could move off in search of work.

The streams of tramps in the 1870–1920 era depended on local government and railroads. Providing the skeleton for travel in search of work, the roles of these two organizations changed simultaneously with the changing travel patterns of the twentieth century. Municipal government operated in its most basic function through the free lodging provided by the police, and railroads supported the network by winking at the tramps stealing rides. For both organizations, tramps were important, even essential. Urban enterprise depended on the fluid labor supply; railroads needed seasonal labor for building and for creating the very goods which the freights hauled.

Cities and railroads needed tramps, and they also needed each other. The symbiotic relationship of cities and railroads is now well understood. Cities attracted and supported railroads by subsidizing capital investment through the issuance of public debt. But the railroads maintained the prosperity which facilitated the repayment of that debt. And they both needed the flexible labor supply provided by the tramps. Both underwrote the costs of moving and housing these traveling workers, thus absorbing the indirect costs generated by seasonal, cyclical, regional, and firm specific variations. Local government and the railroads provided an effective system of adjusting labor supply and demand. Tramps, traveling through the network created by this mix of public and private enterprise, filled an economic function at least as vital as that of the Mexican-American migrant workers in agriculture today. Ironically, few nineteenth century observers ever perceived these systematic interdependencies, elites most often expressing cruel hostility or amusement and disdain, working class observers seeing only the victimization of the workers.

Neither city officials nor railroad officers conceptualized their interdependence on tramps in this way. Railroads held to the official line that riding the rails was theft, pure and simple, and sometimes tramps shared this view. Hence the term "beating" the rails, for the traveler had beaten the railroad out of a fare. Obviously, the railroads tolerated tramps only when it was in their interest to do so, keeping their official policy line in reserve for whenever the tramps' nuisance costs exceeded their productive value. By the end of the nineteenth century, this happened. The system of tramping became less vital to the economy; railroads began to enforce their rules against tramping.

They focused particularly on the damage tramps did to freight, often throwing things off to make room in boxcars or burning down cars when their warming fires got out of control. One of the most famous writers on tramps at the end of the century, Josiah Flynt Willard, turned his expertise at beating the railroads, gaining the confidence of other tramps, and writing about the details of the tramps' life into a profession. He became a detective and antitramp consultant to several different railroads, doing his best to bring to an end the era which had provided him his literary livelihood.

A handful of tramp letters from 1912, preserved in the Northern Pacific's archives, illustrates the cool attitude this company had concerning tramps. Several men from various towns in the West, evidently preparing to meet their maker and wishing to settle earthly debts, either sent payment for rides stolen or asked to be forgiven for beating the rails in the 1890s. Although the company did accept payment when it accompanied the letters, it did not ask for specific reimbursement, even when the writers detailed the trips taken and the damage done. Instead, it magnanimously responded: "We are glad to know that you have learned you were in the wrong and we will call the account square."[10] Tramps were a necessary nuisance: ones who knew their place were tolerated.

As the need for tramps declined, so did tramping. After 1893, some cities (most notably New York) ended their "no strings attached" police station lodging, building instead municipal lodging houses which required either a payment or a few hours of labor to compensate the municipality for the night's rest and a breakfast. This policy change, motivated by notions about how best to control the poor, would in the next two decades spread across the country. But it was not dysfunctional; reformers were not cutting off their noses to spite their faces. In order to best untangle the elements contributing to the end of the publicly and privately supported tramping era, we must first remember that the agricultural aspects of tramping, while changing, had never completely disappeared.

Douglas Jones shows in his contribution to this book how the seasons of preindustrial tramping had been attuned to the planting and harvesting of the agricultural cycle, with other economic seasons—those of fishing and oceanic shipping—in the late eighteenth century moving tramps away from a purely agricultural orientation. This seasonal component persisted in tramping even in industrial times. In the late nineteenth century, for instance, the jail and lodging records of Red Wing, Minnesota, a small river city offering both manufacturing employment (shoes and pottery) and a rich agricultural hinterland, demonstrate the overlay of agricultural and urban/industrial cycles. In this city, the changing seasonal usage of the jail as both a place of punishment and a place of sustenance encapsulates the demise of industrial tramping.

That a small city like this should even have housed tramps in the municipal jails shows the official ambivalence to and support of tramping. Most places had vagrancy ordinances, so that were they a real nuisance, the tramps could have been arrested easily. (In the early decades of the twentieth century, especially, as the need for them declined, they often were arrested as vagrants.[11]) But because both farmers and local industry needed them, the city boarded them. As a consequence, in the 1890s, the seasonal patterns of lodging and arrests were almost the exact opposite of one another. In the fall and spring, the jails filled with tramps taken in as lodgers. In the summer there were almost no tramps, and instead the jails served for coercive social control, staying busy with local farmers recovering from drunken sprees. The strong and statistically significant inverse relationship between these two usages of the jail in the 1890s disappeared in the first two decades of the twentieth century, the two seasonal patterns merging with one another in the first decade and showing no relationship by the second decade (see Table 1). One can clearly see the function of the local jail changing as local and regional labor demands changed. The utilitarian tolerance of the 1890s was reversed: the city still paid for the housing of tramps but also arrested them, thus beginning the separation of the arrest process and crime control from the city's obligation to house the homeless poor.[12]

Of course the changed seasonal relationship between jailings and tramp lodging did not instantly end tramping, nationally or regionally. Red Wing, for instance, continued to house some tramps until at least World War II. That this small city did not end its jailhouse lodging of tramps while larger cities often did suggests that tramping, and also the governmental response to it, varied in scale and kind by locale. While impossible to prove, the fragmented information left to us implies that there were three tiers of tramping in the industrial period. First, there was a local tier of unskilled workers moving within a small, fixed territory. To continue with the Red Wing example, many tramps had come from Lake City, a day's walk away. Probably this local tier was the busiest, because the most casual. Above this tier was a regional one, where workers moved through adjacent states in the regional economy. And above this was the national tier, where the skilled workers particularly moved. The two articles in this book by Jules Tygiel and Patricia Cooper show how carpenters and cigar makers kept abreast of changing news of opportunities and of depressed

Table 1: Pearsonian Correlation of Number Lodged and Number Jailed, 1896–1961, Red Wing, Minnesota.

Date	R	N	Sig.	R^2
1896	−.679	10	.10	.46
1897	−.775	12	.01	.60
1904	.534	8	ns	.28
1905	.220	12	ns	.05
1906	−.381	12	ns	.14
1907	−.217	12	ns	.05
1910–11	.052	5	ns	.003
1916	−.164	12	ns	.03

Source: City of Red Wing, Minnesota, *Jail Register*, Tramps Lodged, 5 vols., 1896–1916, in the City of Red Wing Records. Minnesota State Archives, Minnesota Historical Society.

areas across the whole country through the medium of their union journals. Their organization made rational and national circulation feasible. On the other hand, regional travel may well have exhausted the informational resources of less skilled and less organized workers. Because the unskilled would have the least to gain in even regional travel, they would therefore have been the most likely to restrict their range. Clearly, regional shifts would distort this pattern, but it does locate tramping during "normal" times.

Hard and systematic data to support this scheme cannot be established easily. A comparison of the occupations of the tramps in Red Wing and those staying in a Washington, D.C. station house in the 1890s is suggestive. Almost all of the Red Wing lodgers listed their occupation simply as laborer, as opposed to over half of the D.C. lodgers, who gave their occupations as something more specialized and skilled than laborer. Most likely, the tramps staying in D.C. represented a confluence of men, some following local routes, others following regional or national quests. Some came from nearby small towns, some from regional centers like Baltimore and Richmond, and some from national cities like New York and Philadelphia. Those in Red Wing for the most part followed a local circulation pattern. Of all tramps staying in the city jail between 1896 and 1907, slightly less than 10 percent came from further than one state away from Minnesota.[13] My article in this book explores the dynamics of regional effects and transportation access on a larger scale to show how these nested tiers of travel operated within a broad set of national factors. The primary determinant, in fact, of the per capita number of tramps in any one city was its location in the national railroad network, and region made much less of a difference in tramping levels than one might have predicted.

At the same time that the skill levels of the tramps moving throughout these tiers varied, other things remained surprisingly constant. Most tramps were men. As the articles by Priscilla Ferguson Clement and Douglas Jones demonstrate, such had not been the case in the earlier part of the century. Then the tramps were the traveling poor, and a greater proportion of nuclear families, women, children, and black people moved about in search of work. But by the period of heaviest industrial tramping, these proportions had declined considerably. Those women who did tramp faced considerable obstacles, as Lynn Weiner's article makes grimly clear. Very few black people tramped in this period, partly because so few southerners of any race tramped, and partly because by this time tramps no longer represented the most oppressed persons in American society. The absence of many black tramps indicates that to be forced to tramp meant that the individual had expectations of survival, some hope that work or welfare could be found at the destination. For black people in the late nineteenth century, these were not realistic expectations. Thus the massive black migration that had begun was from the South to established black communities in cities, in the South and North, but not out on the chancy tramp trail.

The world peopled by tramps in the period from 1870 to World War I was one of neither outcasts nor deviants. John Schneider argues in detail how it was in fact a bachelor subculture, deviant only in the sense that it did not represent the mainstream demographic structure. It was surprisingly coherent. Subsections of cities formed temporary neighborhoods for these men. These neighborhoods catered to their needs, serving as information centers, the quintessential urban function. Most tramps were between twenty and forty years old, and because there is no evidence of a changing age structure, we can infer that most tramped only for a portion of their adult lives. Did those who were forced to tramp return to their homes to form nuclear families? We simply have no evidence with which to assert a positive, negative, or mixed answer to this puzzle. Nor can we yet say what proportion of the subculture was gay. The origin of the term "gay" seems to have appeared in the tramp jargon, for some tramps were known as "gay-cats," and older men who traveled with young boys were called "Prussians."[14] Because our knowledge of these terms comes mainly from Josiah Flynt Willard, who himself belonged to the minority of outcasts and deviants contained within the larger tramping population, any definitive discussion of these issues must be tentative. We are best off guessing that a smaller culture of gays and outcasts existed within the larger subculture of traveling workers.

In reading this book it is important to keep in mind the overall shape of tramping in the United States, particularly its periodization. First came the preindustrial period of the wandering poor, down to around the Civil War.

Then followed the age of the industrial tramp, until World War I. And finally came our modern era, with the marginal, defeated, and ill as tramps, and with migrant workers most closely reflecting the economic roles of the earlier tramps. It is most important to remember that the tramps really were the builders of what has become our late twentieth-century world.

Notes

1. For the early relationship between social reformers and tramps, see Paul T. Ringenbach, *Tramps and Reformers, 1873–1916: The Discovery of Unemployment in New York* (Westport, Conn.: Greenwood, 1973). For an accurate and useful description of the urban consequences of the demise of industrial tramping, see Alvin Averbach, "San Francisco's South of Market District, 1850–1950: The Emergence of a Skid Row," *California Historical Quarterly* 52 (Fall 1973), 197–223.

2. A sentimental view of tramp history, accompanied with the excellent photographs of the J. J. McCook Collection, may be found in Roger Bruns, *Knights of the Road: A Hobo History* (New York: Methuen, 1980).

3. For a sensitive and sensible study of contemporary tramping, see James T. Spradley, *You Owe Yourself a Drunk: An Ethnology of Urban Nomads* (Boston: Little, Brown, 1970). For a perceptive photo essay, see Michael Mathers, *Riding the Rails* (Boston: Houghton Mifflin, 1974).

4. On the strikes of 1877, see Robert V. Bruce, *1877: Year of Violence* (Indianapolis: Bobbs, Merrill, 1959); for Coxey's Army, see Donald L. McMurry, *Coxey's Army: A Study of the Industrial Army Movement of 1844* (Boston: Little, Brown, 1929).

5. For a discussion and refinement of the literature on mobility, see Michael B. Katz, Michael Doucet, and Mark Stern, "Migration and the Social Order in Erie County, New York: 1855," *Journal of Interdisciplinary History* 7 (Spring 1978), 669–701.

6. Frederick Jackson Turner, "The Significance of the Frontier in American History," in *The Frontier in American History* (New York: Holt, 1921), 1–38.

7. The *Minneapolis Tribune* (July 30, 1878, 3) echoed the hostility of the *Chicago Tribune* towards tramps in reprinting an article discussing a Minnesota farmer's murder of two tramps. Although one may question whether the editors sincerely meant to murder all tramps, it is clear that their hostility to tramps knew no bounds. The article cited with vigorous approval the intent of a group of farmers to "fertilize their land with their [the tramps'] dead bodies . . . as a radical and permanent cure for the evil complained of. . . . Not that we put a low estimate on human life" (citation supplied by Lynn Weiner). The *Railroad Gazette* (1879) re-printed an article from the *St. Louis Times-Journal* which stated, "A wrecked freight car invariably means a dead tramp. It's an expensive but effective way of getting rid of a very undesirable class of nuisances" (353). In its own article nine years later, "Tramps and Train Wrecking" (November 23, 1888), the *Railroad Gazette* took an equally vicious attitude, calling on localities to "exterminate these pests" (773). (Even as this is being written, 21 February 1983, the *Los Angeles Times* carries stories of nineteenth-century type welfare systems being reintroduced, systems designed to discourage tramping and the poor from making their poverty visible— as in the Sacramento "poorhouse," in actuality a municipal lodging house.)

8. For one attempt to estimate the actual numbers of tramps, see Eric H. Monk-konen, *Police in Urban America, 1860–1920* (New York: Cambridge University Press, 1981), 93–96. For the census data see Frederick H. Wines, *Report on the Defective, Dependent, and Delinquent Classes . . . Tenth Census,* v. 21 (Washington: GPO, 1888, Table 136, 566–74; Wines, *Report on Crime, Pauperism, and Benev-olence . . . Eleventh Census: 1890,* v. 3, pt. 2 (Washington: GPO, 1895), Appendix: Police Statistics of Cities, 1023–35. Because neither census contains complete returns, the reported figures have been adjusted by estimating the numbers of tramps in the nonreporting cities. As the smallest cities tended to be the non-reporters, the adjustments take cognizance of the declining quality of reporting by city size. For instance, in 1880 all of the ten largest cities reported, while 69 percent of those between ranks eleven and fifty-five reported, and only 25 percent of the smaller ones reported. The actual number of lodgers reported for 1880 and 1890 was 557,760 and 469,443. It is not clear if the police reported the annual number of lodgings which they provided or if they reported the number of individuals—a significant problem. For those two lodger lists I have examined, Red Wing and Washington, there were two different recording procedures. Red Wing listed only the actual number of individuals, while Washington listed the number of lodgings—about 20 percent of whom were repeaters. Of course, those persons staying in several cities would be doubly counted by the national survey also. Therefore the quality suggests this numerical index must be used with great caution.

9. Walter Van Brunt, *Duluth and St. Louis County, Minnesota: Their Story and People* (Chicago: American Historical Society, 1921), 243–44.

10. Letter from R. W. Clark to William Weir (Islandale, Washington), May 18, 1912, in Northern Pacific Company Records, Minnesota Historical Society.

11. William J. Chambliss, "A Sociological Analysis of the Law of Vagrancy," *Social Problems* 12 (Summer 1964), 67–77.

12. For an analysis of the decline of police welfare in particular, see Monkkonen, *Police,* 86–128.

13. For more detail on Washington, D.C. tramp occupations, see my article in this book, Table 5. Figures for Red Wing were calculated from the *Jail Register,* Tramps Lodged, City of Red Wing Records, Minnesota State Archives, Minnesota Historical Society.

14. The standard dictionary of tramp argot is in Josiah Flynt Willard, *Tramping with Tramps: Studies and Sketches of Vagrant Life* (New York: Century, 1899). For details of Willard's peculiar life, see also his *Notes of an Itinerant Policeman* (Boston: Page, 1900) and *My Life* (New York: Outing, 1908).

Part I: The Beginnings of Industrial Tramping

Douglas Lamar Jones

The Strolling Poor: Transiency in Eighteenth-Century Massachusetts

In 1790, William Bentley, the Salem diarist, observed two of the dominant changes occurring in Massachusetts society during the eighteenth century: the transiency of the poor and increased migration of economically diverse segments of the population.[1] Bentley noted that the Salem Selectmen debated "whether [or not] to warn Strangers out of Town in order to save the Town from the charges of the Poor. It is found in fact that the greater part of the whole property is in the hands of persons not Town born, and in the best streets even a majority of freeholders [are newcomers]."[2] To Bentley, migration had become a way of life in eighteenth-century Salem, and one result was a realignment of the rules for defining the social order. One could no longer expect that one's neighbors were, in Bentley's felicitous phrase, "Town born," and had grown to adulthood within the same town and presumably with the same set of values.

Bentley's observations of a changing social order were not simply the particularistic sentiments of a local diarist; they were the articulation of the passing of traditional Massachusetts society and the emergence of a more modern one.[3] This process of modernization in Massachusetts was by no means abrupt or dramatic. Indeed, it is more useful to view the middle and late decades of the eighteenth century as a period of transition. During this transitional stage, structural change, social values, and personal behavior fluctuated amidst the demands of passage from the more simple, face-to-face society of the seventeenth century. This essay seeks to examine three aspects of transiency migration during this transitional stage: the magnitude of transiency during the eighteenth century; the social and economic characteristics of transients; and the legal response to increasing numbers of transient poor persons.

During the eighteenth century, an increase in the number of transients in eastern and western Massachusetts coincided with the secular trend in westward migration and declining levels of residential continuity. This transition to increased mobility during the eighteenth century became even more firmly established during the nineteenth century. Mostly poor and of lower-class origins, eighteenth-century transients were found in both the congested eastern Massachusetts counties and the frontier. Moving very short distances from town to town and job to job, this class of

Table 1: Rates of Persistence in Selected
Communities in Premodern New England[a]

Decade	Community[b]	Rate of Persistence	N	Range	Mean
				52–83%	67%
1643–53	Rowley, Mass.	59%	(54)		
1648–60	Dedham, Mass.	52%	(98)		
1660–70	Dedham	78%	(91)		
	Hingham, Mass.	73%	(96)		
1676–86	Windsor, Conn.	57%	(165)		
1680–90	Dedham	73%	(113)		
1686–96	Manchester, Mass.	61%	(34)		
1687–95	Boston, Mass.	53%	(1224)		
1690–1700	Dedham	83%	(125)		
				50–69%	60%
1723–33	Dedham	55%	(204)		
1731–41	Wenham, Mass.	68%	(99)		
1741–51	Beverly, Mass.	50%	(302)		
	Wenham	58%	(113)		
1751–61	Beverly	58%	(304)		
	Wenham	53%	(105)		
1754–65	Hingham	69%	(331)		
1761–71	Beverly	64%	(368)		

continued

transients confronted traditional communities with mounting problems of social welfare and control. The process of increased migration caused the towns to live in uneasy tension with a growing class of poor persons for several decades during the eighteenth century.

In response to this class of transients, new legal mechanisms were developed to limit their impact on the traditional towns. The towns relinquished some but not all of their customary responsibilities for the transient poor while society at large gradually assumed a greater proportion of the duties of care and control. These new legal mechanisms did not completely alter the care provided by families and towns, but they did make clear that Massachusetts society required more routinized means

Table I *Continued*

Decade	Community[b]	Rate of Persistence	N	Range	Mean
	Wenham	59%	(99)		
1780–90	Boston	56%	(2225)		
1790–1800	Hingham	68%	(347)		

(a) Computation of the persistence statistic displayed in this table was based on a determination of the number of persons listed in the first time period, and then a ratio of the persons who continued to the following time period was calculated. All persistence statistics in this table have been standardized to fit this method.

(b) Sources, in order of listing, calculated by the author from *The Early Records of the Town of Rowley, Massachusetts, 1639–1672* (Rowley, Mass., 1894), pp. v–x; Kenneth A. Lockridge, "The Population of Dedham, Massachusetts, 1636–1736," *Economic History Review* 19 (1966), 322; Daniel Scott Smith, "Population, Family, and Society in Hingham, Massachusetts, 1635–1880," (Ph.D. dissertation, University of California, Berkeley, 1973); Linda Auwers Bissell, "From One Generation to Another: Mobility in Seventeenth-Century Windsor, Connecticut," *William and Mary Quarterly* 31 (1974), 79–110, Table VIII; calculated by the author from *Manchester Town Records, 1636–1736* (Salem, 1889), 30–31, 73; James A. Henretta, "Economic Development and Social Structure in Colonial Boston," *William and Mary Quarterly* 22 (1965), 74–92; tax list and reconstitution data of Wenham, Massachusetts; tax list and reconstitution data of Beverly, Massachussets; Allan Kulikoff, "The Progress of Inequality in Revolutionary Boston," *William and Mary Quarterly* 28 (1971), 402.

All towns listed are located in Massachusetts unless otherwise noted.

Table 2: New and Subdivided Settlement Formation
in Massachusetts, 1621–1860, by Geographic Region[a]

Region and type of settlement	1621–1660 Percent	N	1661–1700 Percent	N	1701–1740 Percent	N
East[b]						
New settlements	75	(36)	52	(14)	14	(8)
Subdivisions	19	(9)	22	(6)	48	(28)
East—Total	94	(45)	74	(20)	62	(36)
West[c]						
New settlements	6	(3)	19	(5)	20	(12)
Subdivisions	—	(0)	7	(2)	19	(11)
West—Total	6	(3)	26	(7)	39	(23)
Massachusetts, all						
New settlements	81	(39)	70	(19)	34	(20)
Subdivisions	19	(9)	30	(8)	66	(39)
Grand Total		(48)		(27)		(59)

	1741–1780 Percent	N	1781–1820 Percent	N	1821–1860 Percent	N
East						
New settlements	—	(0)	—	(0)	—	(0)
Subdivisions	10	(10)	42	(22)	68	(21)
East—Total	10	(10)	42	(22)	68	(21)

continued

for sustaining social order than face-to-face, local society offered.[4] Thus the appearance of a visible class of transients and the rationalization of legal means of welfare and control during the eighteenth century represent aspects of the transition from traditional to modern American society.

In premodern Massachusetts, there was a remarkably wide divergence in the rates of population persistence, ranging from 50 to 83 percent (see Table 1).[5] This broad pattern of residential continuity was accounted for, however, by the first generation of settlers. Their rates of persistence

Table 2 *Continued*

West						
New settlements	40	(38)	11	(6)	3	(1)
Region and type	1741–1780		1781–1820		1821–1860	
of settlement	Percent	N	Percent	N	Percent	N
Subdivisions	50	(48)	47	(25)	29	(9)
West—Total	90	(86)	58	(31)	32	(10)
Massachusetts, all						
New settlements	40	(38)	11	(6)	3	(1)
Subdivisions	60	(58)	89	(47)	96	(30)
Grand Total		(96)		(53)		(31)

(a) Compiled from Kevin H. White, *Historical Data Relating to Counties, Cities and Towns in Massachusetts* (The Commonwealth of Massachusetts, 1966). As used in this table, "date of settlement formation" is based on dates of founding of towns, districts, and plantations. In order to generate the most accurate time series of population dispersion using settlement formation as the index, I tried to use the earliest date of formation, particularly of districts and plantations. This definition of settlement formation—which focuses on the social organization of communities—offers the most useful way of portraying the dispersion of organized society by geographical area.

(b) Eastern Massachusetts includes all counties to the east of, but excluding, Worcester County: Barnstable, Bristol, Duke's, Essex, Middlesex, Nantucket, Norfolk, Plymouth, and Suffolk.

(c) Western Massachusetts includes all counties to the west of, and including, Worcester County: Berkshire, Franklin, Hampden, Hampshire, and Worcester. Several counties in Maine also received out-migrants, but they were omitted from this tabulation. Their inclusion would increase the proportion of new and subdivided settlements formed outside of eastern Massachusetts.

(from available local studies) ranged from 52 to 83 percent. As time passed and the population expanded, the range of persistence in eighteenth-century Massachusetts narrowed to 50 to 69 percent. While the minimum rate of population continuity in premodern Massachusetts never fell below 50 percent, the maximum range varied quite dramatically over time. By the mid-eighteenth century, the overt residential stability found in some Massachusetts towns a century earlier had disappeared; taxpayers and their families began to move at a faster pace.

This mobility quickened even more during the early nineteenth century, as the secular patterns of persistence declined more sharply. From a longitudinal perspective, the decreased rates of the eighteenth century should be viewed as a transition to the more volatile rural and urban populations of nineteenth-century America.[6]

A useful index of eighteenth-century population redistribution through migration is the proportion of settlement dispersion occurring by geographic region. During the seventeenth century, almost all new settlements were formed in eastern Massachusetts. The western part of the colony remained relatively untouched except around Springfield and Northampton (see Table 2). By 1740, however, there was an absolute decline in settlement formation in the eastern counties as the white population began to shift to the west and the north. Almost 90 percent of the settlements founded between 1741 and 1780 were in the western counties.

Not all of the western settlements formed after 1741 were new; many were subdivisions which split off from older towns. While we normally think of the congested eastern towns as having to subdivide, the reverse was true between 1741 and 1780: almost no towns subdivided in the east. Out-migration was the primary response to population growth in many eastern towns during the transitional period. (There were, however, rural-urban differences in the extent of out-migration in the east.) Ultimately, western migration declined after 1781 as economic adjustments were made and higher population densities accepted. But the transition to increased mobility had been made during the eighteenth century.

Migration increased during the eighteenth century as a natural but unwanted response to demographic pressures on available economic resources.[7] This change to greater geographic mobility was neither abrupt nor dramatic. It was a slow process intimately related to population growth and the need for land in traditional, agricultural society. Migration became a stopgap attempt to limit the population sizes of many Massachusetts towns, particularly the older farming towns in the eastern counties. Not until family limitation emerged during the nineteenth century as a more effective control on population size was geographic mobility loosened from its mechanistic relationship to population growth.

Precisely during the peak periods of eighteenth-century migration and settlement formation, the number of unwanted persons—transients—in two representative Massachusetts counties, Essex and Hampshire, increased dramatically (see Table 3). In Essex, located to the north of Boston along the coast and established during the seventeenth century, the rate of increase in the number of transient households doubled in each of the two decades following 1739–43 (from 56 percent in 1750–54 to 112 percent in 1760–64). Despite the higher absolute number of transients in Essex County, a rapid increase in the proportion of transients was common in Hampshire as well.

Located in western Massachusetts, Hampshire County underwent a substantial population growth during the eighteenth century. But during the early 1760s, Hampshire witnessed a phenomenal increase in the proportion of persons warned out as transients. The rate of increase was so

Table 3: Number of Transient Households Warned Out
of Essex and Hampshire Counties, 1739–74, and the Rate of
Increase or Decrease from the Previous Time Period

| | Households warned and the rate of increase or decrease from previous time period | | | | Average increase or decrease |
| | Essex County[a] | | Hampshire County[b] | | |
Dates	Percent	N	Percent	N	Percent
1739–43	n.a.	(257)	n.a.	(50)	n.a.
1750–54	56	(400)	76	(88)	+58
1760–64	+116	(862)	+248	(306)	+139
1770–74	−93	(58)	−60	(122)	−85

(a) Taken from the Court of General Sessions of the Peace, 1726–96, Essex County, Massachusetts, Clerk of Courts Office, Salem, Massachusetts.

(b) Taken from the Court of General Sessions of the Peace, 1735–81, Hampshire County, Massachusetts, Clerk of Courts Office, Northampton, Massachusetts.

Note: The designation n.a. means that the proportional increase for the given time period was not available.

much greater than in any other time period in either Hampshire or Essex that it suggests that the impact of a growing class of transients occurred later in the demographic history of this frontier county.[8] Once this time lag is accounted for, the ratio of transients in 1760–64 to the total population in 1765 in each county was almost identical (.106 in Essex and .104 in Hampshire). By the 1760s social exclusion of the poor was as common on the frontier of Massachusetts society as in the older, more established, eastern counties.[9]

The migration transition in eighteenth-century Massachusetts involved both an increase in general population redistribution and a rise in transiency mobility. The wandering poor person was not a completely new "type"; transients were found in smaller numbers in seventeenth-century towns. What was new, however, was the existence of a class of the transient poor who required economic assistance. This swelling population of dependent poor, many of whom were single persons, confronted the traditional towns with problems of poor relief. The visibility of eighteenth-century transients implicitly challenged the traditionalism of the communal society; unemployment, single-person households, and residential mobility were not accepted patterns of behavior.

During the eighteenth century, towns began to follow the practice of presenting the names and prior residential origins of transients to the courts of general sessions of the peace. Parents, their children, and servants (if any) were grouped together in the warnings which were prepared by local constables for the legal identification of all transients. Single persons were usually listed separately. The social unit warned out was the household, which consisted variously of a family, a single man or woman, or, more rarely, a family with a servant or slave.

The most distinctive feature of transient households in Essex and Hampshire counties was the high proportion of single persons (see Table 4). The total proportions of single transients in Essex County ranged from 52 to 62 percent, while in Hampshire County there was a greater variation across time (from 26 to 54 percent). Although we do not know the ages of these single transients, their large proportion of the total suggests that many may have been young and unmarried—the most common

Table 4: Household Status of Transients in Essex and Hampshire
Counties, Massachusetts, During the Eighteenth Century[a]

Household status	1739–43		1750–54	
	Essex	Hampshire	Essex	Hampshire
Single persons				
Males	27%	28%	38%	33%
Females	27%	26%	30%	14%
Families[b]				
Two-parent	39%	38%	28%	42%
One-parent	7%	8%	4%	11%
Servants[c]	—	—	1%	—
Slaves	—	—	—	—
Total[d]	100%	100%	100%	100%
N	(257)	(50)	(400)	(88)

	1760–64		1770–74	
	Essex	Hampshire	Essex	Hampshire
Single persons				
Males	32%	30%	28%	11%
Females	31%	14%	24%	15%
Families				
Two-parent	29%	45%	40%	68%
One-parent	6%	10%	9%	6%
Servants	1%	—	—	1%
Slaves	1%	—	—	—
Total	100%	99%	101%	101%
N	(862)	(306)	(58)	(122)

(a) Taken from the Court of General Sessions of the Peace, 1726–96, Essex County, Clerk of Courts Office, Salem, Massachusetts; Court of General Sessions of the Peace, 1735–81, Hampshire County, Clerk of Courts Office, Northampton, Massachusetts.

(b) Almost all one-parent families were headed by females. In Essex County, forty-six of fifty-one one-parent families in 1760–64 were headed by women. In Hampshire, forty-one of the fifty-two one-parent families were headed by single mothers.

(c) Since occupations were not included in the warning out, this is only a minimal estimate of the number of servants.

(d) Percentages may not add to 100 percent due to rounding.

characteristics of migrants.[10] Yet we cannot rule out the possibility that some were older persons, such as widows, who were unemployable and migrating for better living conditions as dependent poor.

Transiency among single persons was not restricted by sex; almost equal proportions of men and women were warned in Essex while in Hampshire, again, there was more variation over time. These regional variations in the numbers of single men and women may be explained by the different demographic histories of the two counties. Essex, a demographically "older" county than Hampshire, had the most unbalanced sex ratio of all Massachusetts counties. In many Essex County towns, native sons migrated during the eighteenth century because of economic and population pressures. This out-migration reduced the supply of males and created a demographic imbalance. Hampshire, however, expanded after 1730, when the number of towns increased sixfold and the number of adult men and women was almost equal.[11] Single transient women were perhaps more welcome in Hampshire because of the need for marriage mates in a developing area. In Essex, transient males were not the solution to a decline in available marriage mates because of their lower-class status. Caught between the pressures of increasing demands on economic resources and legal and moral strictures against the status of the single-person household, unmarried transients formed the major subclass of the dependent population.

The one-parent household was subject to very close scrutiny in eighteenth-century Massachusetts, particularly if headed by a woman. The overall proportion of one-parent families remained at a low level in both Essex and Hampshire, but the number of female-headed families almost tripled during the early 1760s. There may have been an incremental increase in widowhood following the French and Indian Wars which could account for this change.[12] But mothers with illegitimate children also fell victim to banishment by communities attempting to avoid poor relief and enforce moral censure.[13] The late eighteenth century was a period of increased sexual activity, as the rise in premarital pregnancy rates in Massachusetts suggests. Prosecution for illegitimacy also reflected increased sexual activity as well as the moral authority of the towns and county courts.[14] It seems likely that transient single mothers fell within this category of socially excluded persons.

Not all transients were unmarried; families comprised the second largest category of unwanted persons. These transient families generally included only biologically related members: husbands, wives, and their children. Rarely were three-generational households, apprentices, servants, or slaves found among transient families.

Smaller than the average, premodern American family, transient families averaged just about four persons (see Table 5). Since family size is an indication of the relative age of the parents, it seems clear that married transients were as youthful on the frontier as in older, eastern Massachusetts. But there were demographic differences between transient families in each county. Proportionally more transient families lived in Hampshire than in Essex, and the average household size was larger in the west as well. These differences suggest that more families migrated to Hampshire County, presumably for better economic opportunities. Essex County, on the other hand, became more congested during the last half of the eighteenth century.[15] Part of this congestion may have resulted from transients who were trapped geographically and economically by old age, ill health, and poverty.

These distinctions showed also in the type of community more likely to take action against the transients. Since warnings out were related to a town's efforts to avoid the costs of poor relief, we would expect that in Essex County, where the economy was under stress, both the wealthy and poor towns would have warned out transients in equal proportions. The wealthy towns would be motivated by the desire to preserve their wealth and economic order; the less wealthy towns by the need to preserve what wealth was available. This, in fact, was the case in Essex County during the 1760s. There was almost no relationship between per capita warnings and per capita wealth. Transiency migration in Essex County was common to all towns, regardless of their wealth or population size.[16]

But in Hampshire County there was a stronger relationship between per capita warnings and per capita wealth. In part, this relationship reflects greater economic opportunities in Hampshire than in Essex. Transients

Table 5: Average Household and Family Size of
Transients, 1760–64, and of Persons Listed in the Census of
1765, in Essex and Hampshire Counties, Massachusetts[a]

	Average household size	Average family size
Essex County		
1765 Census, whites only	5.34	n.a.
Transients, 1760–64	2.10	4.10
Hampshire County		
1765 Census, whites only	5.95	n.a.
Transients, 1760–64	2.65	4.03

(a) Sources for transients, see Table 3. 1765 calculations are taken from data in Joseph B. Felt, "Statistics of the Population in Massachusetts," *Collections of the American Statistical Association* I, part II (Boston, 1845), 149–51.

Note: Definitions of the relationships among family members are not available in the 1765 Census. For this reason, I have adopted the term "household" to describe the average number of persons within each living unit. From the aggregated data available in the 1765 Census, "household" seems to be a more inclusive definition than the term "family," which was used by the census takers. Within the census category of "family," servants, apprentices, possibly slaves, and three-generational families seem to have coresided together. Also, the term "household" permits us to categorize single individuals into separate households.

The category of "average family size" omits single individuals and employs as the unit of analysis persons who were defined as biologically related members of the same family. While information of this type is not available from the census, it can be found in the warnings out. For a discussion of the definitions of family and household used here, see Peter Laslett, ed., *Household and Family in Past Time* (Cambridge, England, 1972), 28–40.

clearly were attracted to Hampshire County, as its population growth and proliferation of new settlements suggest. Some communities were more attractive than others, but exactly which ones is not clear at this time. For example, the sick, the aged, and widows may have been drawn to those towns with well-developed charitable and institutional support. More generally, younger transients showed some sense of economic advantage in seeking places in Hampshire County, though they were often rebuffed.

Overriding these differences, however, was the fact that transients in both counties came from the bottom of the social scale. Almost all of the Salem transients listed in 1791 (mostly males) were working-class artisans and lower-class mariners and laborers (see Table 6). Only a handful were in higher occupational groups. Compared to the complete occupational

Table 6: Occupational Status of Transients to Salem, Massachusetts, in 1791, by Residential Origins, Compared with the Occupational Structure of Boston, Massachusetts, 1790

Residential origins of Salem transients, 1791[a]

Occupational status	U.S. Percent	N	Foreign Percent	N	Total Percent	N	Boston, 1790[b] All Males Percent	N
Government	—	(0)	—	(0)	—	(0)	3	(67)
Professional	—	(0)	1	(1)	1	(1)	9	(219)
Tradesmen	—	(0)	2	(2)	1	(2)	18	(474)
Clerical	—	(0)	1	(1)	1	(1)	3	(66)
Artisans	51	(59)	15	(12)	36	(71)	49	(1271)
Building crafts		(11)		(1)		(12)		(245)
Cloth trades		(17)		(2)		(19)		(289)
Food trades		(10)		(3)		(13)		(175)
Marine crafts		(6)		(4)		(10)		(219)
Metal crafts		(6)		(2)		(8)		(132)
Wood-workers		(3)		(0)		(3)		(106)
Miscellaneous		(6)		(0)		(6)		(205)
Service	—	(0)	—	(0)	—	(0)	7	(183)
Mariners	24	(27)	61	(50)	39	(77)	5	(117)
Unskilled	25	(29)	20	(16)	23	(45)	7	(188)
Total		(115)		(82)		(197)		(2585)

(a) Calculated from "Salem Warnings, 1791," *Essex Institute Historical Collections* 43 (1907), 345–52. Because of missing information as to occupations or residential origins, twenty-six males, twenty-two single women, and fourteen widows were omitted.

(b) Calculated from Allan Kulikoff, "The Progress of Inequality in Revolutionary Boston," *William and Mary Quarterly* 28 (1971), 411–12, Appendix.

within Massachusetts. Primary economic and population centers such as Salem and Boston received a majority of their transients from within Massachusetts.[18] Smaller inland towns, removed from initial contact with foreign immigrants, also received almost all of their transients from within Massachusetts. The main exceptions were towns which dotted the borders, thus coming into contact with transients from neighboring states such as New Hampshire or Connecticut. Chelmsford, for example, a small, agricultural town located near New Hampshire, received nearly one-fifth of its transients from outside Massachusetts. Cambridge, however, recorded only a bare 2 percent of its transient population as coming directly from outside Massachusetts.

Thus the general pattern of transient migration in eighteenth-century Massachusetts was one of localized mobility, as transients moved from town to town within discrete local areas. The long migratory move—except for foreign immigrants—was rare. More typically, transients circulated among towns within a ten-mile radius. It is important to distinguish between localized mobility among rural and urban (or seaport) towns. Major population sources such as Boston or Salem, with their large and diverse migratory streams, drew transients from distances greater than ten miles. Of the transients entering Boston and Salem, however, about one-half were from within ten miles.[19]

In contrast to the urban areas, two rural Middlesex County towns, Cambridge and Chelmsford, received most of their transients from within ten miles (see Table 7). With its close proximity to Boston, Cambridge was like a way station for transients. Three-fourths of Cambridge's transients came from within ten miles, and a third were from nearby Boston. Boston's transient migration stream seemed to feed directly into Cambridge, as a procession of migrants—many of foreign birth—paused briefly but moved on. Chelmsford, located outside of a large migration stream, experienced even fewer long-distance transients than Cambridge. Indeed, the county boundaries of Middlesex were as useful a guide to the extent of localized mobility into Chelmsford as the ten-mile radius (72 percent from within the county vs. 64 percent from within ten miles). Ultimately, the ten-mile radius provides the most useful measure of transiency migration. The nearer a town was to a major population stream, the more likely it was that the transient would cross a political boundary. Even during the transition from a traditional to a modern society, there was a pattern of rural to urban migration. Artisans, for example, were probably "pulled" across political boundaries to better opportunities; unskilled laborers may have been "pushed" from their jobs by poor working conditions or a declining economy.

Transiency thus reflected important but limited geographic mobility, which followed from frequently intense poverty and physical hardship. Constables and clerks conveyed a sense of poverty in some cases from which escape was almost impossible. William Pickett, for example, had been a prisoner in Canada during the French and Indian War. After suffering hardships of war and captivity, he returned to Springfield without even sufficient clothing. The London-born Pickett had been a servant before his capture during the war.[20]

Given the high proportions of single transients, it is plausible to suggest that many transients were ex-servants. Servitude of whites in Massachusetts usually was not permanent. At the end of their terms of service, men and women were often in their early twenties and ready to begin a new "stage" in their personal and economic growth. For example, over one-fifth of the privates from Essex County who served in the French and Indian War in 1758 were servants. For some, the experience of travelling to other parts of New England during military service may have opened up hitherto unknown opportunities for settlement. One such private, Daniel Buteman from Beverly, eventually appeared on the tax lists there, married a local woman and out-migrated.[21] The case of Buteman is but one example; the important point is that migration and military service were tied to improved economic opportunities for young ex-servants such as Buteman.

Others were less fortunate. Benjamin Baley, his wife, and their three children required poor relief from Topsfield in 1762. Baley bound himself to some Topsfield inhabitants who failed to fulfill their obligations, leaving him without a job, any form of income, and dependent upon the town.[22] Transients such as Baley, encumbered by economic responsibilities to the towns in which they settled, were taxed just as other inhabitants but lacked the ability to pay their shares. Appearance on an eighteenth-century tax list implied neither wealth nor residential stability. Peter Frost, for one, made an extreme choice when he was unable to solve his continuing problems of poverty and personal care. Frost, an Ipswich laborer, bound himself for life in 1700 to William Cogwell, Jr.[23]

Sickness plagued some transients. Reports of clerks commonly referred not only to their poverty but also ill health. The death of transients in unfamiliar towns was common; Samuel Graffam, for example, of Harpswell fell sick in Topsham and died there. In particular, young children were extremely vulnerable to the ardors of repeated migration. Jane Wing, a single mother, lost one of her three children in Bridgewater and the town reluctantly absorbed the cost of the burial.[24] The rigors of transiency—poverty, constant mobility, poor health, the inability to work, and few alternatives for improvement—confronted at least some of the transients of eighteenth-century Massachusetts with a circle of poverty which was difficult to break. Widows, the aged, children, and the mentally ill were most vulnerable to the conditions of transiency.

One ex-servant who fell into distress was Elizabeth Nicholson Stimson. Her history—brief as it is to us—reads like a microcosm of the transient's existence.[25] Elizabeth was born in Salem in 1775 but moved to Andover with her family in 1779. When she was fifteen or sixteen years old, Elizabeth left her family and worked as a "maid servant" for eight years, until 1798, primarily in Middleton but also in Reading. She lived on her wages, completed the term of service, and returned to Salem to live with her aunt. After a few months, she moved again, this time back to her father's home in Andover. There she lived until she married in 1799 at the age of twenty-four. With her husband, probably an itinerant mariner, she lived in Salem and bore three children until the entire family required poor relief in 1807. Elizabeth Stimson's mobility patterns seem typical of eighteenth-century Massachusetts: completely localized within a discrete geographical area. She married at an average age, but only after completing eight years as a servant. Precisely why she and her family required poor relief was not clear, but they, like hundreds of others, turned to the town for assistance in increasing numbers during the eighteenth century. Their ability to cope with poverty and illness depended in part on the institutional responses of the towns, the counties, and the General Court to the plight of the transients.

Both the rising numbers of transients and their economic dependency prompted institutions in eighteenth-century Massachusetts to develop new solutions to social welfare and control. During this transitional period, some continuity in traditional practices of welfare and control remained. But the thrust of the eighteenth-century response to the new class of transient poor was away from the seventeenth-century practices.

The seventeenth-century background of the institutional control of transients (as distinct from welfare) presents an incomplete record, but two themes emerge from the archives of the towns. First, the towns regulated very carefully the admission of new members. Viewed in this sense, close scrutiny of all types of migrants functioned to monitor the quality of potential townsmen and women in order to achieve a cohesive social order.[26] In addition to controlling the quality of new inhabitants, the regulation of transients was rooted in a suspicion of their possible-criminal acts. Salem, for example, did not permit Indians in the town except during daylight hours, and constables were directed by the Selectmen to view as suspicious "night walkers" and others who were awake at unreasonable hours.[27] The most dangerous transients, often called vagabonds, required more specific public control. Persons who were unable to give "a good and satisfactory account of their wandering up and down" were included within this category.[28] They were subject to corporal punishment for their wanderings and returned to their legal residences. In this case, banishment was used because no police force existed which could maintain effective control over the more dangerous transients.

The second rationale for social control was economic; towns tried to minimize transiency in order to avoid responsibilities of poor relief. Theoretically, those persons most likely to require poor relief—foreign immigrants, ex-servants, the wandering poor, and the sick—could gain legal inhabitancy by residing for a specific length of time. Once a needy person was settled, his welfare was normally provided through families.[29] But the seventeenth-century towns took measures to prevent things from going this far. Ipswich, for example, regulated the flow of transients in a 1699 town law because such persons "may prove burdensome in several respects to the town." An earlier law in Wenham required a security bond from transients, while Salem sought to protect itself from economic burdens by permitting two joiners to enter the town in 1661 only because they had secure employment.[30] Employment defused the threat of poor relief, particularly if the transient was a servant and responsible to a master.

Local institutions monitored the activities of transients as well. Seventeenth-century churches and schools limited their participants to personally familiar inhabitants, as opposed to transients. In the 1640s, the elders of the church at Salem advised the newly formed Wenham Church to admit only those individuals "known [personally] to some of the congregation to be in Covenant elsewhere." In the small seventeenth-century communities, where relationships were conducted on a face-to-face basis, the distinction between personally familiar individuals and those without connections within the community was an important boundary between transients and residents. Ipswich went so far as to distinguish formally between the family and friends of town residents and unwelcome "strangers" who were outside of those networks. Even if transients lived side-by-side with local inhabitants, town institutions separated the transient. In Salem, transients could send their children to the local school master, but only at a fee of twice that of full inhabitants.[31]

While most of the evidence indicates that transients in seventeenth-century Massachusetts towns were treated with varying degrees of suspicion, it must be noted that the practice of geographic mobility was also an accepted one. Cambridge acknowledged the passage of travellers through that town by giving permission to Andrew Belcher in 1653 "to sell beer and bread for [the] entertainment of strangers and the good of the town." Such licensing was not uncommon. Similarly, the General Court recognized the status of the nonresident by creating special laws and courts to handle some of their financial and legal situations.[32] While geographic movement was a normal part of the life of some towns, particularly seaports such as Boston, transients held an ambiguous position—neither totally accepted nor completely rejected.

In most towns during the eighteenth century, resident dependents still received care in individual families. For dependents without families or close relatives, the usual practice was for Selectmen or overseers of the poor to pay residents for boarding disabled or indigent persons. Often dependents performed small household chores if physically able. Mary Cue, of Wenham, agreed "to keep" Aaron Jones for one year in 1745, a standard length of time for this contractual service. Her duties included providing Jones with food, "both in sickness and in health," as well as mending his clothes. For these services, the town paid her about four pounds and absorbed all medical expenses. By 1788 in Wenham, the care of local dependents remained with individual families but the town took steps to rationalize the economics of poor relief. Placement of dependents occurred through bidding, with the poor going to the family with the lowest bid. Wenham obtained care but at minimal public cost.[33]

Assistance of local dependents was an integral part of life in the Massachusetts towns, but these functions were performed with varying degrees of success and motives. On the one hand, care was extended to nonresidents such as widow Mercy Fiske, who entered Wenham without permission of the Selectmen in 1694. They nevertheless paid for a doctor and nurse to care for her.[34] Similarly, the smaller agricultural towns such as Manchester, Topsfield, and Wenham agreed to raise money to donate to the poor of Boston during the Revolution.[35]

On the other hand, disputes between towns and between individuals and towns over the responsibility for the care of the poor were common. The poor law of 1794 attempted to alleviate some of these questions of care by providing poor relief of up to three months for all persons. Indeed, one of the most striking features of the revised poor law was its meticulous provision for resolving disputes between towns. Usually the point of contention was the precise residential origin of the persons in need of care. Gloucester and Wenham, for example, disagreed over the legal residence of an "idiot boy" named Nathan Rolings, with Wenham claiming that he was brought into the town illegally.[36] The plight of Rolings, who required some form of permanent care, suggests that social welfare by families in colonial Massachusetts also had its problematic side. One can easily imagine a boy like Rolings having been buffeted from town to town and family to family.

Even families did not always care for their own relatives who were in need. Wenham and Beverly had to negotiate a contract in order to force a nonresident son to care for his widowed mother. Also, the overseers of the poor of Marblehead petitioned the Court of General Sessions of the Peace in 1752 to force the relatives of two "aged" women to care for them.[37] Avoidance of familial responsibility, while not the usual practice, clearly was a part of the colonial experience.

With overseers of the poor empowered to bind out transients as well as children, social welfare and social control converged. In both rural and urban towns, overseers bound children of the poor and idle into service. Boston's and Wenham's overseers turned naturally to the servant and apprenticeship system. Children as well as adult transients received food, shelter, clothing, perhaps some form of training, and varying degrees of emotional relationships.[38] What must be understood here, though, was the conjunction of family life and its values and the community's resolution of economic dependency through the labor system. Not only did overseers minimize their relief expenses; they maximized social order by dispersing potential transients into the community.

Another alternative—formal institutionalization—was not used extensively in Massachusetts until the early nineteenth century. But the practice of grouping dependents under the same roof existed throughout the eighteenth century. Early forms of institutionalization were found not only in large population centers such as Boston or Salem; small agricultural towns such as Manchester, Wenham, and Ipswich also experimented with group housing.[39] Known as a workhouse or poorhouse, the typical eighteenth-century institution frequently housed the local poor and transients together. Also, towns combined the use of houses for transients and the poor with family welfare. As early as 1719, Ipswich built a poorhouse but in 1734 recommended that the poor be placed in private homes and employed outside. The use of workhouses for both the housing and employment of "idle and indigent" persons became widespread enough in Massachusetts by 1750 to require the General Court to regulate their operations. This law permitted the housing of poor, vagrant, and idle persons because all were deemed socially harmful.[40]

Transients who did not work had long been a source of intense concern to the General Court. The court labelled transient vagrants as disruptive persons, accusing them of luring children and servants away from their "callings and employments." As early as 1682, the court singled out Boston as a haven for "idle persons in families as well as single persons."[41] Transient vagrants who required specific controls were not only perceived as bad in themselves but as menaces to others and to the social order. This control was not confined to the large eastern towns. The General Court passed a special act at the end of the eighteenth century for the removal of vagrants and "strolling poor people" from the District of Marshpee on Cape Cod. Marshpee, according to the court, had become a place of shelter for the transient poor, and was populated primarily by Indians and blacks.[42] And generally the more traditional forms of social welfare and control which relied on personal familiarity and residential continuity provided a stark contrast to the needs of a growing class of transient poor during the eighteenth century. Despite the continuities of care on a local level, the more complex and routine legal mechanisms of the eighteenth century represented a shift from traditional approaches to welfare and control.

As the eighteenth century progressed, the control of transiency depended less on each town as a unique social entity and more on the legal administration of a routine system of welfare and control. The customary statutory settlement laws before 1739 permitted a legal settlement if an individual resided in a town for a specified number of months. After 1739, residency requirements stiffened. Legal residency required the agreement of the town meeting or the Selectmen; even the payment of taxes did not create a de facto form of legal residence.[43] In practice, the control of the movement and settlement of eighteenth-century transients was an integral part of the social order. The granting of poor relief, the laws of settlement, and the practice of warning transients to leave town were interrelated aspects of the legal structure employed by towns in Massachusetts to preserve their social order.

Who held the responsibility for discovering the presence of transients and informing them that they had to leave a particular town? This important question of the legal responsibility for the detection of transients changed over the course of the eighteenth century. The purpose of the settlement and poor-relief laws—the social control of unwanted persons—remained substantially the same, but the methods for dealing with transients were transformed. While each town originally was accountable for discovery and notification, by the end of the eighteenth century the town no longer had the sole responsibility for transients in its midst. By focusing closely on the process of discovery and the burden of notification of the warnings-out system, we can ascertain the shifting legal relationships between the transients, the towns, and the county courts.

In 1692, the Province of Massachusetts enacted a settlement law which provided that persons not legally warned out of a town within three months became inhabitants, and entitled to poor relief.[44] This statute was a more formalized statement of seventeenth-century settlement laws passed by individual towns; however, it added several features to the legal process of the control of transiency and of poor relief. First, the burden of discovering the presence of transients was placed on the towns themselves. Eager to avoid poor relief, warnings were returned by towns to their county courts as proof that the town had warned out all transients. These procedures meant that the costs of the discovery of transients and the legal notification of their presence became functions of the town governments and secondarily of the county courts. In most towns, populations were small and transients easily identifiable. But in more populous towns, or those with a greater turnover of new persons such as Boston and Salem, identification of transients required more than the customary reliance on the face-to-face encounters of the agricultural villages. As early as 1670, the Salem Selectmen hired Thomas Oliver to go to each house once a month to inquire about the presence of "strangers."[45]

During the late 1720s and 1730s, the General Court altered the settlement and poor-relief laws by shifting the burden of discovery of the transients from the towns themselves to the local inhabitants who provided them with food and shelter.[46] Called "entertainment" laws, these statutes provided that transients could not remain in a particular town longer than twenty days without special permission from that town.

Inhabitants who housed transients were required to give the town clerk a written description of the transient's personal characteristics or be subject to a forty-shilling fine for noncompliance. As a device for the control of transiency and reduction of poor relief, warnings out were used contemporaneously with the "entertainment" laws. The former prevented the transient from becoming a legal resident; the latter provided a source of indemnity against the poor relief of transients. This dual form of control regulated not only the transients but also cautioned local inhabitants before they rented rooms to transients.

The operation of this law was straightforward and local inhabitants seem to have cooperated. For example, in 1738, Richard Dodge, a lifelong resident of Wenham, notified the Selectmen that he had "taken in" Thomas Colwell, his wife, and their three children. The Colwell family migrated to Wenham from New Hampshire, were given a dwelling house by Dodge, and probably hired as servants. Because this family was employed, they were exempted from the twenty-day restriction. It was not unusual for Dodge to hire a servant family. Married in 1724, Dodge's wife Mary gave birth to seven children by 1738—but only one was alive by the end of that year. Without maturing children in an agricultural economy, Richard Dodge was labor poor and in a position to need hired help for his farm.[47]

By 1767, the General Court removed the burden of discovery of transients from the towns and their inhabitants alike, placing it directly on the transients themselves. Instead of relying on local constables to warn transients through the county courts, the 1767 statute required all transients to inform the Selectment of their presence as they entered a town. Responsibility for being a transient came to rest with each migrant; status as a nonresident meant that persons were to submit themselves voluntarily to physical removal back to their towns of legal residence.[48]

Known transients were removed on authority of a warrant from a justice of the peace. Constables secured transients by warrants, and returned them from town to town until the transients reached their legal residences. If possible, the transient paid for the cost of this removal; otherwise, the town of legal residence bore the expense.[49] The General Court absorbed the costs of persons to destinations outside of Massachusetts. One important exception to this law exempted apprentices and servants from removal if attached to a master or family; the labor system remained intact while physical removal controlled potentially harmful transients. An important implication of this statute was the decline of the system of warnings out processed through the county court. Legal notification that transients were nonresidents was no longer necessary under the 1767 law.

Not until the 1790s did the General Court fully rewrite the settlement and poor-relief laws in operation during the middle years of the eighteenth century. Indeed, it seems as though the Revolution and its aftermath temporarily interrupted—rather than caused—revision of the policies regulating transients. Drawing on the principles of the 1767 statute, the revision of 1794 provided for an even more routinized procedure for the removal of transients.[50] The 1767 statue in effect had eliminated the warning out as a device for controlling transiency, but some towns continued the practice both through the county court and local overseers of the poor. However, the 1794 statute specifically ended the warnings-out system, substituting a comprehensive procedure for the return of transients to their legal residences. With this added power of removal came expanded responsibilities; each town had to provide care and immediate relief for all persons regardless of resident status for a period of up to three months.

The shifting burdens of legal responsibility for the transients of eighteenth-century Massachusetts culminated in this statute of 1794. Poor transient persons became fully integrated into the legal structure but not the social order. Towns became legally responsible to the transients' need for care; yet these same towns also could employ removal procedures practiced earlier in the century. The difference was that the new procedures for removal provided the most efficient and least expensive method of removing transients and reducing the work of the county courts. Transients received some increased procedural rights, such as an appeal to the court for common pleas to contest removal, but the statute focused most extensively on the procedural aspects of removal, the control of dependent persons, and the arbitration of disputes among towns over questions of legal residences of transients. This revised law of 1794 clearly revealed continuities with past practices, but it also reflected divergences, particularly more precise, rational forms for the administration of poor relief. For while the 1794 poor law was a "legal institutionalization" of the transient poor, it also, paradoxically, maintained a resolution of dependency which relied heavily on the family.

By the end of the eighteenth century, local systems of welfare and control ultimately became integrated into the larger structure of Massachusetts society. The implications of this process of integration (by the General Court, the county courts, and the towns) suggest that the familiar communal assumptions of life in the premodern town experienced severe testing under the reality of increased transiency migration and economic stratification. Late eighteenth-century Massachusetts society was a dynamic one in transition; it was not a fixed, flat, "colonial" one. David Rothman, in his recent analysis of nineteenth-century penal and welfare practices, uses a "noninstitutional" counterpoint based on a motionless view of colonial America as a contrast to the nineteenth-century society which "discovered" the asylum.[51] This leaves the impression that before 1800, social welfare was an unchanging, idyllic blend of assistance from one's family and neighbors. Rothman's point about the development of institutionalization during the nineteenth century is astute; the counterpoint, however, does not explain transitional change within the history of premodern systems of welfare and control. Rather than stressing a dichotomy between "colonial" and "Jacksonian" policies of social welfare and control, we must recognize a transitional period from the traditional forms to the more modern ones of the nineteenth century.

The eighteenth-century legal process of social control activity involved both the town and the county court. The role of the county court, however, did not supersede that of the town; the two interacted defensively in attempts to monitor transient migration, minimize poor relief, and preserve the social order. The decline in the use of warnings in 1767 and their disappearance from the revised poor law of 1794 as a technique of social and economic control represent part of the rationalization of the legal sanctions on transiency in Massachusetts. These more predictable, routine methods of limiting the economic and social impact of transients are characteristic of more modern societies.[52]

Social solidarity did not disappear as the towns shared their political authority with the county courts, but the boundaries of social interaction were redefined.[53] Localism, or the "Town born" in Bentley's words, was no longer a guarantee of homogeneity. The emerging social order in late eighteenth-century Massachusetts required support from general laws which defined transients as deviants from the cultural and economic norms of family life, residential stability, and secure employment. Banishment could no longer satisfy the needs of a transitional society. Increasing levels of transiency migration and reciprocal legal means of control indicate that premodern Massachusetts had passed from an explicitly communal society to a more complex, modern one. This transition was by no means complete by 1800. Yet the tensions of the structural change and legal adjustments pointed more in the direction of modern nineteenth-century America than toward communal continuity.

Notes

Financial support for the research cited below was provided by an Irving and Rose Crown Fellowship, Brandeis University, and the National Science Foundation, grant #35051. I am indebted to Linda Bissell, Michael Hindus, Allan Kulikoff, Elizabeth Pleck, and David Reed for criticisms made during revision of this essay. Valuable suggestions for changes were made by John Demos and David Fischer. Parts of this analysis employed computer programs written by Joseph H. Pleck.

1. The term "transient" appeared in eighteenth-century court records to describe unwanted persons. Other variations on the same term were "non-inhabitant," "vagrant," and "low and poor." In this essay, I have used "transient" to describe all unwanted persons. Most of these persons were of low economic status, including the "poor," the "near poor," and persons of working-class status. Examples of the terminology used to characterize unwanted transients may be found in the Court of General Sessions of the Peace, Hampshire County, Clerk of Courts Office, Northampton, Massachusetts, 1758–62, 247; 1762–64, 49–50, 88, 163.

2. William Bentley, *The Diary of William Bentley* (Salem, Mass.: The Essex Institute, 1905–14), vol. 2, 188.

3. Several recent historical analyses of the trend towards modernization have appeared: Kenneth A. Lockridge, "Land, Population, and the Evolution of New England Society, 1630–1800," *Past and Present* 39 (1968), 62–80; Richard D.

Brown, "Modernization and the Modern Personality in Early America, 1600–1865: A Sketch of a Synthesis," *Journal of Interdisciplinary History* 2 (1972), 201–28; and Lockridge, "Social Change and the Meaning of the American Revolution," *Journal of Social History* 6 (1973), 403–39. Many of the issues of modernization in early American history are discussed in Daniel Scott Smith, "Population, Family and Society in Hingham, Massachusetts, 1635–1880," (Ph.D. dissertation, University of California, Berkeley, 1973).

4. For a general discussion of the changes in legal structures in modernizing societies, see Marc Galanter, "The Modernization of Law," in Myron Weiner, ed., *Modernization: The Dynamics of Growth* (New York: Basic Books, 1966), 153–65.

5. In determining trends of geographic mobility before 1800, in- and out-migration statistics are the most useful because they permit the direct control of mortality. But because source materials are sparse and normally underrecorded, complete measurement of migration for a substantial number of New England towns is not yet possible. In order to circumvent these problems, we must turn to the persistence statistic. As defined here, persistence rates apply to male tax-payers or landholders who appeared on consecutive lists of inhabitants at regularized time intervals. Not pure measures of migration, persistence rates permit us to understand the extent of residential continuity, and by implication, discontinuity.

6. Persistence rates in rural communities, 1800–1890, displayed a much lower range (21 to 59 percent) than in eighteenth-century New England; the range of persistence in nineteenth-century urban communities was also low (30 to 64 percent). The nineteenth-century data are most conveniently summarized in Stephan Thernstrom, *The Other Bostonians: Poverty and Progress in the American Metropolis, 1880–1970* (Cambridge, Mass.: Harvard University Press, 1973), 221–32, Tables 9.1 and 9.2.

7. Population growth in colonial New England came from within, due primarily to low age at marriage, generally uncontrolled fertility practices, and healthy conditions. For a discussion of the growth rate of New England's white population, see Daniel Scott Smith, "The Demographic History of Colonial New England," *Journal of Economic History* 32 (1972), 174–83. The limitations of migration as a means of controlling family and population sizes have been discussed by Nathan Keyfitz, "Migration as a Means of Population Control," *Population Studies* 25 (1971), 63–72. Some Massachusetts towns overtly attempted to rationalize the process of resettlement of younger sons or the generation of revenue from land ownership by petitioning the General Court to expand their boundaries or acquire new land. See petition of 27 November 1729, *Journal of the House of Representatives of*

Massachusetts 9 (1729–31), 134; *Wenham Town Records* (Wenham, Mass., 1940), III, 25; and Thomas Franklin Waters, *Ipswich in the Massachusetts Bay Colony* (Ipswich, Mass.: The Ipswich Historical Society, 1917), vol. 2, 398–401.

8. It is possible that a cyclical pattern of transiency migration occurred within the general secular trend of the eighteenth century. Definitive statements on this issue are difficult to make because of the type of records from which transient migration is drawn. Warnings out were legal actions taken by individual towns, and therefore reflected the values of each town as well as the needs and behavior of transients. Also, transients undoubtedly were warned more than once from nearby towns. This problem of recidivism in legal records further complicates any relationship between cyclical fertility patterns and levels of transiency migration. On cyclical issues in early American history, see P. M. G. Harris, "The Social Crisis of American Leaders: The Demographic Foundations," *Perspectives in American History* 3 (1969), 159–344.

9. About 1770, warnings out processed through the county courts declined because of a change in the statutory law. The 1767 settlement law no longer required notification of the presence of transients. Since this law was slow to take effect, some towns continued to warn transients according to the old practice; see *Massachusetts Acts and Resolves,* vol. 4 (1757–68), 911–12.

10. The youthfulness of migrants in industrial society is well documented; see Henry S. Shryock, Jr., *Population Mobility Within the United States* (Chicago: Community and Family Study Center, University of Chicago, 1964), 346–58; Sidney Goldstein, *Patterns of Mobility, 1910–1950: The Norristown Study* (Philadelphia: University of Pennsylvania Press, 1958), 203–6. But the dominant pattern of migratory young persons, especially males, was found in a preindustrial English village; see R. S. Schofield, "Age-Specific Mobility in an Eighteenth Century Rural English Parish," *Annales de Demographie Historique* (1970), 262–74.

11. The adult sex ratios, that is, the number of men for every 100 women, in 1765 and 1800 in Essex County were 84 and 82 respectively; in Hampshire County, they were 99 and 98. For a delineation of the increasing pressure of population in one Essex County town, see Philip J. Greven, Jr., *Four Generations: Population, Land, and Family in Colonial Andover, Massachusetts* (Ithaca: Cornell University Press, 1970); for a suggestive formulation of the issues of population pressure and land supply, see Lockridge, "Land, Population, and Evolution." The critical issue, however, may not have been a persistent shortage of land, but the problems of transition to new types of agricultural methods as well as increasing commercialization.

12. For example, the proportion of widows taxed in Wenham increased from 3 percent to 8 percent from 1751 to 1761.

13. One witness in a divorce case in Boston testified against a single mother who was a servant, saying that he "got her warned out of Town because she was with child to prevent charge." Suffolk County Court Files, Divorce Cases, No. 129749, 112. I am indebted to Nancy F. Cott for bringing this case to my attention.

14. Daniel Scott Smith and Michael S. Hindus, "Pre-marital Pregnancy in America, 1640–1971: An Overview and Interpretation," *Journal of Interdisciplinary History* 5(Spring 1975), 537–70. Prosecutions for the crime of fornication in Middlesex County during the period 1760–74 accounted for 65 percent of all cases in the Superior and General Sessions Courts; see William E. Nelson, "Emerging Notions of Modern Criminal Law in the Revolutionary Era: An Historical Perspective," *New York University Law Review* 42 (1967), 452. Of course, premarital pregnancy rates and fornication prosecution rates are not identical; they only illustrate the increasing sexual activity of the eighteenth century. What is not clear, however, is if the incidence of prosecution compared favorably with the total pattern of premarital pregnancy.

15. The congestion in Essex County may be seen in its crowded housing patterns. Essex had an average of 7.6 persons per house in 1765, while Hampshire had only 6.7; this difference continued through the century. Yet the average household size was smaller in Essex than in Hampshire. It seems possible that some of this crowding was the result of transients sharing houses with local residents. For the analysis of persons per house and per family, see Philip J. Greven, Jr., "The Average Size of Families and Households in the Province of Massachusetts in 1764 and in the United States in 1790: An Overview," in Peter Laslett and R. Wall eds., *Household and Family in Past Time* (Cambridge, England,: Cambridge University Press, 1972), 545–60; see also Table 5.

16. In order to measure the relationship between transients, population size, and wealth of the towns in Essex and Hampshire Counties, I used a rank-order correlation test. To control for population size, I employed correlations based on per capita number of warnings per town and per capita wealth per town. This test measures the strength of the relationship between two ranked variables. The conclusions in this paragraph and the following are based on the following correlations of per capita wealth during the early 1760s: Spearman's R for Essex County = +.070; for Hampshire County +.456. Population figures for 1765 were taken from Joseph B. Felt, "Statistics of the Population in Massachusetts," *Collections of the American Statistical Association* (Boston, 1845), vol. I, part II: 149, 151, 211–12. Wealth rankings are from the proportion of county taxes assessed for each town within each county; see Court of General Sessions of the Peace, Essex County, 1764–77, 211; Court of General Sessions of the Peace, Hampshire County, 1758–

62; 196. Transients for the period 1760–64 were used in order to provide a sufficient number of transients to rank per town; for sources, see notes to Table 3.

17. On English tramping, see E. J. Hobsbawm, *Labouring Men: Studies in the History of Labour* (New York: Basic Books, 1965), 41–72. For a discussion of vagabonds in Elizabethan England, see A. L. Beier, "Vagrants and the Social Order in Elizabethan England," *Past and Present* 64 (1974), 3–29. For a comparison of the changes in the laws affecting vagrants in England and America, see William J. Chambliss, "A Sociological Analysis of the Law of Vagrancy," *Social Problems* 12 (1964), 67–77. Chambliss argues, incorrectly in my view, that American vagrancy (i.e., transiency) laws were merely adaptations of their English counterparts. This interpretation of similarity fails to take into account the fact that Massachusetts laws were specific reactions to social change within the American experience. Clearly, increased regulation occurred in both England and America; but criminal sanctions against transients were more common in England than in Massachusetts.

18. In Boston, 28 percent of the transients warned in 1791 by the Overseers of the Poor were from foreign countries; 71 percent arrived from towns within Massachusetts. Boston figures are for the total population of transients, not households; see Kulikoff, "The Progress of Inequality in Revolutionary Boston," 400–401, Table X.

19. Of the Salem transients who entered from within Massachusetts, 57 percent came from within ten miles. Forty-six percent of the Massachusetts transients who migrated to Boston were from within ten miles; see ibid., 401, Table X.

20. Court of General Sessions of the Peace, Hampshire County, Massachusetts, 1758–62, 247.

21. Computed from Beverly reconstitution data from Eben Putnam, "Soldiers in the French War from Essex County, 1755–1761," *Essex Institute Historical Collections* 29 (1892), 169–76.

22. *Town Records of Topsfield, Massachusetts* (Topsfield, 1917), vol 2, 217–18, 222, 229.

23. Waters, *Ipswich*, vol. 2, 391–92.

24. *Topsham v. Harpswell, 1 Mass. Reports* 517 (1805); *Bridgewater v. Dartmouth, 4 Mass. Reports* 273 (1808); *Quincy v. Braintree, 5 Mass. Reports* 86 (1809); *Town Records of Topsfield*, vol. 2, 225.

25. *Salem v. Andover, 3 Mass. Reports* 436 (1807).

26. For examples see Waters, *Ipswich*, vol. 2, 386, 392–93; *Wenham Town Records*, vol. 1, 5; *The Records of the Town of Cambridge, 1630–1703* (Cambridge: City Council, 1901), 24, 108, 155, 193; *Town Records of Salem, Massachusetts* (Salem, 1913), vol. 2, 112; S. A. Bates, ed., *Records of the Town of Braintree, 1640–1703*

(Randolph, Mass.: D. H. Huxford, 1886), vol. 2, 19–20; Josiah Henry Benton, *Warning Out in New England* (Boston: W. B. Clarke, 1911). Various types of controls of access to the community were used: Braintree limited land ownership and sale to approved persons, while Cambridge even fined one of its own inhabitants for "entertaining" his son.

27. *Town Records of Salem,* vol. 2, 303–4.

28. *The Charters and General Laws of the Colony and Province of Massachusetts Bay* (Boston, 1814), ch. 99 (1662), 200. David J. Rothman, *The Discovery of the Asylum* (Boston: Little, Brown, 1971), 1–29, provides a discussion of some of these issues.

29. For discussions of the family as an institution of social welfare in seventeenth-century Massachusetts, see John Demos, *A Little Commonwealth: Family Life in Plymouth Colony* (New York: Oxford University Press, 1970) and Edmund S. Morgan, *The Puritan Family: Religion and Domestic Relations in Seventeenth-Century New England* (New York: Harper, 1966).

30. Waters, *Ipswich,* vol. 2, 392–93; *Wenham Town Records* (Wenham, Mass., 1930), vol. 1, 5; *Town Records of Salem,* vol. 2, 50.

31. Diary of John Fiske, 1637–75 (typescript copy), 44–49, Essex Institute, Salem, Massachusetts; Waters, *Ipswich,* vol. 2, 393; *Town Records of Salem,* vol. 2, 50.

32. *Records of the Town of Cambridge,* 100; *Charters and General Laws,* ch. 92 (1641), 191–92; ch. 21 (1665), 72–73; ch. 31 (1639), 91.

33. *Wenham Town Records,* vol. 3, 81–82; vol. 4, 81, 89. The Selectmen of Worcester also expressed concern that the poor of that town were placed "to the best advantage and Saving to the Town." *Worcester Town Records, 1784–1800* (Worcester, 1890), 146.

34. *Wenham Town Records,* vol. 1, 135–59.

35. Ibid., vol. 4, 11; *Town Records of Topsfield,* vol. 2, 344; *Manchester Town Records, 1718–1769* (Salem, 1889), vol. 2, 147.

36. *Wenham Town Records,* vol. 3, 99; see also ibid., vol. 4, 160, for another example of conflict over the legal residence of a transient.

37. Ibid., vol. 4, 80; Court of General Sessions of the Peace, Essex County, Massachusetts, petition dated December 1752, 115.

38. A systematic study of the apprenticing of children in eighteenth-century Boston reveals that one-half of all children bound between 1734 and 1805 were between the ages of five and nine years, while the median age was nine. Potential transients or dependents, these children were apprenticed to families both within and outside Boston. A small rural town such as Wenham also apprenticed children, but with less of a geographic dispersion than Boston. See Lawrence W. Towner, "The Indentures of Boston's Poor Apprentices: 1734–1805," *Publication of the*

Colonial Society of Massachusetts 42 (Boston, 1966), 417–68; and *Wenham Town Records,* vol. 4, 196–98, 206, 213.

39. See *Town Records of Manchester,* vol. 2, 105, 114; *Wenham Town Records,* vol. 3, 188; *Records of the Town of Braintree,* 236, 281–82.

40. Waters, *Ipswich,* vol. 2, 396–97; *Mass. Acts and Resolves,* vol. 3 (1742–56): ch. 12, 108–11.

41. *Charters and General Laws,* ch. 99 (1662), 200; ch. 53 (1682), 128; see also *Mass. Acts and Resolves,* vol. 3 (1742–56): ch. 43, 926; and ibid. (1792–93), ch. 59, 479–93.

42. *Mass. Acts and Resolves* (1796–97), ch. 23, 52–53.

43. Ibid., vol. 2 (1715–41): ch. 9, 995.

44. Ibid., vol. 1 (1692–1714): ch. 28, 64–68.

45. *Town Records of Salem,* vol. 2: 112.

46. *Mass. Acts and Resolves,* vol. 2 (1715–41): ch. 6, 386; ch. 8, 616; ch. 9, 994–95; ch. 16, 835–36.

47. *Wenham Town Records,* vol. 3, 40, and reconstitution data. For other examples of compliance and enforcement of "entertainment" laws, see "Persons 'Warned Out' of the Town of Newbury, 1734–76," *Essex Institute Historical Collections* 69 (1933), 36.

48. *Mass. Acts and Resolves,* vol. 4 (1757–68): ch. 17, 911–12.

49. Examples of physical removal may be found in *Worcester Town Records,* 66, 81, 91, 121, 174–75; and *Wenham Town Records,* vol. 4, 57.

50. *Mass. Acts and Resolves* (1792–93), ch. 59, 479–93.

51. Rothman, *The Discovery of the Asylum,* especially 3–56.

52. For example, the "instrumental conception" of early nineteenth-century American law fits this pattern of predictability; see Morton J. Horwitz, "The Emergence of an Instrumental Conception of American Law, 1780–1820." *Perspectives in American History* 5 (1971), 287–326.

53. Michael Zuckerman, *Peaceable Kingdoms: New England Towns in the Eighteenth-Century* (New York: Knopf, 1970), has made the argument that the towns were the centers of a broad range of political, legal, moral, and social authority. His analysis has been faulted by legal historians in particular, who have argued implicitly and explicitly that there was more conflict and court participation in the affairs of eighteenth-century New England towns; see L. Kinvin Wroth, "Possible Kingdoms: The New England Town from the Perspective of Legal History," *American Journal of Legal History* 15 (1971), 318–30; and David Grayson Allen, "The Zuckerman Thesis and the Process of Legal Nationalization in Provincial Massachusetts," *William and Mary Quarterly* 39 (1972), 443–60, and Zuckerman's reply in ibid., 461–68. It seems to me, however, that we should not frame the question in terms of power located in either the town or the court system; to do so means any answer would have to overlook the complexity of shifting trends in authority and conflict. The more likely explanation is that which is suggested below: that power was becoming shared as demographic and economic changes posed shifts in the basic social order.

Priscilla Ferguson Clement

The Transformation of the Wandering
Poor in Nineteenth-Century Philadelphia

In the early nineteenth century Americans called them vagrants and, after the Civil War, tramps, but quintessentially they were the wandering poor. Men and women, young and old, black and white, native and foreign-born, they drifted in and out of farm communities and cities across America seeking work. Not surprisingly, expanding urban centers which offered job seekers a variety of opportunities, especially in manufacturing and construction, served as magnets for the nation's wandering poor. Such a center was Philadelphia, the third largest city in the country in the last century. With its diversified economy, it attracted a varied population, including many of the tramping fraternity. By definition the wandering poor are among history's most inarticulate classes and therefore pose a particular problem for the historian who wishes to study them. However, for the city of Philadelphia, which retains excellent records of its public institutions, it is possible to study those wandering poor who came in contact with city asylums such as the Prison, the House of Correction, the Almshouse, and the police station.[1]

On 4 February 1808, a constable apprehended Sara Bird, brought her before a city magistrate, and charged her with vagrancy. The constable then conducted her to the Walnut Street Prison which, from 1784 to 1821, was Philadelphia's only prison; it housed both convicted criminals and vagrants like Sara Bird. There she remained for exactly one month, the typical prison term for most vagrants in antebellum Philadelphia. On 14 February 1823, when Peter Prince was taken into custody on similar charges, he was committed by the mayor for a one-month term to the new Arch Street Prison at Broad and Arch Streets, which had opened six months earlier. This prison accommodated vagrants and untried prisoners. It had been constructed in the depression years of the early 1820s when members of both the Board of Inspectors of the Prison and the Philadelphia Prison Society (a volunteer prison reform group) grew alarmed about the extraordinary number of wandering poor in Philadelphia and demanded a separate facility for vagrants.[2] However, by the early 1830s overcrowding at and deterioration of both the Walnut and Arch Street prisons prompted officials to authorize the construction of a new prison in the "style . . . of the castles of the middle ages" one mile south of the city at Moyamensing. In 1835–36 it became the city's place of imprisonment for both convicted felons and vagrants.[3]

Neither Sara Bird at Walnut Street, nor Peter Prince at Arch Street, nor any of the vagrants sent to Moyamensing were forced to do much labor during their prison terms. In fact, Josiah Flynt, a writer turned tramp, reported that Pennsylvania jails had a reputation for being comfortable places of abode where little work was required of inmates.[4] Thus when Moyamensing became somewhat congested in the 1850s and 1860s and Philadelphia prison authorities resolved to build a larger city asylum exclusively for vagrant, drunk, and disorderly persons, they determined to alter the benevolent image of Pennsylvania asylums for vagrants by making the new House of Correction a place of punishment. All vagrants apprehended in the city from 1874 through the rest of the century were sent to the House of Correction, where they were often treated quite harshly. For example, in 1876 inmate Thomas Stafford was forced to work quarrying stone and pumping water even though he had both a fractured collarbone and a hernia. Another inmate had a revolver put to his head by a guard who threatened to shoot if the inmate refused to do as he was told.[5]

Throughout the nineteenth century, not only the prisons and House of Correction but also the Almshouse admitted some vagrants. Wandering poor persons could be dispatched to any of these asylums by a magistrate, the mayor, a poor relief official, or they could come of their own accord. Typically, authorities sent able-bodied, healthy vagrants to the prisons or to the House of Correction and committed ailing or handicapped tramps to the Almshouse.[6]

Figure 1:   Vagrants per Thousand in Philadelphia Prison,
House of Correction, 1805–99

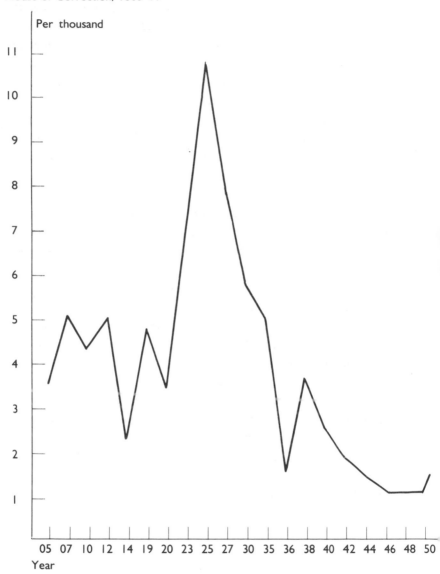

Note: City population figures between censuses were determined by linear interpolation.

Sources: Figures for 1805–22 and 1828–35 are drawn from PCA, Philadelphia County,
Prison, Vagrancy Docket. I counted the number admitted each year and then reduced that
number by 33 percent to account for recidivism. (Samples from various years, taken by using
the alphabetical index at the front of some volumes, indicated that 33 percent was the typical

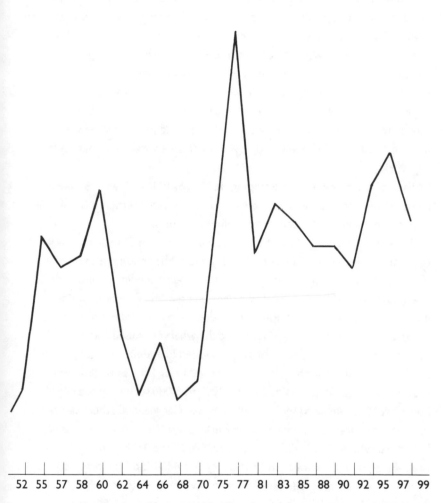

52 55 57 58 60 62 64 66 68 70 75 77 81 83 85 88 90 92 95 97 99

recidivism figure.) Figures for 1823–27 are from Samuel Hazard, *Hazard's Register of Pennsyl-vania* (Philadelphia: W. F. Geddes, 1828), vol. 1, 240, 244. Figures for 1836–71 are from the Prison Inspectors, *Annual Reports* (vagrants only). Figures for 1875–99 are from the Managers of the House of Correction, Annual Reports, in the *Annual Messages of the Mayor of Philadelphia*.

tramps stopped last before moving to the city and probably where many of those leaving stopped first. Were farmers there affluent and in need of farm labor, or were they facing economic constraints which made them unwilling or unable to hire the wanderer in search of a job? (3) Job opportunities in agriculture, construction, and mining elsewhere in the region. Could tramps who left the city be assured of work on one of the state's many wheat farms, or of jobs in canal or railroad building or coal mining? Or were such jobs so scarce as to drive many persons to the city in search of work as well as to hold there many others who might have migrated? (4) The existence of wars and the consequent enlargement of the army and and the navy, which furnished paying jobs to persons who might otherwise have been unemployed and likely to wander about seeking work.

Each of the three eras of tramping, 1805–35, 1836–72, and 1873–99, had a unique conjunction of these four factors which interacted to influence the number of wandering poor in Philadelphia.

Between 1805 and 1835, the number of tramps in Philadelphia was larger than it would be again until the very end of the century because of a combination of economic crises in the city and surrounding countryside. The Embargo of 1807 precipitated a depression in the economy of Philadelphia, which was then profoundly dependent on commerce and trade with other nations. Laboring jobs around the wharves vanished, and sailors searched in vain for berths. Mariners petitioned President Thomas Jefferson for aid "that means may be had to prevent our families beging [sic]." No assistance was forthcoming for the 4,000 to 5,000 seamen in the city.[12] Some left Philadelphia to seek seafaring jobs in Canada, but others stayed on and were joined by many common laborers from New York and Baltimore who found "living was cheaper" in Philadelphia. Eventually, in 1808–9, a construction boom in the city provided jobs for many such men.[13] However, a decade later a more severe depression, which succeeded the Panic of 1819, led to an even larger aggregation of vagrants in the city prisons. This depression came about when American ship captains failed to recapture trade they had lost during the War of 1812 and when American consumers once again were able to purchase European manufactured goods and rejected comparable American products. Philadelphia commercial interests suffered, as did the owners and employees in the many new manufactories erected in the city during the war. Private charity officials were acutely aware of the growing economic distress and in 1821 observed that "the absence of useful employment is the fruitful parent of poverty." In 1824 concerned citizens noted that there were still enormous numbers of hungry and unemployed poor wandering the city streets.[14]

While the city endured several economic downturns in this era, the farming areas immediately adjacent to Philadelphia (Chester, Delaware, Montgomery and Bucks counties) were in grievous economic straits throughout the years in question. During the last third of the eighteenth century, the choicest farm land in these counties had been cleared and divided into the smallest economical-sized farms. The consequent population pressure often led fathers to bequeath land to their eldest sons only (violating the long-held American belief in partible inheritance). Younger sons either rented land, moved west, or migrated east to Philadelphia. Those who became tenant farmers had large families, and by the second decade of the nineteenth century, their children were of age, many of them no doubt on the road seeking work.[15] Moreover, at this time farms in this part of the state were continuously cropped. Farmers rarely practiced soil conservation, nor did they use fertilizers.[16] As a result, many young people emerged from these farm counties near Philadelphia with no land of their own and little opportunity to secure employment on infertile neighboring farms. They swelled the tramping population in Philadelphia. When there were economic crises in the city, these youths and others who were urban born could not move out to local farms and there find jobs. This double economic crunch, in the city and surrounding countryside, inflated the tramping population in Philadelphia from 1805 to 1835.

Still, there were some bright spots in these years. In western Pennsylvania, wheat farming was the foremost enterprise and it was quite profitable, especially during the War of 1812. The diminution of the tramping population in the city in 1813–14 was probably partly due to the plentiful supply of jobs on western Pennsylvania farms, and partly to the war itself, which kept employed persons who might otherwise have wandered through the city in search of work.

However, after the war, during the 1820s, there was an abrupt reduction in farm prices and depression throughout Pennsylvania agriculture. This factor, along with the depression in the city and surrounding countryside, helped to make the whole state in the 1820s a "poor man's land."[17]

In contrast, from the 1830s until the depression of 1873, the agricultural outlook throughout the state brightened. In the counties nearest to Philadelphia (the very same areas from which most of the city's wandering poor came), farmers finally began to use lime, making it possible for them to raise more clover and grass for livestock. They also began to collect manure and apply it to their fields. In consequence, their properties became more fertile and fruitful and they required more farm help.[18] In addition, in the 1830s and 1840s, many new well-paying jobs became available in western Pennsylvania coal mining, as well as in the construction of the Main Line Canal and the Pennsylvania Railroad.[19]

Statewide prosperity helped to hold down the tramping population in Philadelphia from 1836 to 1872. Even during the depression which began in 1837 after the demise of the Second Bank of the United States, the prison vagrant population expanded only slightly in 1838–39 and then declined considerably throughout the rest of the depression which lasted until 1845. In 1842 city newspapers reported that many of the unemployed had departed the city for the "west," probably to take jobs on canals, in coal mines, or on farms where the harvests were "abundant."[20] The recession of 1855 and the depression from 1859–60 did result in a growth in the number of tramps incarcerated, but these increases were not nearly as great as those in the city prison population in the 1820s. Again the reason seems to be that even if jobs were not available in the city, they were in other parts of the state. Moreover, workers enjoyed better access to such employment once the Main Line Canal system opened in 1834 and the Pennsylvania Railroad opened in 1852.

Finally, wars also served to diminish the city's tramping population between 1836 and 1872. The Mexican War of 1848–49 and, most important, the Civil War drew many wanderers off the roads and into army camps instead.

Post–Civil War prosperity ended in 1873 with the failure of Jay Cooke and Company in Philadelphia, which set off a commercial slump in the city which lasted until 1879. Officials noted an alarming accretion in the numbers of unemployed "mechanics and laborers" who, unwilling "to burden their families or friends," committed themselves to the House of Correction during this depression. These same officials were delighted to report that the business revival of 1879 occasioned a drop in admissions, but they lamented that, when depression recurred between 1893 and 1897, commitments to the House of Correction were almost as great as they had ever been previously.[21]

Meanwhile, farm prices took a sudden downturn in 1873 and remained low for the rest of the century. The most astute farmers in the state earned only a 3 percent profit in these years. Two-thirds of Pennsylvania's rural counties lost population—to the West and to Philadelphia as well. When farm jobs were available in these hard times, they paid little.[22]

Thus, the situation in Philadelphia and Pennsylvania mirrored what it had been in the first thirty-five years of the century. Unemployment in both city and countryside drove many to tramping and thousands into seeking aid from Philadelphia welfare authorities. The years 1876 and 1877 were particularly grim because the centennial celebration in Philadelphia attracted many out-of-work farm laborers to the city, where they found a depressed economy and few jobs. Meanwhile, the Philadelphia police pursued an aggressive policy of rounding up every sleeper on every park bench to keep the city "clean" for the country's one-hundredth birthday.[23] As a result, the number incarcerated in the new House of Correction expanded abruptly, a sobering salute to a century of independence.

Those poor who wandered in and out of Philadelphia in the nineteenth century were an ethnically diverse lot. (See Table 1.) A sample of tramps in the city Almshouse between 1822 and 1840 reveals that 24 percent were foreign-born—a sizable number for a city where in 1830 only 10 percent of the population had been born abroad.[24] From the 1870s until the end of the century, the proportion of foreign-born among city vagrants remained roughly twice that of the proportion of foreign-born in Philadelphia itself.

Table 1: Sexual, Racial, and Ethnic Composition of Vagrant Population in Philadelphia Prison, House of Correction, Nineteenth Century, Selected Years

Year	# W. Male	# B. Male	# W Fem.	# B. Fem.	% Fem.	% Blk.	% F. Born[a]
1823	256	250	200	200	44	51	—
1825	360	400	335	380	49	53	—
1826	437	240	220	313	46	46	—
1847	161	7	143	35	51	12	—
1848	238	26	138	21	37	11	—
1853	439	12	350	28	46	4.7	—
1858	1594	55	970	96	39	5.5	—
1861	1300	65	1246	53	48	4.4	—
1863	545	33	1152	53	67	4.8	—
1865	453	18	538	26	54	4.2	—
1868	580	26	478	9	45	3.2	—
1871	634	15	399	11	39	2.0	—
1876	6302	175	1489	108	20	3.5	48
1882	4217	135	1291	44	23	3.1	43
1887	4124	224	1371	122	26	5.9	38
1889	3526	168	896	77	21	5.2	47
1895	5866	486	1008	186	16	8.9	34
1899	5582	505	919	131	15	9.1	30

(a) The percentage of foreign-born vagrants was not officially recorded until the Managers of the House of Correction initiated their annual reports in the 1870s.

Sources: Figures for 1823–26 are in *Hazard's Register*, vol. 1, 240, 244. Figures for 1847–71 are in Prison Inspectors, *Annual Reports*. Figures for 1875–99 are in Managers of the House of Correction, Annual Reports, in the *Annual Messages of the Mayor of Philadelphia*.

(See Table 2.) Of course, many other vagrants in city institutions may have been the sons and daughters of persons born abroad. In the absence of recorded data on parental birthplaces the number of such second generation Americans among vagrants is difficult to calculate.

The Irish were, throughout the century, Philadelphia's biggest immigrant group. Their agrarian origins and their lack of marketable skills led the men to seek out farm, canal, or railroad laboring jobs and to migrate back to the city principally in the winter or when farm prices were low or construction jobs scarce. Irish men and women constituted five-sixths of the foreign-born vagrant population in the Almshouse between 1822 and 1840 and 63 percent of the immigrants in the House of Correction in

1875. Germans, Englishmen, and Scotsmen made up the remainder of foreign-born vagrants in these city asylums at this time.[25]

In the nineteenth century, not only were there numerous immigrant tramps in Philadelphia, so too was there a substantial number of female wandering poor. (See Table I.) Between 1823 and 1861 women constituted almost one-half of the vagrant population in Philadelphia, and, in the Civil War years, over 50 percent. Prison officials attributed this growth to the war itself which, while providing work for many formerly unemployed male tramps, also separated husbands from wives and led many women, "deprived of the control of their ordinary protectors," to "vagrancy and crime."[26] Yet throughout the antebellum years, the percentage of women tramps in Philadelphia was remarkably high; it was roughly equal to the proportion of women in the total state population. In an era when women's "separate sphere" was presumably in the home, it is peculiar to find so many of them on the road.[27]

Perhaps there were numerous women in Philadelphia asylums for va-

Table 2: Blacks and Foreign-Born: Proportion in Philadelphia and in Philadelphia Vagrant Population for Selected Years

Year	% Black in Prison or House of Correction	Year	% Black in City	Year	% For. Born in House of Correction	Year	% For. Born in City
1823	51	1820	8.8				
1826	46	1830	8.3				
1850	5.0	1850	4.8				
1860	3.0	1860	3.9				
1870	2.0	1870	3.3				
1881	4.0	1880	3.6	1879	43	1880	24.2
1891	4.6	1890	3.8				
1899	9.1	1900	4.8	1899	30	1900	22.8

Sources: The sources for the percentages of blacks and foreign-born in the Prison and House of Correction are the same as cited in Table I above. For the percentages of blacks and foreign-born in the city see Table I, 465 in Theodore Hershberg et al., "A Tale of Three Cities: Blacks, Immigrants, and Opportunity in Philadelphia, 1850–1880, 1930, 1970," in Hershberg, *Philadelphia in the Nineteenth Century*.

grants because city officials more willingly sent male tramps on their way with just a warning, but adjudged any female without a home or family to be more in need of institutional reform. Still, such an explanation cannot completely account for the remarkable number of female vagrants in city asylums at this time. A sample of wandering poor in the Almshouse between 1822 and 1840 reveals that most of these women resembled Hannah Bowman, a twenty-one-year-old, illiterate, unmarried, childless wanderer in search of a domestic service job. Hannah had been born in Northhampton County, Pennsylvania, where her family lived in a "log cabin" and her father and brothers were "labouring men." She had left home at age eighteen and in the next three years held six different jobs and never remained in one place longer than six months.[28] Most of Hannah's fellow female vagrants in the Almshouse in the 1830s and 1840s were, like herself, uneducated, unskilled, young, and single. Three-quarters of them were illiterate; virtually all did only "housework," had a median age of twenty-three, and were neither wives nor mothers. In addition, most, like Hannah, left home at eighteen and held upwards of four jobs between their late teens and early twenties. Thus in antebellum Philadelphia the woman most likely to tramp was native-born, young, and uneducated; she had broken family ties and was on the road seeking employment as a servant—then about the only respectable employment open to women except sewing.

Significantly, in the postbellum years between 1876 and 1899, the proportion of females among Philadelphia's wandering poor dropped sharply to 25 percent or less. (See Table 1.) There were no changes in laws which explain this singular decrease in female vagrancy. Admittedly, between 1869 and 1871 Prison officials endeavored to impose harsher discipline on female vagrants after the huge upsurge in women's admissions in the Civil War years. These officials attributed the slight reduction in females committed to the Prison for vagrancy at this time to these stricter policies. However, after the House of Correction opened in 1874, officials there actually welcomed female inmates because they performed essential institutional maintenance chores.[29] Nonetheless the proportion of female tramps in the House of Correction between 1876 and 1899 remained less than half what it had been in the Prison from 1823 to 1868. (See Table 1.)

A more probable explanation for the diminution of female tramps in Philadelphia after the Civil War is the improvement in occupational opportunities for women at this time. Female labor force participation of young, single women (those who, like Hannah Bowman, had previously constituted the majority of female wandering poor) expanded not only in domestic service but also in manufacturing.[30] A sample of women admitted to the House of Correction in 1875 corroborates this dramatic change. The proportion of single women among female vagrants declined from 61 percent between 1822 and 1840 to 22 percent in 1875, while their median age rose from twenty-three to thirty-three over this same time span. In 1875 the typical female vagrant resembled Martha Robinson, a forty-year-old, widowed Irishwoman with two grown children who had been two months in Philadelphia seeking work as a domestic servant before being picked up for vagrancy and sent to the House of Correction.[31] Native-born, single women were a rarity among institutionalized vagrants after 1875, presumably because of enlarged employment opportunities for them in the city. Instead, foreign-born, middle-aged, unskilled, married women who, like Martha Robinson, were widows (or whose husbands had deserted them) with children who were old enough to be indentured or self-supporting, predominated among homeless females late in the century. While in the antebellum era women tramped in their youth before becoming wives and mothers, in the postbellum years women tramped later in life, after their marriages and families had broken up.

Just as there was a marked change in the number and kind of female tramps in Philadelphia in the course of the nineteenth century, so was there also a sizable shift in numbers of black wandering poor. From 1823 to 1826 black vagrants amounted to between 43 and 53 percent of those in Prison, and between 1822 and 1840 they were 31 percent of the wandering poor in the Almshouse. (See Table 1.) Yet black Philadelphians accounted for just 8 percent of the city's population in these years. (See Table 2.) Actually, it is not especially remarkable that so many blacks were compelled to tramp, for they were then excluded from most well-paying jobs, denied apprenticeships, and rarely permitted to practice the skills they possessed. The meager economic prospects of black Philadelphians did not improve much in the antebellum era, yet the proportion of blacks in the city's vagrant population did taper off substantially by the late 1840s. Not black prosperity but rather a rising tide of racism in Philadelphia and Pennsylvania accounts for this decline. Between 1829 and 1839 there were several antiblack riots in the city, and by 1838 the new Pennsylvania state constitution disenfranchised black voters. Racism probably influenced the directors of the new Moyamensing Prison, opened in 1836, to admit fewer black vagrants than had the inspectors of the Arch Street Prison, where tramps were incarcerated in the 1820s. It is also likely that the intense wave of prejudice against blacks in the fourth and fifth decades of the century frightened many into remaining in one place or at least outside of Philadelphia, where racial confrontations were unusually bitter. The threats and discrimination of the era probably goaded many young black males to quit the city, and young males were the most likely to tramp. The diminution of young black men is supported by the fact that more black female than black male tramps were admitted to the Prison between 1847 and 1865, although in the years when black vagrant admissions had been highest in the 1820s and 1830s, more colored male than colored female wandering poor had entered the Prison and the Almshouse. Industrial opportunities for blacks in Philadelphia apparently improved slightly late in the century, attracting many young black men back to the city.[32] In addition, acute racism in the South, particularly in the 1890s, propelled many blacks, particularly young males, north to cities like Philadelphia. In any case, the composition of the tramping population of the city shifted; the absolute number and proportion of blacks in the House of Correction (especially black males) rose in the 1880s and most particularly in the 1890s. While the percentage of black vagrants incarcerated rarely matched the percentage of blacks in the total city population between 1850 and 1880, by the late 1890s the proportion of black tramps in the House of Correction grew to approximately twice the proportion of blacks in the entire city of Philadelphia. (See Table 2.)

This broad sketch of the kinds and numbers of the wandering poor in Philadelphia in the nineteenth century demonstrates the profound impact of agricultural change, labor force composition, and racism on the poor. For a closer look at the indigent homeless, we may analyze two remarkable surveys of Philadelphia's vagrant poor. Both surveys were begun at times when there were considerable numbers of wandering poor in the city: the first in the 1820s and the second in the 1870s. Each reflects official concern about the growth of tramping through the city.

Between 1822 and 1840 Almshouse officials recorded interviews with inmates who were not residents of Philadelphia.[33] The original intent of these inquiries was to chronicle the inmate's life history and thereby determine if there was one place he or she had lived long enough (usually one year or more) to establish legal residence. If such a place could be ascertained, then Almshouse officials were permitted by law to return the inmate to this place of residence, or to ask his or her home town to forward payment for the inmate's care. Either way, Philadelphia officials escaped financial responsibility for the "nonresident." These interviews provide us with a unique, systematic insight into the lives of poor people on the move.

In contrast, the second later survey probed less deeply into the lives of Philadelphia's vagrants, although it is still very useful. This survey recorded all of the persons admitted during the first year of operation (1874–75) of the Philadelphia House of Correction. In spite of the different intents of these surveys, they were similar enough in terms of types of information collected to make it possible to use them to compare the Philadelphia vagrant population before and after 1850.[34] Moreover, both appear to be fairly representative of the Philadelphia tramping population. Vagrants incarcerated in the poorhouse were somewhat unique in that they usually required some kind of medical attention, although nearly all suffered from minor complaints. Those admitted to the House of Correction were all healthy and able-bodied.

From the Almshouse data of 1822–40, there emerge three distinctive profiles of different types of tramps. The first group consisted of native-born tramps of whom John Kerby is representative. Kerby was twenty-six years old when he entered the Almshouse. He had been born in Philadelphia, but when he was a young boy he and his family relocated first in the state of Delaware and later in rural Pennsylvania. At the age of nine Kerby was indentured to a tavern keeper with whom he remained until he was sixteen. Thereafter he removed to another small Pennsylvania town to learn shoemaking from one James McClure. After a year of apprenticeship, Kerby accompanied McClure to the Cumberland Valley, where Kerby abandoned his master within six months. The young man moved about the state, but nowhere did he live more than one year. Unmarried, illiterate, and only semiskilled at shoemaking, a trade that in Philadelphia all too many men followed, Kerby came to the city, could not find work, and soon took up residence in the Almshouse.[35]

Although John Kerby was an adult white male, the general outline of his life history differed in very few particulars from that of other American-born vagrants, including blacks and females. Like Kerby, most native-born tramps left their families or masters in their late teens or early twenties. Kerby took to the road at about the age of seventeen, although most young men departed a little later at age twenty and most young women when they were eighteen years old. While Kerby remained unattached and childless during his tramping years, so too did most other native-born vagrants. Kerby was twenty-six when he entered the Almshouse, close to the median age of twenty-seven for native-born white males, and just a few years older than most American-born tramping women: their median age was twenty-three. Kerby and other wandering poor born in America tramped principally when they were young (only 12 percent were over forty-one years old). Youthful, with no families to tie them down, it is not surprising that they were also a very footloose group. Like Kerby, the longest most had spent in any one place was a year or less, and the majority had held at least four different jobs between their late teens and early twenties.

Perhaps few remained on any one job for long partly because they lacked skills. Most, like Kerby, were illiterate. Among all American-born females, and among black male tramps, three-quarters could not sign their names. Native white males fared only slightly better: 61 percent were illiterate. These illiteracy figures are remarkably high. Kenneth Lockridge has estimated that among the Revolutionary War generation of adults, just one-quarter were illiterate. In 1850 in Pennsylvania only 3 percent of whites over the age of twenty and seventeen percent of adult free blacks could not read and write. Females constituted roughly two-thirds of those who were illiterate in the state.[36] Blacks and females in Pennsylvania and in the nation were the least likely to be educated because they were viewed as inferior and not as much in need or deserving of schooling as were white males. Still, all groups in Philadelphia's tramping population between 1822 and 1840 were much more likely than their counterparts in the state population at large to be unable to write their names.

Not only did they have little education, the majority of wandering poor in the Almshouse did not possess any special job skills. Virtually all females were servants, and most males were either farm or day laborers or, like Kerby, were only semiproficient at a craft. These tramps formed an uneducated underclass of Americans who, at least in their youth, drifted about from one low-skilled job to another.

Thus in Philadelphia between 1822 and 1840, the typical native-born tramp was young, single, childless, illiterate, and constantly on the move. Like Kerby, such tramps were not yet able or ready to settle down, to establish a stable home. In all probability, for the American-born wandering poor tramping was a life style followed temporarily between the time a person left home and the time he or she earned enough to settle down to marry and form a family.

A somewhat different life course characterized a second group of wandering poor in Philadelphia between 1822 and 1840. These were foreign-born men like Archibald Barr, who was single and between thirty and forty years of age when he entered the Almshouse. Barr had migrated to this country from Ireland in his twenties. He landed in New Jersey but soon relocated in Philadelphia, where he resided for five or six years. Later he moved out into Philadelphia County for a year, then back to the city, and again to the county, where he dwelt for three years and worked for a tavern keeper. Finally, he returned to Philadelphia and after a few months sought admission to the Almshouse, where he was able to sign his name to the record of his interview with asylum officials.[37]

In common with Archibald Barr, most Irish and other foreign-born men among the wandering poor arrived in America and began to tramp in their early twenties, customarily did not marry or form families, and moved around a great deal, taking one low-skilled job after another. In these particulars they were not unlike most native-born vagrants in Philadelphia between 1822 and 1840. However, Barr and his fellow immigrant tramps were unique in that they were older than most native-born vagrants. Since the median age of foreign-born male tramps in the Almshouse was thirty-seven, most were fully a decade older than their American-born counterparts. Moreover, many male wanderers born in Ireland, Germany, England, and Scotland continued to tramp into their forties (41 percent were over the age of forty-one). Few native-born vagrants tramped for such a large portion of their lives.

Barr and other male vagrants born abroad also differed from the wandering poor born in America in that fully 63 percent of these foreign-born men were literate. This finding is not altogether unexpected since various studies have shown that men (but not women) who migrated long distances to new lands were quite likely to be literate. For example, among the Irish-born in Hamilton, Canada in 1861, just 20 percent were illiterate, yet in their homeland in 1841, 54 percent were unable to read and write. Among English migrants in Hamilton in 1861, 3.2 percent were illiterate, but in England in the same year, the illiteracy rate was 30 percent.[38] Evidently, the most educated European men had the courage and the wherewithal to migrate far from their homelands to North America. Thus, the greater degree of literacy among foreign-born male tramps in the Almshouse is explained by the high level of literacy among all immigrant men. Nonetheless, these figures reveal that the foreign-born man's ability to read and write did not ensure him a secure job nor spare him from a wandering life. Apparently, literate native-born men did not have to tramp, but literate foreign-born men often did.

Immigrant tramps also were more likely than native-born wanderers to settle down, and many, like Archibald Barr, lived well over a year in one place. They probably preferred a steady, secure life style. Nevertheless, most drifted about for a good part of their lives. Tramping was a more enduring occupation for the foreign-born than it was for their native American brother tramps. Seemingly, discrimination against them in this country prevented them from ever finding a permanent place to settle and raise a family.

Finally, the third distinctive group among the wandering poor in the Almshouse before mid-century encompassed foreign-born females like Ann McGowan. When she came to the poorhouse, McGowen was a fifty-five-year-old widow with three grown children. She had been born in Ireland and had arrived in the state of Delaware in her twenties. From there she moved on to Philadelphia, where she met and married John McGowan. For the next eight years the McGowans lived in the city and began a family. They then migrated to the rural Pennsylvania town of Mt. Vernon, where John worked at an iron furnace for four years. Later the family moved on to Carlisle, Pennsylvania, where John worked in construction for the nine years prior to his death. Her children now grown and her husband dead, Ann McGowan "broke up House Keeping" and became a live-in servant in the homes of various farmers around Carlisle. She visited Philadelphia for six weeks, worked for five weeks in New Jersey, and then moved back to the Carlisle area. Four weeks previous to her admission to the Almshouse, she had again traveled to Philadelphia. At the time of her interview with Almshouse officials, she could not sign her name.[39]

Foreign-born female tramps, most of whom, like Ann McGowan, hailed from Ireland, were distinct and unlike both immigrant men and native-born male and female vagrants. Such women usually arrived in America in their late teens, soon married, had children, and settled down to live several years in one place. They did not tramp in their youth but rather took to the road when they were in their late twenties or older (63 percent were between the ages of twenty-four and forty-four) and their families had broken up due to death or desertion. Three out of four female immigrant vagrants in the Almshouse were, like McGowan, illiterate, and nearly all were, also in common with her, unused to performing any labor except housework. Such women apparently became wanderers out of necessity. Uneducated, unskilled, often homeless, they had to move about in search of work.

Although in many ways so disparate, Kerby, Barr, and McGowan had one thing in common: all had traveled relatively short distances to reach Philadelphia. Over half of all tramps (regardless of sex, race, ethnic, or age differences) had moved to Philadelphia from a point thirty miles or less from the city. Moreover, 80 percent arrived in the city from destinations one to 100 miles away.[40] One explanation for this pattern of movement has to do with the limitations of transportation in this era. Although turnpike roads between major cities in Pennsylvania had been in existence for some time, canals and railroads were just being constructed in the state in the years between 1822 and 1840.[41] Hence, most tramps probably journeyed to the city on foot, and, travelling by this means, they could not have come too far. Students of migration patterns have noted that in the first half of the nineteenth century most persons moved not direct from farm to city, but from farm to small town and then perhaps to a larger city.[42] Evidently this was the pattern with Philadelphia's wandering poor between 1822 and 1840. Two-thirds of those who migrated to the city from a point thirty miles or less away were not born in these areas, a fact which indicates that for most, their relocation to the countryside around Philadelphia was transitional, soon to be followed by another move to the city itself.

Let us now turn to the sample of tramps in the Philadelphia House of Correction in 1874–5, where once again it is possible to discern three distinctive groups of itinerant poor.

The first consisted of women, both native and foreign-born. As we have seen, by the 1870s the typical female vagrant most closely resembled the minority of foreign-born (principally Irish) women tramps in the Almshouse previously. The middle-aged, married woman with a husband who had died or deserted her, and with children who were old enough to be on their own and self-supporting, predominated among females late in the century. Men tramped before or instead of marrying. Women tramped after marriage.

The second comprised native American men like Benjamin Kitts, who had been born in New Jersey and was twenty seven years old when he entered the House of Correction. Kitts was single and childless. He had acquired some education and knew how to both read and write. Moreover, he was not without some occupational skills and testified to officials that he was a "stairbuilder."[43]

In several ways Kitts and his fellow American-born tramps in the House of Correction in the mid-seventies were like their counterparts in the Almshouse a half-century before. In both institutions, in both eras, most native-born male vagrants were unmarried without families dependent upon them and relatively young: the median age of such men was twenty-seven. They tramped largely in their youth (in 1874–75 over half were under the age of thirty). In addition, both samples indicate that American-born men usually gave up the wandering life in their thirties (in 1874–75 only 20 percent were over the age of forty).

However, in two ways Benjamin Kitts and others like him differed from their brother American tramps who took refuge in the Almshouse earlier in the century. First, by the later era, the typical native-born male tramps was no longer illiterate. In 1874–75, 71 percent were, like Kitts, able to read and write. The greater accessibility of public education in Pennsylvania and in adjacent states probably accounts for this change. Nonetheless, even though the illiteracy rate among tramps in Philadelphia declined by 1875, it was still almost four times that of the general population of the state and nation. In1880 in Pennsylvania only 8.1 percent, and, in the United States, just 8.7 percent of white adults could not read or write.[44] Lack of education continued to bar many from all but itinerant labor. On the other hand, the majority of all Philadelphia's male wandering poor were literate, proving that in a depression decade like the 1870s, a basic grounding in reading and writing was not enough to secure a person a stable job.

There were also significant occupational differences between the wandering poor in Philadelphia early and late in the last century. While 58 percent of American-born men in the House of Correction in 1874–75 were, like their predecessors in the Almshouse between 1822 and 1840, unskilled, a significant minority of men (42 percent) in the later era had acquired some occupational training and might be classed as artisans. Earlier, among the Almshouse wandering poor, there had been no such artisan minority. Yet the trades most of these "skilled" workers practiced were not particularly in demand nor very high-paying. Only 14 percent had jobs in construction, like Kitts, or in printing or metal work, then the most lucrative of skilled laboring positions. Moreover, artisans in these very trades which were so well-paying had a tradition of tramping.[45] Thus it is not remarkable that such skilled craftsmen, between jobs, took up residence with their fellows of the "tramping fraternity" in the House of Correction.

The third distinct group of tramps in the House of Correction in 1874–

75 included foreign-born men like James Richardson. When he was committed as a vagrant, Richardson was thirty-five years old, single, and childless. He had been born in Ireland and knew how to both read and write.
Officials recorded his occupation as "laborer."[46]

Richardson and other Irish, German, English and Scots tramps of the
1870s were remarkably like foreign-born men on the move a half century
before. Not only in the Almshouse in 1822–40 but also in the House of
Correction in 1874–5, immigrant male wanderers were typically about a
decade older than their fellow American-born tramps. (In 1874–75 the
median age of foreign-born males was 36.2.) As in the antebellum era, in
1874–75, male tramps born abroad, like James Richardson, rarely married
and settled down to hearth and home but roamed constantly until they
were well along in years (34 percent were over the age of forty-five). In
addition, most male immigrant tramps, both early and late in the century,
resembled Richardson in that they were literate, although also like him,
most were unskilled laborers. However, in the 1870s, among foreign-born
as well as among native-born men on the move, there was a sizable
minority (one-third of the foreign-born males) who were artisans. Still,
such immigrant tramps, like skilled native-born vagrants of the same era,
either did not ply the most lucrative of trades or were engaged in crafts
where tramping was customary.

The ebb and flow of tramps through the city depended upon economic
conditions in Philadelphia, its surrounding countryside, and in the state at
large. In two periods, 1805–35 and 1873–99, Philadelphia retained comparatively large numbers of wandering poor in her institutions largely
because of depressed conditions in both the city and the agricultural areas
surrounding it. However, in the period from 1836–72, prosperity on
Pennsylvania farms and a plentiful supply of construction jobs throughout
the state offset the effects of city depressions and held down the number
of tramps in Philadelphia.

The foreign-born tramp (typically of Irish extraction) was always a
common sight among Philadelphia's vagrant poor. On the other hand,
while female and black vagrants were also common early on, by the end of
the century they had begun to fade from sight.

The basic characteristics of Philadelphia's wandering poor changed somewhat in the years before and after mid-century, especially in the increased rate of literacy and degree of occupational diversity. More important, however, is the fact that throughout the century native and foreign-born tramps followed contrasting life courses. For the native-born, especially men, tramping was a temporary life style pursued largely when fairly young and single. In contrast, for the foreign-born male, tramping seems to have been more a life-long vocation, while for the foreign-born female, and, by the late nineteenth century, the native-born woman as well, it was a way of life to be pursued only after she was widowed or separated from her husband and family.

Notes

1. John Daly, *Descriptive Inventory of the Archives of the City and County of Philadelphia* (Philadelphia: City of Philadelphia, 1970). For a more complete description of records of the poor in the Philadelphia City Archives see Priscilla Ferguson Clement, "Paupers and Public Relief: Studying the Poor in Nineteenth Century Philadelphia," *News Letter of the Philadelphia City Archives* 34 (June, Oct., 1978).

2. For a discussion of the places where Philadelphia housed vagrants over time see Negley K. Teeters, *The Cradle of the Penitentiary, The Walnut Street Jail in Philadelphia, 1773–1835* (Philadelphia: Pennsylvania Prison Society, 1955), 104–9. For the records of Sara Bird and Peter Prince see Philadelphia City Archives (hereafter referred to as PCA), Philadelphia County, Inspectors of the County Prison, Vagrancy Docket, volumes for 1808 and 1823. For the typical periods of incarceration for vagrants see the Vagrancy Docket, 1805–70.

3. *First Annual Report of the Inspectors of the Philadelphia County Prison* (Harrisburg: J. M. G. Lescure, 1848), 3–4, 9.

4. J. F. Willard [Josiah Flynt], *Tramping with Tramps* (New York: The Century Co., 1899), 99.

5. For complaints of prison officials about overcrowding see *Fifth through the Twenty-Fifth Annual Reports of the Inspectors of the Philadelphia County Prison* (Philadelphia: Crissy and Markley, 1852–57, 1859–61, and J. B. Chandler, 1858, 1862–72). For a description of the purposes and programs of the House of Correction see the reports of the managers of the House of Correction in the *Annual Message of the Mayor of Philadelphia for 1874, 1875, 1879, and 1889* (Philadelphia: E. C. Markley, 1874, 1875, 1879 and Dunlap and Clark, 1889). On Thomas Stafford see *Phila-*

delphia Telegraph, 19 June 1876 in PCA, House of Correction, Scrapbook. On the armed guard and the vagrant see the same volume, *Philadelphia Press,* 30 Sept. 1875.

6. Laws on vagrancy include: Chapter DLV, Acts of the General Assembly, 21 Feb. 1767; No. 68, 13 June 1836; No. 240, 21 Mar. 1866; No. 56, 3 May 1878; No. 96, 13 June 1883 in *Laws of Pennsylvania,* vols. for 1700–1781, 1836, 1866, 1878, 1883; and No. 126, 8 May 1876 in Pennsylvania, *Laws of the General Assembly,* 1876.

7. For statistics on "lodgers" in police stations see the reports of the superintendent of police in the *Annual Messages of the Mayor of Philadelphia, 1859 through 1899* (Philadelphia: n. p., 1859–73, E. C. Markley, 1875–80, J. Spencer Smith, 1881–82, Dunlap and Clark, 1884–90, 1891–1900, Dando Printing, 1890). For information on privately maintained lodging for vagrants see Pennsylvania Society for Organizing Charity, *Annual Report, 1902,* Appendix C. "Notes on an Amateur Wayfarer," 40–44.

8. *First through the Twenty-Fifth Annual Reports of the Inspectors of the Philadelphia County Prison;* reports of the House of Correction and of the police in *Annual Messages of the Mayor of Philadelphia, 1859–99.* (Quote in the 1879 House of Correction report.)

9 Allan Pinkerton, *Strikers, Communists, Tramps and Detectives* (New York: Arno Press, 1969; reprint of 1878 ed.), 62.

10. Paul T. Ringenbach, *Tramps and Reformers, 1873–1916: The Discovery of Unemployment in New York* (Westport, Conn.: Greenwood Press, 1973), 10.

11. These trends are not simply an artifact of the sources used. If they were, we might expect to see a sharp increase in vagrant admissions every time a new asylum for them opened. Such was not the case when the Moyamensing Prison opened in 1836. Regardless of the enlarged facilities for tramps there, vagrant admissions remained quite low in the 1830s and 1840s. A decided rise in admissions did occur when the Arch Street Prison opened in 1822 and the House of Correction in 1874, but this growth was probably as much the result of economic depressions in the 1820s and 1870s as it was of the appearance of new institutions for vagrants. Neither do differing reporting procedures in the documents used account for the trends in tramping patterns. The Prison Vagrancy Docket is available for 1805–71, and the methods of recording data on vagrants in it do not alter. I have not used the Vagrancy Docket to compute admissions to Moyamensing, 1836–71, simply because the annual reports of the prison inspectors are easier to use. However, I have, for selected years, compared the numbers of vagrants admitted according to the Vagrancy Docket and according to the prison inspectors' reports, and they do not differ once recidivism in the Vagrancy Docket has been taken into consideration. As for the reporting procedures of the House of Correction, they seem to have been roughly the same (although more information was recorded for each vagrant) as those for the Prison. Confirmation of the rise in the number of tramps in America in the late nineteenth century can be found in the historical accounts of Ringenbach and of Donald L. McMurry, *Coxey's Army: A Study of the Industrial Army Movement of 1894* (Boston: Little, Brown, 1929). Contemporary concern about tramps is revealed in Willard, *Tramping with Tramps* and John McCook, "A Tramp Census and Its Revelations," *Forum* 15 (Aug. 1893), 753–56.

12. Louis Martin Sears, "Philadelphia and the Embargo: 1808," *Annual Report of the American Historical Association for the Year 1920* (Washington, D.C.: Government Printing Office, 1925), 255–56.

13. Herman LeRoy Collins, *Philadelphia: A Story of Progress* (New York: Lewis Publishing Co., 1941), I, 179–80. Quote from the *Philadelphia Directory* (Philadelphia: Woodhouse, Kite, Woodward, 1809), xiv. Sears, "Philadelphia and the Embargo," 256–60.

14. Samuel Rezneck, "The Depression of 1819–1822, A Social History," *American Historical Review* 39 (1933–34), 28–34; *Poulson's*, 7 April 1821, 13 Jan. 1824.

15. Bruce Laurie, *Working People of Philadelphia, 1800–1850* (Philadelphia: Temple University Press, 1980), 9. For the severe economic problems of the laboring poor in the city from 1750 to 1800 see Gary B. Nash, "Poverty and Poor Relief in Pre-Revolutionary Philadelphia," *William and Mary Quarterly* 33 (Jan. 1976), 3–30; Billy G. Smith, "Death and Life in a Colonial Immigrant City: A Demographic Analysis of Philadelphia," *Journal of Economic History* 37 (Dec. 1977), 863–89; John K. Alexander, *Render Them Submissive: Responses to Poverty in Philadelphia, 1760–1800* (Amherst: University of Massachusetts Press, 1980).

16. Stevenson W. Fletcher, *Pennsylvania Agriculture and Country Life, 1840–1940* (Harrisburg: Pennsylvania Historical and Museum Commission, 1955), I, 317–18 and II, 24.

17. Ibid., I, 320–21. Quote from *United States Gazette*, 23 March 1821.

18. Fletcher, *Pennsylvania Agriculture*, I, 129–30, 137, II, 364–66.

19. William A. Sullivan, *The Industrial Worker in Pennsylvania, 1800 to 1840* (Harrisburg: Pennsylvania Historical and Museum Commission, 1955), 73. James M. Swank, *Progressive Pennsylvania, A Record of the Remarkable Industrial Development of the Keystone State* (Philadelphia: J. B. Lippincott, 1908), 145; R. D. Billinger, *Pennsylvania's Coal Industry* (Gettysburg: Pennsylvania Historical Association, 1954), 4–15.

20. *Public Ledger*, 7 Dec. 1842; Charles Lyell, *Travels in North America in the Years 1841–42* (New York: Wiley and Putnam, 1845), I, 172; Richard McLeod, "The Philadelphia Artisan, 1828–1850," (Ph.D. dissertation, University of Missouri, 1971), Table I, 43, cited in Laurie, *Working People of Philadelphia*, 108.

21. Reports of the House of Correction in the *Annual Messages of the Mayor of Philadelphia,* 1876, 1083; 1879, 1093; 1893, IV, 346; 1896, IV, 341; 1897, IV, 322.

22. Fletcher, *Pennsylvania Agriculture,* II, 366–68, 78.

23. Report of the House of Correction in *Annual Message of the Mayor of Philadelphia,* 1876, 1083–84. Annual reports of the police through 1899 do not indicate that there were any other years when police policy toward vagrants altered as much as it did during the centennial.

24. John McCook in his famous "A Tramp Census," 756, found 44 percent of the tramps he studied to be foreign-born. On the proportion of foreign-born in Philadelphia see Laurie, *Working People of Philadelphia,* 12.

25. On the Irish in Philadelphia early in the century see Edward C. Carter, III, "'Wild Irishman' Under Every Federalist's Bed: Naturalization in Philadelphia, 1789–1806," *Pennsylvania Magazine of History and Biography* 94 (July 1970), 331–46. For a description of the Irish in the city later see Bruce Laurie, Theodore Hershberg, and George Alter, "Immigrants and Industry: The Philadelphia Experience, 1850–1880," in Theodore Hershberg, ed., *Philadelphia: Work, Space, Family, and Group Experience in the 19th Century* (New York: Oxford University Press, 1981), 109–13. The figures on the Irish in the Almshouse and House of Correction are based on sample populations which are described in more detail below.

26. *Seventeenth Annual Report of the Inspectors of the Philadelphia County Prison,* 7.

27. Nancy F. Cott, *Bonds of Womanhood: Women's Sphere in New England, 1780–1835* (New Haven, Conn.: Yale University Press, 1977).

28. PCA, Guardians of the Poor, Almshouse, "Examinations of Paupers," 1831–39 vol., 206.

29. *Twenty-Second and Twenty-Fourth Annual Reports of the Inspectors of the Philadelphia County Prison,* 8 (1869), 15 (1871); Report of the House of Correction in *The Annual Message of the Mayor of Philadelphia,* 1875, 1249.

30. On work opportunities for women in the late nineteenth century see Carl Degler, *At Odds: Women and the Family in America from the Revolution to the Present* (New York: Oxford University Press, 1980), 375.

31. PCA, Philadelphia County, House of Correction, Description Docket, 1874–75, No. 4192, admitted 20 Feb. 1875.

32. For figures on blacks in Philadelphia see Theodore Hershberg *et al.,* "A Tale of Three Cities: Blacks, Immigrants, and Opportunity in Philadelphia, 1850–1880, 1930, 1970," 470; and Theodore Hershberg, "Free Blacks in Antebellum Philadelphia: A Study of Ex-Slaves, Freeborn, and Socioeconomic Decline," 370, 375 in Hershberg, *Philadelphia in the 19th Century.* Chapters by Schneider and Monkkonen in this volume confirm the small number of blacks on the road in the late nineteenth century.

33. This analysis is based upon a random sample of 300 such interviews drawn from PCA, Guardians of the Poor, Almshouse, "Examinations of Paupers," 1822–40.

34. A random sample of 300 was also drawn from PCA, Philadelphia County, House of Correction, Description Docket, 1874–75. While both surveys contain information on sex, race, marital status, number of children, birthplace, age, literacy, and occupation, only the Almshouse data include information on indentured servitude, number of places each inmate had lived before incarceration, age at which the inmate first left home (or came to America), and the longest time the inmate spent in any one location.

35. PCA, Guardians of the Poor, Almshouse, "Examinations of Paupers," 1826–31 vol., 93.

36. Kenneth Lockridge, *Literacy in Colonial New England: An Enquiry into the Social Context of Literacy in the Early Modern West* (New York: W. W. Norton, 1974), 87. Figures on illiteracy in Pennsylvania are from the seventh census, 1850. In that year nationally, 10 percent of native-born whites and 43 percent of free blacks were illiterate. Harvey Graff, in his study of three Canadian cities in 1861, also found that women and blacks predominated among the illiterate. See his *The Literacy Myth: Literacy and Social Structure in the Nineteenth Century City* (New York: Academic Press, 1979), 58, 62. It should also be noted that for poor persons, learning was hard to acquire in the years under discussion since Pennsylvania did not establish a public school system until 1834. Philip S. Klein and Ari Hoogenboom, *A History of Pennsylvania* (New York: McGraw Hill Co., 1973), 214–15.

37. PCA, Guardians of the Poor, Almshouse, "Examinations of Paupers," 1826–31 vol., 131.

38. Graff, *The Literacy Myth,* 65–67. Graff also found that in Canada most foreign-born women were illiterate. The same was true of foreign-born female tramps in Philadelphia. Timothy L. Smith has shown that in 1900 there was a much higher degree of literacy among Croatian and Slovenian migrants in America than in their homeland. See his article in Michael Katz, ed., *Education in American History: Readings on the Social Issues* (New York: Praeger, 1973), 240–41.

39. PCA, Guardians of the Poor, Almshouse, "Examinations of Paupers," 1831–39 vol., 54, 203.

40. The last residences of all inmates in the Almshouse sample (except those who came directly from Europe) were coded by distance into three groups: (1) Those that lived thirty miles or less from the city, who included those that came from counties immediately surrounding Philadelphia or from northern Delaware or western New Jersey. (2) Those that previously dwelt thirty one to 100 miles from the city, who encompassed those from a number of counties in Pennsylvania as well as migrants from New York, southern Delaware, eastern New Jersey, and Maryland. (3) Those who had lived most recently 101 miles or more from Philadelphia, who included those from western Pennsylvania and from all other states besides New York, Maryland, Delaware, and New Jersey.

41. Swank, *Progressive Pennsylvania,* 104–5, 145, 149; Klein and Hoogenboom, *Pennsylvania,* 179–84.

42. John Modell and Lynn H. Lees, "The Irish Countryman Urbanized: A Comparative Perspective on the Famine Migration," 357–58 in Hershberg, *Philadelphia in the 19th Century;* John Modell, "The Peopling of a Working-Class Ward: Reading, Pennsylvania, 1850," *Journal of Social History* (1971), 71–95.

43. PCA, Philadelphia County, House of Correction, Description Docket, 1874–76, No. 1088, admitted 11 June 1874.

44. On the development of public schooling in this era see William Bullough, *Cities and Schools in the Gilded Age: The Evolution of an Urban Institution* (Port Washington, N.Y.: Kennikat Press, 1974) and David Tyack, *The One Best System: A History of American Urban Education* (Cambridge: Harvard University Press, 1974). Figures on illiteracy in Pennsylvania and the United States are from the tenth census.

45. Laurie, Hershberg and Alter, "Immigrants and Industry," 102–9 in Hershberg, *Philadelphia in the 19th Century.* See also chapters by Tygiel and Cooper in this volume.

46. PCA, Philadelphia County, House of Correction, Description Docket, 1874–75, No. 224, admitted 6 March 1874.

Part II: Organized Labor and Tramps

Jules Tygiel

Tramping Artisans:
Carpenters in
Industrial America,
1880–90

Over a quarter of a century ago, E. J. Hobsbawm wrote a provocative article describing the tramping system that emerged among skilled artisans in nineteenth-century Great Britain, detailing the travel habits of craftsmen and the practices established by the trade unions to accommodate them.[1] In contrast, social historians in the United States have paid increasing attention to measuring the mobility of Americans in the industrial age without examining the institutional mechanisms delineated by Hobsbawm. Studies of persistence have demonstrated the prominence of transience in working-class life in the United States, creating what Stephan Thernstrom and Peter Knights called a "floating proletariat."[2] Despite this growing body of scholarly literature concerning the dimension of geographic mobility, however, we know far less about the travel patterns of particular American artisan groups than we do of those studied by Hobsbawm. Why, when, and where they moved remain, for the most part, unknown. Nor is there a great deal of information describing the ways in which itinerancy affected the lives and and institutions of American workers. This study of one group of tramping artisans in the United States, the carpenters, shows how they created traditions of migration and complex communication networks which facilitated their accommodation to a fluid and mobile economic system in the late nineteenth century. Moreover, the problems of itinerancy actually fostered the organization of a national federation of carpenters unions in 1881.

Itinerancy had long been associated with the carpentry trade. "There is a streak of the nomad in every carpenter," wrote Robert Christie, "and itinerancy has in some measure characterized the trade since guild carpentry."[3] Although some historians have argued that the high level of blue collar transiency in the United States has been an impediment to labor organization, carpenters, despite their tradition of tramping, were usually among the first groups of workers to successfully form unions in most cities. Their national body, the United Brotherhood of Carpenters and Joiners, became one of the most powerful labor federations in the nineteenth century.

Nor were the carpenters distinct in this respect. Other groups of skilled workers, most notably those in the building, printing, and metal trades, overcame the existence of a mobile constituency to form both local and national unions. Geographic mobility was only one of many factors affecting the ability of a group of workers to engage in collective activities. The success or failure of union efforts in a given trade often rested more with technological developments and market conditions than with the level of residential permanence attained by the workers. Indeed, the problem posed by intinerancy spurred the expansion of the United Brotherhood of Carpenters and Joiners and other national federations in the 1870s and 1880s.[4]

Carpenters took to tramping for a variety of reasons, but for the most part they responded to market conditions and unemployment. The seasonal and temporary character of labor in the building industry often forced these artisans to travel long distances, as well as short, to procure jobs. As a poet carpenter from Poughkeepsie wrote, "Often when the house is built,/Then tramping is our luck. . . ." Describing the paths the artisan must follow, he rhymed,

> From shop to shop, from town to town,
> We oft-times have to go it.
> 'Tis not all honey in our trade,
> I wish you friends to know it.[5]

Although carpenters in the preindustrial United States had often been migratory, several major developments in the latter half of the nineteenth century transformed the market situation for carpenters, increasing both the scope and scale of itinerancy. The first was the extension of the transportation and communication facilities in the United States and the corresponding integration of the national economic network. The post–Civil War spread of the railroad placed virtually all cities within easy reach of the tramping artisan, while better communication links informed him of building booms and job opportunities.

The course of westward expansion and urban growth also created conditions conducive to itinerancy. The construction of new communities and the sporadic expansion of older ones launched building booms which increased job opportunities in a given city. Once a local boom had run its course, most of the carpenters were no longer needed to meet the normal demands of the local market. But often as employment declined in one area, the cycle was repeated in another. The vicissitudes of a growing urban nation buffeted building tradesmen from place to place.[6]

A third related change involved the technology of carpentry itself. The introduction of machine-made millwork in the 1870s and the high speed construction of commercial and dwelling units in the growing cities transformed artisan work patterns. As ready-made parts came streaming out of the mills, the work of the carpenter required less skill. Since a lengthy apprenticeship or training period was no longer necessary to master the craft, entry into the trade opened to more workers. Old-time carpenters frequently complained of the "saw and hatchet brigade" or "botches" who were invading their profession and lowering the standards of the craft. The increased number of carpenters, the national character of the labor market, and the boom and bust cycle of the building industry created what Lloyd Ulman has termed "a chronic oversupply of labor at the local level."[7] As a result, carpenters were often forced to travel to procure employment.

The Carpenter, the journal of the United Brotherhood of Carpenters and Joiners, often reported the movements of union members. Sometimes the moves were short as men traveled to neighboring or suburban towns. In July 1885, for example, The Carpenter reported that "Bro. L. W. Davidson is again in Boston after being away on a job in Beverly Farm, Mass." while A. D. Bruce of Battle Creek, Michigan had moved to Jackson, Michigan. Long-range moves, however, were not uncommon. John S. Gillespie, one of the first members of the Philadelphia chapter in 1881 and a member of the General Executive Board of the United Brotherhood, moved to Los Angeles in 1887. A dispatch from the Baltimore local in February 1884 demonstrated the long- and short-haul travels of its members. Of the four men who had drawn travel or withdrawal cards during that month, one was heading for Centerville, Maryland, another for Washington, D.C., a third was reported to be in New Orleans, while the final traveler made his way to San Francisco.[8] Items of this kind were common in *The Carpenter.*

For these artisans, *The Carpenter* recorded no more moves, but one cannot be sure how many changes each man actually made during his working life. On the other hand, several carpenters left records of extensive travels, stopping at as many as nine places within a decade. John Bystead, for example, joined the union in San Francisco in 1883 and moved across the bay to Oakland the next year. In 1885 the local in Des Moines admitted him. Shortly thereafter he died of consumption at the age of forty-one in Chicago. And L. E. Pake left his mark in Chicago, Albuquerque, and San Bernadino, California before settling in Colton, California.[9]

Biographies of union officials also demonstrated the mobility of the carpenters. P. J. Wellin, a vice-president of the United Brotherhood, was born in Ireland and apprenticed in New York City. As a young man, he tramped in the East before setting out for San Francisco in 1861, passing through Panama on the way. For two years, he "followed the gold fever through California, Nevada, and Idaho" before returning to San Francisco and the carpentry trade. Wellin played a prominent role in the labor affairs of that city for the next twenty-five years. In 1882 he was one of the founders of the local chapter of the United Brotherhood. In 1886 *The Carpenter* reported that Wellin had "gone to Santa Barbara to reside permanently." Four years later, however, he was back in San Francisco when he was elected to national office.[10]

W. T. Dukehart also displayed a detailed itinerary. He was born in Emmitsburg, Maryland, in 1855 and served his apprenticeship in Waynesboro, Pennsylvania. In 1885, he journeyed to St. Louis and "drifted about in various western towns for two years." During this period he joined the union in Wichita and became vice-president of that local. In 1888 Dukehart moved to Nashville, where he apparently settled. Very influential in organizing a carpenter's union in that city, Dukehart became the southern representative on the General Executive Board.[11]

The most mobile carpenter to leave a record of his travels was E. L. Malsbury. Apprenticed to the trade in 1882 in Kansas City, he was initiated into the union in Los Angeles in 1886. His tramping took him through Oregon, Washington, Idaho, and Montana. In 1890 he was a member of Union 351 in Seattle before joining Local 22 in San Francisco. Two years later he returned to Kansas City, where he remained for eleven months before heading back to San Francisco. In both of these cities he held positions in the union—as a walking delegate in Kansas City and a district organizer in California. His high office in the latter instance did not put an end to Malsbury's travels. At the time his biography was printed in 1896 he was living in Arizona.[12]

The tramping of carpenters at times took on an international character. In 1881 The Carpenter reported that "hundreds of skilled hands in the past two years have gone to the Sandwich Islands, where considerable improvements are going on." In 1888, George Huber, a member of Union 22 of San Francisco, died while bathing at San Jose de Guatemala, and two years later ten New York carpenters, four of whom were union members, journeyed to Greytown, Nicaragua, to work at Camp La Fi for seventy-five dollars a month.[13] One of them sent back the following menu from Central America: "Turtles are plenty; we get mock turtle, turtle soup, turtle hash, turtle steaks, turtle pie, turtle boiled, baked and fried, turtle's eggs and turtle egg cake, turtle fritters, turtle tripe, and some turtle dishes I have not found a name for to date."[14] Occasional reports in The Carpenter listed conditions in Canada, Mexico, England, Australia and on one occasion union members were warned, "Don't go to Capetown, South Africa."[15]

As these examples illustrate, traveling carpenters had a wide variety of destinations both near to and far from their points of origin. The question remains as to how typical itinerancy was for carpenters in the late nineteenth century. The absence of any systematic documentation of this matter makes a definitive assessment impossible. Other evidence, however, also indicates that tramping was widespread. Persistence studies have consistently demonstrated a high degree of mobility among skilled workers. Less than half the artisans in any given city remained there for as many as ten years.[16] An analysis of the records of another group of craftsmen, the printers, lends further credence to this hypothesis. Between 1857 and 1892 the International Typographical Union reported the number of travel cards it issued. Tramping among the printers increased dramatically during this period. By the early 1890s the number of travel cards drawn each year equalled almost two-thirds of the total national membership. While many of these cards were doubtless issued to the same people, tramping appears to have been quite common among printers.[17] It can be assumed that the carpenters, given the nature of the construction industry and the numerous references to traveling members in their journal and records, had similar traditions.

The quest for work created a great flow of carpenters and other laboring men in and out of cities. Ideally, this mobility should have redistributed labor into areas in which opportunities for employment were greatest. But, of course, this only worked when the total number of jobs was greater than the number of travelers. Often, particularly during times of depression, men traveled from place to place unable to secure steady work. This posed a hardship both for the tramping artisans and for those who remained at home and saw outsiders vying for the handful of local jobs.

Sometimes unions noted the outward flow of their membership. In 1883 San Francisco carpenters were said to have "gone to the interior of the state, also to Oregon and the Territories." Two years later, nearby Alameda reported, "Several of our members have gone to the country in search of work," while Tacoma, Washington reported, "Trade in this city is dead; men are leaving here constantly." The seasonal as well as cyclical nature of the trade accounted for a great deal of travel. During the winter, building activities were usually slack. "The months of January, February, and March are always dull months with us," noted the San Francisco local. In the Northeast and Midwest, the off season lasted even longer and workers would often head south for the winter in hopes of finding work. "Many of our members have strolled away down South," reported the Chicago union in February 1884. Even in Charleston, South Carolina, carpenters were said to "have gone to Florida and other points further South." In 1892 the union in Jacksonville, Florida issued the following appeal: "Brothers do not come South this winter. Every winter brings suffering and want to the home mechanic and the stranger."[18]

The exodus of some carpenters from urban areas was often more than amply matched by the influx of others. "The city is flooded with carpenters from other cities," lamented a Kansas City correspondent in 1882. In Cleveland that year "there were more men out of work . . . than at any time in the past three years; not because of a scarcity of work, but we have hundreds of strangers."[19] Local reports to The Carpenter frequently featured complaints about "strangers," "traveling chips," and "tramps."

Large urban areas seasonally attracted the artisans of nearby farms, villages, and secondary cities, and many carpenters called attention to the problem. They complained about the "influx of 'haybacks' or country men who sport the saw and hatchet," or "Buckwheaters" who "work at carpenter work in the summer, and then go home in the winter and live on the buckwheat their families have raised when they were away in the summer." As a consequence, in 1882 Robert Stoffel of St. Louis called for "strenuous efforts to organize the small towns everywhere. . . . We are constantly overrun in this city with carpenters from small towns to the injury of union men." A month later, the Philadelphia local reported, "The Lord only knows how many countrymen from the backwoods of Pennsylvania and Delaware" were in the city. In 1884, Chicago was "deluged by the floating labor of the whole Northwest," while San Francisco was hit by "the influx of carpenters from the country and cities along the coast."[20] Often, this migration was seasonal, as rural workers flooded cities when agricultural work was scarce.

Formal and informal communication networks helped synchronize the migration decisions of carpenters. In an effort to attract traveling members as well as exercise some level of control over the flow of labor in the nation, The Carpenter, like other union journals, provided several services for tramping artisans. Lists of the secretaries of local unions were published each month "as an aid to our traveling brothers, so that when they come to any of the cities on the list, they will know where to inquire for the meeting place of the union, etc."[21] The secretaries also sent in reports of conditions and wages in each city as a guide to where work was and was not available. These dispatches provided a counterweight to advertisements placed by employers to draw surplus carpenters to their building sites.

The reports usually consisted of one-word summations of the local hiring market. The trade in cities was frequently described as "dull," "over-stocked," or, at best, "improving" or "satisfactory." At times, however, the secretaries would go into detail and report items like the following: "Trade very bad; 3500 carpenters in the city and barely 1000 at work. . . . Traveling carpenters had better steer clear of this place as it is overrun." Some accounts mimicked real estate advertisements. "There is plenty of land (rent dear), lots of climate, and an abundance of air, but not much work in this city," wrote a cynical San Francisco correspondent.[22]

One might question the accuracy of these reports in many instances as it was clearly in the interest of the carpenters of any city to keep the labor supply down by discouraging the migration of other skilled workers. While many reports in the late nineteenth century were negative, however, others would indicate that the local carpenters were not always reluctant to reveal good conditions to their fellow workmen. "Our unions are building up grandly," was the northern California report in June 1895, "and a splendid feeling exists among the men favorable to thorough organization. Some prospects for better wages."[23] In addition, a regular reader of these columns of The Carpenter could readily distinguish how desperate the situation was from the tenor of the dispatch. "Dull" was clearly not as foreboding as "overstocked," which paled in comparison to the exhortation, "For God's sake keep away from the city." Despite any shortcomings in the accuracy of the trade reports, they provided the traveling carpenters of the nation with an alternative view to the optimistic picture often painted by builders, speculators, and railroad men in other newspapers of the day.

For the most part, tramping in nineteenth-century America was not a random phenomenon in which artisans and other workers drifted aimlessly in hopes of finding a job. Economic historians have demonstrated that the work force as a whole generally drifted into areas with higher wages and better job opportunities.[24] Carpenters usually traveled to places where they thought work was available or wages were higher. Rumors and word of mouth were sources of information for the unemployed. Sometimes circulars printed by real estate and building interests advertising job opportunities provided more tangible, though not necessarily more reliable, sources of knowledge. Boom sites usually promised ample openings and good wages to traveling carpenters. Often such promises turned out to be crafty deceptions. In 1890 *The Carpenter* contended, "Real estate sharks, land speculators, and men of kindred low characters are advertising in every direction for carpenters to get the labor market in these cities overstocked and thereby reduce wages." A dispatch from Manitoba, Canada, reported that a "state of misery has been provoked by the fraudulent advertisements and glowing promises of railroad speculators and land agents, who got thousands to break up their comfortable little homes here and in Europe to perish like rotten sheep in the cold winds of Manitoba." At one point in the 1880s, *The Carpenter* published a column entitled "False Frauds and Inducements," listing cities from which allegedly mendacious circulars had been issued.[25]

This problem proved particularly severe on the Pacific Coast, described by one carpenter as the "promised land of the disinherited." California locals repeatedly warned other carpenters of misleading advertising. In 1883, San Francisco carpenters described "glowing inducements" promising four or five dollars a day. "Whenever you see such a report, stamp it as a lie!" they asserted. Across the bay, the carpenters of Oakland complained of "Emigration Bureaus" that "swindle and dupe workmen to come here from the East to get work." Ten years later, a report from San Francisco charged that, "Hundreds are in this city today who a few years ago had comfortable homes in eastern states, but were induced by the lying statements of the press in the interests of the railroads, land sharks, and other speculators to sell all and rush here to find themselves duped and defrauded."[26] Nineteenth-century carpenters attempted to balance employer advertisements with denials in the trade journals, thus helping readers choose the most promising destinations.

National depressions put unusual pressure on the system of traveling, where in city after city traveling artisans found a surplus of labor and a scarcity of jobs. Arthur Vinette, a Los Angeles carpenter, described one such hypothetical journey:

The plundered victim of greed bade adieu to friends and kindred, took a last look at boyhood's home and started on his weary march to the Occident. From Ohio to Missouri, tramping over the plains, scaling the snow-clad Rockies, a pitiless fate follows in his footsteps. Now he takes a spin into the Black Hills, now he turns to Carbonate Camp and again he is in New Mexico.

   He follows the wide valleys, he is on the line of every railroad, but somehow or other, there is always a surplus crop of his tribe. . . . With his face toward the setting sun he renews his toilsome march and finally reaches the Pacific shore. . . . Here he finds a population enacting the same scene he has witnessed every-where. . . . Alas, the promised land is a myth.[27]

   These lengthy treks in search of work introduced carpenters and other workers to the fact that national rather than regional or local forces governed the economy. During periods of depression there was little hope that employment could be found in another city. In England, accord-ing to Hobsbawm, this growing realization led to the decline of tramping, but without absolute figures it is difficult to determine whether this was also the case in the United States.[28] As early as the depression of the mid-1880s, however, the United Brotherhood urged carpenters, "Stay where you are and don't tramp off expecting trade is better somewhere else than where you are. It is bad everywhere and tramping around only helps to reduce wages and make things worse."[29] In the years after World War I, blue collar transiency did decline, though it is not clear whether a growing awareness of the national nature of economic fluctuations was responsible.[30]

   Although most significant, the search for employment was not the only reason for itinerancy. To some extent, tramping was a young man's pas-time, a function of the life cycle. Many carpenters in their twenties took to the road before they settled down. The case of Louis Kalkbrenner pro-vides a good illustration. Kalkbrenner learned the trade from his father in Belleville, Illinois and joined the local union there in 1889 when he was nineteen. Later that year, he moved to East St. Louis, Illinois, where he remained for two years before moving on to San Francisco. During the next three years he was affiliated with unions in Lewiston, Maine; Duluth, Minnesota; and Chicago. Finally, in 1895, he returned to Belleville. At the age of twenty-five, Kalkbrenner had already toured the nation, belonging to six unions in a period of six years before returning to his point of origin. Two years later, he was still in Belleville, the financial secretary of Local 433.[31]

Kalkbrenner's experience was probably not exceptional. P. M. Wellin was reported to have "traveled considerably in his early days," and W. T. Dukehart had reached thirty-three when he ceased roving and settled in Nashville. In Europe artisans were known to make the grand tour in their early years, and in England it was said that "no man knows his ability or what he is worth until he has worked in more than one town."[32] The same sentiments also existed in the United States. Tramping provided the young, single artisan with the opportunity to see the country and learn different techniques of his trade before the responsibilities of a family restricted his travels. Some wanderers stayed on the road until they found a place where they would like to settle, while others, like Kalkbrenner, ultimately returned home.

Marriage limited, but did not necessarily bring an end to, a carpenter's travels. Studies of persistence have demonstrated that in general single men were less likely to remain in a city than were their married counterparts.[33] Samples drawn from the 1880 and 1900 manuscript census schedules for San Francisco suggest that carpenters with children were not likely to make frequent or long-range moves. By examining the places of birth of an artisan's children, one can get a rough approximation of his family's mobility. If all were born in the same state, one can infer that little or only short-term mobility was experienced. In those households in which the birthplaces of the offspring differed, one can conclude that during at least one stage of the child-rearing process the family had transplanted itself. While this measure is inexact (children could have been born in different places within the same state or there may have been several moves made between the birthdates of the children), it does provide some insight into family mobility patterns.[34]

The most striking feature of the data on place of birth is the overwhelming proportion of children born in the home state. (See Table I.) In 1880, 77 percent of the offspring of San Francisco carpenters were born in California, while in 1900 this figure had risen to 82 percent. This suggests that family units were not prone to travel from place to place, but settled in one area during the child-raising phase of life. This can be further illustrated by examining the statistics for individual families. In 1880, only 35 percent of carpenters' households had any children born outside of California. In less than a quarter of the cases did two different birthplaces appear within a family, and the instances in which more than two states were recorded were extremely rare. This pattern grew even stronger in 1900. Only 11 percent of the sample families had multiple birthplaces in the latter year, while 75 percent of the households with two or more children exhibited no other stopping point than California. It would appear that most workingmen with families did not uproot themselves and their relations and make long-distance residential changes with great frequency. The childbearing years were spent, if not in one city, at least in one state.[35]

The fact that these working-class households reveal little residential mobility does not necessarily mean that wage earners did not leave their

Table I: The Birthplaces of Carpenters' Children,
San Francisco, 1880–1900, as Percentages

	1880	1900
Born in California	77%	82%
Born in other states	18%	13%
Foreign-born	5%	5%
	(N = 434)	(N = 417)
By Family		
All children born in California	65%	75%
All born in one place not in California	13%	14%
Mixed birthplaces	22%	11%
	(N = 145)	(N = 162)

Source: Computed from samples drawn from the 1880 and 1900 manuscript census schedules. For further information on sampling technique see my dissertation, "Workingmen in San Francisco, 1880–1901" (University of California, Los Angeles, 1977).

home cities to seek employment. Sometimes unemployment forced a laboring man to leave his family behind as he traveled to find a job. After being blacklisted, Frank Roney, a San Francisco labor leader, found work near Pioche, Nevada. Roney described this experience in his autobiography: "To leave my family penniless was more than I wished to do, but in my straitened circumstances, I called upon Henry Paulsen, a German grocer in the neighborhood, who assured me that during my absence they would not want for anything that money could buy. . . . In the three months I was there, I sent more than $300 to my wife."[36]

Not all of the families whom the carpenters left behind, however, fared as well as did Roney's. Advertisements in *The Carpenter* often sought information about men who had left their homes in search of work and failed to return. These pleas also shed light on their wide-ranging destinations and suggest the family strain caused by traveling. In 1889, the patient Mrs. James Rea asked for "tidings" of her husband, who had left Chicago for the Black Hills twelve years earlier. In the same issue, Mrs. Charles James of Boston inquired for her spouse, who "at one time worked in New York City, but is possibly in the western states now." In 1898 the following item appeared: "Mrs. James Vicker, 1810½ Broderick Street, San Francisco, California would like to know the whereabouts of her husband. He was a member of 'Frisco Union 22 since 1888 and left there last April for Sonora and Truckee, California. He is a native of Pennsylvania and was out of employment. His wife thinks he may possibly be in Montana." Following the San Francisco earthquake in 1906, Mrs. Charles Beaver, "facing want and misery as a result of the horrible catastrophe which has befallen San Francisco," sought her carpenter husband through the national journal. She thought he had gone to Kansas City, Missouri. In subsequent issues he was traced to Los Angeles and San Pedro in California, and Topeka and Kansas City, Kansas. Whether or not she actually found him went unreported.[37]

These instances of mobility after marriage actually reinforce rather than contradict the image of the geographically stable family unit conveyed by the data. While men tramped looking for work, their families remained at home. Only in atypical cases did a man's family travel with him from city to city as he searched for work or did a man with a wife and children change residence from one state to another. Stephan Thernstrom and Peter Knights have suggested the existence of a "floating proletariat" in the United States during the nineteenth century, "a group of *families* who appear to have been *permanent* transients."[38] The experience of the carpenters should modify this notion on two counts. For many people, itinerancy was not a permanent state but rather more characteristic of the early, rather than the later, years of the worker's life. In addition, the levels of persistence that were typical of blue collar Americans in the nineteenth century were to a large extent the product not of the working-class family man, but of the young, unmarried, childless workers who had yet to settle down.[39]

Thernstrom has also argued that the high degree of geographic mobility among American workingmen impeded the formation of working-class movements in the United States. He contends that the stability of the labor force within a given city "would seem to be a minimal necessity if mere complaints are to be translated effectively into class grievances and to inspire collective protest."[40] In the case of the carpenters and other skilled workers in the 1880s, however, the absence of a stable labor force encouraged the formation of a national union, while the travel habits of the artisans were incorporated into the union's practices and in many instances used as organizing tools.[41]

There can be little doubt that, despite their reputation for tramping, skilled artisans in the nineteenth century were less mobile than nonskilled workers. Recent persistence studies have consistently demonstrated higher levels of stability among craftsmen. It is unlikely, however, that these differences accounted for the varying degrees of labor organization between members of one occupation and another. It is significant to note that only a modest gap in the levels of persistence between skilled and unskilled workers existed. In almost all of the examples of blue collar mobility presented by Thernstrom in *The Other Bostonians,* less than half of either group remained in the city over a ten-year period in the decades prior to 1920. In only two of the ten instances cited by Thernstrom did the difference amount to greater than 8 percent. Thus, it would seem to be unlikely that the greater ability of skilled workers to form labor unions in the late nineteenth and early twentieth centuries came from these relatively narrow variations.[42]

What would appear to be a more important consideration than the stability of the labor force in a given *locale* would be the perceived permanence of a group of workers in a given *occupation*. Two frequently cited examples of workers who did not organize, the Lowell mill girls and immigrant steelworkers in the years before World War I, provide cases in point. Both of these groups of employees demonstrated high rates of job turnover and physical mobility. The crucial bar to organization, however, was their psychological attitude toward their jobs rather than their geographic impermanence. In both cases the workers planned to stay in their given occupations for a limited time—the Lowell girls until they had married, the steel workers until they could return home to Europe. Neither group perceived greater control over working conditions in the industry as beneficial to their long-range interests.[43]

The situation of the carpenters and many other American craftsmen in the 1880s is more directly comparable to that of the glassworkers of Carmaux, France described by Joan Scott. The mechanization of the French glassworks during the latter part of the nineteenth century diminished entrepreneurial opportunity for the artisans while opening the craft to additional workers through skill dilution. While itinerancy did not disappear, geographical stability became more common among glassworkers with secure employment. It was among these men, cut off from traditional channels of occupational mobility and now permanently established in a particular locale, that labor organization among French glassworkers had its origin.[44]

A similar set of circumstances transformed the world of skilled workers in America. Changes accompanying industrialization led many artisans to perceive themselves as permanently locked into one occupation. This was particularly true for the carpenters. In earlier decades the designation had not been a fixed one. The average carpenter frequently had been able to cross over the line between skilled artisan and contractor and back again. Social mobility, both upward and downward, was a common feature of the trade. As late as 1884, John Swinton had complained that carpenters would not join a union because "every mother's son of them expects to become a boss." But, with the rise of machine woodworking, high-speed residential construction, and larger buildings, large-scale enterprise replaced the sometimes individual contractor. Opportunities for the building tradesman to become an employer diminished. The awareness grew that no matter where one traveled, his role as an employed carpenter had become more permanent. The carpenters, unlike the immigrant steelworkers or the women at Lowell, therefore developed an occupational identity which encouraged them to concentrate on improving and controlling working conditions wherever they might be employed.[45]

Of course, not all workers whose avenues of advancement were blocked by industrial change were able to organize. Industrial relations studies have demonstrated that for those wage earners employed in local market industries where there could be no importation of goods made by cheaper labor in other cities, labor organization was more successful than in comparable enterprises competing on a national level. Workers in both types of industry were highly mobile, but only in the former instance could they sustain collective action. The building trades provide the ideal example of a local market industry.[46]

Tramping did pose several difficulties for labor organizers similar to those suggested by Thernstrom. Carpenters frequently complained that the impermanence of the labor force created obstacles to union formation. A report from Cheyenne, Wyoming in 1882 lamented that "it is a hard matter to start [a union] up owing to the roving disposition carpenters get after coming West." The correspondent, who was a member of a Washington, D.C. local, claimed that there were probably fewer than a dozen carpenters who had been in the city longer than he had. Union 50 in Portland, Oregon came close to extinction in 1885 because "members have gone elsewhere for want of work."[47] In these cases geographic mobility did block organizational efforts.

The success of local unions, however, depended not upon the absence of member mobility, but rather upon the presence of a permanent core of workers who saw their occupational status as fixed and their interests best served by organization. For fledgling unions, the problem was not so much that of members leaving for other cities as it was one of obtaining and sustaining improved conditions in the face of *in-migration*. The fluidity of the labor supply undermined local gains. Unions criticized "tramp carpenters" who went "from place to place pulling down wages." The gains of organized labor or superior employment opportunities in one city led to an influx of craftsmen seeking to better their own fortunes at the expense of the permanent residents. "A few good jobs going on" was the report from Detroit in 1884, "but what good are they when so many come in from the country towns and take the place of the men who live here with families?"[48] It was existence of a floating labor supply and the need to control the flow of workers as much as any other factors which ultimately encouraged the merger of carpenters' unions into a national federation in 1881.

The impetus for the establishment of a national organization of carpenters came from the St. Louis union led by P. J. McGuire. The carpenters' local in that city had won increased wages and control over piecework, only to find their gains undone by incoming craftsmen. The plight described by the St. Louis carpenters paralleled that of artisans in other cities: "It was discovered that our advance in wages would soon be lost through the influx of men from cities where wages were lower. Day after day men came from other states where wages were $1.75 to $2. Then it was that we concluded the only resort was to form a national union, unite all local unions, organize the low-paid towns and then raise wages to a general standard throughout the country."[49] The St. Louis experience, combined with the urgings of other frustrated union leaders, moved McGuire to action. He issued a call for local carpenters' unions to send delegates to a convention in Chicago on 8 August 1881. McGuire also initiated the publication of *The Carpenter*, designed to provide a regular means of communication among members of the trade. The United Brotherhood of Carpenters and Joiners was thus born out of a need to deal with the problems of itinerancy.[50]

Skilled workers organized several national unions in the late 1870s and early 1880s. All of these fledgling bodies addressed the central issue of the transiency of the labor force. By devising a means of attracting tramping artisans to join, the union could control the flow of workers into high-wage cities and protect local organizations. An arrangement had to be made whereby workers would freely transfer membership from one branch to another without incurring added expense in the form of initiation fees or duplicate dues. All of the national unions, including the carpenters', adopted the travel card as a solution.[51]

"When members start out to travel," warned *The Carpenter,* "they should take traveling cards with them or else they will have trouble and be looked on as scabs."[52] Its first constitution established the tramping policy of the United Brotherhood. When leaving the jurisdiction of his home union, the carpenter would apply for a traveling card which would be honored by all other branches. This allowed the tramping carpenter to travel freely and extensively without having to pay a new initiation fee in each place he stopped and at the same time encouraged union membership. It also permitted local organizations to bar nonunion itinerants from the trade.[53]

During the first seven years of the Brotherhood's existence, the national union experimented with several ways of enforcing the travel card system. In the beginning, the union devised a complex system of identifying tramping carpenters. Upon departure, a carpenter secured a traveling card from his home union as well as instruction in the national password, signs, grip, and "secret Work." These latter features illustrate the fraternal, as opposed to the strictly economic, aspects of the early unions. The financial secretary issued the travel card and the local president countersigned it; the members did not need to vote. The traveler signed his name to the card when he received it. When he found work in another city, the carpenter reported to the conductor of the new local, who tested him on the various rituals and compared his signature to that on the card.[54]

Confusing and not very effective, this system elicited a great many protests and questions from the local unions. Several union leaders complained that men arrived with their working cards but not their traveling cards, or with the traveling card but without the proper password and tests. Reports of "frauds and deadbeats" who had learned the rituals and entered unions only to disappear with money loaned from members also appeared.[55] By 1886, the national union eliminated the secret work, grip, and signs in favor of a password issued quarterly by the general president to the local unions, which along with the traveling card admitted a member to all branches of the Brotherhood.[56]

From 1886 to 1888 the carpenters' experimented with a two-card system which distinguished between itinerants and those moving from one specific place to another. The former would be issued a travel card which was good for up to three months; the latter received a "transfer card" which specified a given destination and was issued for only one month. Members paid dues in advance. This two-card system proved highly unsatisfactory and the union quickly abandoned it. This system also failed among the printers' and bricklayers' unions, the two other national unions which employed it.[57]

Finally, in 1888, the traveling system of the United Brotherhood took the form that it maintained for the next quarter of a century. One card, known as a "clearance card," took the place of the travel and transfer cards. Issued for a period of up to three months, this card had to be renewed or deposited with a new local, or the United Brotherhood suspended the member. Once the card was deposited with a second union, the traveler became a citizen of this local and worked under their rules, though he was not immediately eligible for sick benefits. The carpenter had thirty days after his arrival in a new city in which to deposit his card or clearance would be forfeited. A separate article of the constitution dealt with "Visiting Members" and allowed any carpenter with a present membership card and knowledge of the quarterly password to attend meetings of other unions, though he could not vote or speak out without permission from a majority of those present.[58]

The adoption of the clearance card in 1888 did not eliminate all of the problems inherent in the travel system. It did, however, provide a means by which the national federation could retain the membership of those carpenters traveling from city to city and maintain some element of discipline over them. This system succeeded because it combined the ability of the local unions to monopolize employment in their respective jurisdictions with the power of the national union to impose punishments on those who failed to deposit their cards as they traveled. Although the

United Brotherhood never totally eliminated the nonunion itinerant, the policies of the national union in this area marked a vast improvement over the futile efforts of isolated unions in the earlier era.[59]

The survival of the travel card system and the United Brotherhood itself depended on the recruitment of itinerant carpenters. In its earliest years, the national union therefore incorporated the travel habits of the craftsmen into their organizational efforts, provided numerous services for the tramping artisan, and urged him to act as a traveling organizer. As the union became more firmly entrenched, however, there emerged among its leadership a growing disenchantment with the fabled "tramp carpenter," and by the turn of the century the itinerant had fallen into disfavor with the new class of professional labor bureaucrats.

The first issues of *The Carpenter* portrayed the United Brotherhood as beneficial not only for the permanent population, but for the "floating proletariat" as well. In 1884, when *The Carpenter* listed the accomplishments of the early years of the Brotherhood, it included the tramping system. "Wherever our members travel," claimed the journal, "they are received with open arms as union men, and assisted to obtain employment." Addressing a meeting of Baltimore carpenters in 1888, General Secretary P. J. McGuire was even more effusive, telling the artisans, "You can go to Nova Scotia, or to Florida, or to British Columbia, and if you have a card of this union, you can get a job."[60] In a land with extensive mobility these arguments provided powerful inducements for recruitment.

In England, according to Hobsbawm, the tramping artisan spread trade unionism, "founding local branches on his travels . . . passing on information about local wage rates, advising upon the best times to start a wage movement, a walking encyclopedia of comparative trade-union knowledge."[61] In the United States, the national union encouraged traveling carpenters to further the cause of organization wherever they went. The union told itinerants that "like the apostles of old" they should become "proselytes for the cause." "No matter where you travel," implored an early issue of *The Carpenter,* "do your level best to organize a carpenters' local union." The newspaper urged men on the road to "organize unions wherever you go. We want every member of our Brotherhood to be a missionary to our cause. . . ."[62]

Many carpenters aggressively followed this advice. In 1886 the *Workingman's Advocate* reported that newly arrived carpenters in New Haven had spearheaded the drive for a United Brotherhood local, noting, "It seems strange that our fellow citizens, the local carpenters, should leave it to outsiders to do this important act."[63] *The Carpenter* always had special praise for those who organized when they changed residence or traveled from place to place. In July 1885, it singled out three such cases, including that of T. B. Foster of New Orleans, who had helped to establish a union in Mobile, Alabama while working there. "If every traveling brother would show the same zeal as Brother Foster in organizing new unions in their travels," the paper commented, "we would then have a host of Traveling Organizers."[64] These rank and file members carried the union with them, not as organizers but as itinerant workers.

Tramping artisans served the union cause even where organization was not possible. In 1883 a correspondent from "Tulsa, Indian Territory," filed the following account: "On the journey from Ritchie, Mo. to this place I noticed that there were lots of new buildings in the course of construction. . . . There were about 35 carpenters from all parts and I am passing out your papers and appeals among them. I hope to get them stirred up and thinking so that when they get home . . . they may do something in favor of our organization among carpenters."[65] Where a traveling craftsman was unable to start a new local, he was instructed to record the names of the carpenters and forward them to the United Brotherhood, which would endeavor to organize a union.[66]

For organizing purposes the United Brotherhood stressed the benefits of the national union for a mobile work force. At the same time, however, the federation often expressed disapproval of the floating carpenter and attempted to discourage his travels. In an early issue of *The Carpenter*, workers were requested to "stay where you are and raise wages by organized unity and not fritter away time and money by continually moving." In October 1884, an editorial entitled "Stop Tramping Around" distinguished between those traveling who "start unions wherever they go" and the "cold selfish characters, or else wild, reckless natures who have no intelligent desire to advance the interests of their fellows." The latter group was seen as tools of the bosses "to the injury of men with homes and families," and were advised to "organize and strive to better their condition and not be running off on a 'wild goose chase.' "[67]

Hostility toward itinerant carpenters grew as the Brotherhood and its affiliates established a firm organizational base and as a professional labor leadership emerged on both the local and national levels in the 1890s.[68] For all labor federations organized during this era, the coordination of the traveling network had posed problems regarding initiation fees, benefits, and admission of members. Some national bodies imposed uniform standards to avoid conflicts, but the carpenters left these matters to the discretion of the local unions. Requirements therefore varied from chapter to chapter, yet a worker accepted into one branch had to be welcomed into another even if he did not meet the skill and character requirements of the second local or had paid a lower initiation fee.[69] With the unions no longer struggling for survival, the jurisdictional and disciplinary problems posed by the floating artisans began to outweigh the necessity to court the itinerant. There developed an increasing opposition to tramping, particularly among the emerging class of labor bureaucrats, and rules regulating travelers reflected a growing stringency.

The United Brotherhood instituted changes in the 1890s which made traveling and transfering affiliations more difficult, thereby discouraging tramping among carpenters. In 1891, the Brotherhood cut the maximum period for which a travel card could be issued to thirty days from three months, granting clearance only to those who had belonged for at least three months; all others had to pay a five-dollar fee. (In 1903 it extended the waiting period to six months.) In 1893 it established a system of fines for people who worked without depositing their clearance cards.[70] In the face of the depression, however, the Brotherhood dropped these fines and urged unions to be "as indulgent as possible with traveling members."[71] In addition, the Brotherhood no longer demanded the thirty-day grace period for depositing a card in a new city, instead stipulating that the carpenter attend a meeting immediately after procuring employment.[72] In 1896 it made the method of acceptance into local unions more difficult. Previously the traveling member had been tested and passed upon by a local officer upon deposit of his clearance card; now local presidents had to appoint a committee of three to examine the applicant. Their report would then be presented to the membership, who had to approve the itinerant by a majority vote.[73]

Local unions made repeated efforts to charge tramping carpenters for the right to work in their jurisdiction. Some unions sought to require carpenters from neighboring areas who had secured temporary work to pay for new working cards. In 1890, when D. Remer of Findlay, Ohio secured work in Columbus, the Columbus union demanded a ten-dollar fee for a working card. Remer appealed to the national organization, which ruled in his favor. At the same time, however, the Executive Board sanctioned the more moderate two-dollar charge for outside carpenters.[74] The situation was complicated where one local charged a higher initiation fee than another. In New York City in 1900, five locals raised their fees from five to twenty dollars. This was well within their rights, but when they insisted on charging traveling members the difference between the old and new fee, the Brotherhood suspended them.[75] After 1907 the Brotherhood required travelers to pay the difference in initiation fees if the amount charged by the new union amounted to more than five dollars over that of the original chapter.[76]

Local unions frequently made suggestions to the Executive Board for new rules governing visiting members. Complaints of "country carpenters . . . who make no effort to better the condition of their craft in their own places—get a clearance card from their union and rush into town and create a glut on the labor market" led to a tightening of the tramping system in 1891. A New York chapter called for a provision preventing carpenters from collecting sick benefits for a year after they had joined. This responsibility was to be retained by the local issuing the clearance. The more stringent examination procedures instituted in 1896 were originally proposed by Union 88 of Anaconda, Montana.[77]

The effects of these efforts to control the flow of labor were no doubt limited. Strong locals, like the one in San Francisco, afforded some measure of protection against the nonunion itinerant. In most communities, however, the flood of outside carpenters remained a problem. In times of depression, the great stream of artisans weakened control even among the most dominant local unions. The failure of these local efforts to deal adequately with itinerancy increased the hostility of labor leaders. Whereas the founders of the Brotherhood had emphasized the important role that the tramping artisan would play in the new union, the rising labor professional who came to dominate the Brotherhood and other national unions saw him more as an administrative problem.

By the late 1890s, few items in *The Carpenter* praised the itinerant. Those that did appear presented a less favorable image. An 1896 piece characterized the union man's life as "eight hours a day, steady work, highest wages, a cheerful home, and manly independence." The phrases describing the unorganized were "ten or twelve hours a day, piece work, low pay, often idle, and on the tramp."[78] From the point of view of the now well-established union, stability, not itinerancy, had become the preferred mode of existence for the union man. The national federation sought to replace the easy interunion flow proposed in the 1880s with new barriers designed to discourage the itinerant. Nonetheless, the tramping carpenter remained not only a mythic symbol of the trade, but a persistent problem for the United Brotherhood, and no one, at least in print, suggested the total abandonment of the travel system.

Because transiency was a prominent characteristic of the United States in the late nineteenth and early twentieth centuries, it is necessary to incorporate it into our view of American life. Frequent uprooting represented the normal pattern of the life course in the United States during the industrial era, and any study of the period must analyze this aspect of working-class existence, examining the ways in which people integrated transiency into their lives and how communities and institutions adapted to the realities of a mobile society. The case of the carpenters illustrates both the complexities of travel habits among American workers and the manner in which itinerancy could be integrated into trade unions. The travel patterns of the carpenters reveal a wide array of motivations and destination. The seasons and life cycles as well as employment opportunities and economic fluctuation affected transiency. For some, it was a temporary expedient, for others a way of life. The general fluidity of the labor force affected the experiences of all carpenters, even those who

lived in one place and did not take to the road. The interaction of permanent and transient elements in the community profoundly tempered local
conditions.

Itinerancy did indeed pose obstacles to union formation, but not insur-
mountable ones. Technological developments and market conditions had
greater impact on success or failure of organization in a given trade than
did persistence. Nor do high levels of out-migration appear to have been a
major barrier to collective activities. The downgrading effects of a fluid
surplus labor supply had far more significance. The resulting need to
control the inward flow of artisans at the community level actually encouraged organization on both the local and national levels. Furthermore, the
national unions pitched their appeal to transient as well as settled workers
and used the tramping artisans as traveling organizers. Although these
efforts met with mixed success and labor leaders grew increasingly hostile
to tramp labor, geographic mobility may have served more as a stimulus to
the formation of trade unions than as an impediment.

It must be noted, however, that trade union consciousness is not
synonymous with class consciousness. Skilled workers did not automatically translate their organizational ability to overcome and even incorporate transiency in their unions into cooperation with workers in other
industries. In several cities, the well-organized building trades remained
disdainfully aloof from the efforts of other wage earners to better their
fortunes, representing a conservative "labor aristocracy." Thus it may have
been possible that among other groups of workers the instability of the
labor force did act as a decisive factor in their inability to act collectively.
But for the carpenters, tramping was a fixed institution in the late nineteenth century, creating opportunities and adventure for the younger
worker while strengthening the preliminary organizing efforts of the
Brotherhood.

Notes

1. E. J. Hobsbawm, *Labouring Men: Studies in the History of Labour* (New York: Basic
Books, 1965), 41–74. According to Hobsbawm, the English tramping system operated in the following manner: "The man who wished to leave town to look for

work elsewhere, received a 'blank' or 'clearance' or 'document', showing him to be a member in good standing of the society. This he presented to the local secretary or relieving officer in the 'lodge house' or 'club house' or 'house of call' of the strange town . . . receiving in return supper, lodging, perhaps beer, and a tramp allowance. If there was work to be found, he took it. . . . If there was none, he tramped on. Should he not get permanent enough work to transfer to a new union branch, the traveler would in due course return to his home town. . ." (41).

2. The first work in this area was Stephan Thernstrom, *Poverty and Progress: Social Mobility in a Nineteenth Century City* (New York: Atheneum, 1964). A more recent work by that author is *The Other Bostonians: Poverty and Progress in an American Metropolis* (Cambridge: Harvard University Press, 1974). Additional works dealing with this problem are Howard Chudacoff, *Mobile Americans: Residential and Social Mobility in Omaha, 1880–1920: A Study in City Growth* (New York: Oxford University Press, 1971); and Michael B. Katz, *The People of Hamilton Canada West: Family and Class in a Mid-Nineteenth Century City* (Cambridge: Harvard University Press, 1975). See also Paul B. Worthman, "Working-Class Mobility in Alabama, 1880–1914," and Stephan Thernstrom and Peter R. Knights, "Men in Motion: Some Data and Speculation About Urban Population Movement in Nineteenth-Century America." Both of these articles appear in Tamara Hareven, ed., *Anonymous Americans: Explorations in Nineteenth-Century Social History* (New Haven: Yale University Press, 1969). For a view of geographic mobility in the eighteenth century, see Douglas Lamar Jones's essay in this volume.

3. Robert A. Christie, *Empire in Wood: A History of the Carpenters' Union* (Ithaca: Cornell University Press, 1956), 14.

4. For the role of itinerancy in the formation of the United Brotherhood of Carpenters and Joiners, see Christie, 23–25. A discussion of other national unions can be found in Lloyd Ulman, *The Rise of the National Trade Union: The Development of Its Structure, Governing Institutions, and Economic Policies* (Cambridge: Harvard University Press, 1955).

5. *The Carpenter,* June 1890.

6. Ulman, 59–60.

7. Ibid., 59. For the impact of technological change on carpentry, see Christie, 19–28 and 61–78; Jules Tygiel, "Workingmen in San Francisco, 1880–1901" (Ph.D. dissertation, University of California, Los Angeles, 1977), 101–27.

8. *The Carpenter,* July 1885, November 1887, February 1884, November 1886, and December 1884.

9. Ibid., November 1886 and December 1884.

10. Wellin's biography appeared in the *Official Journal of the United Brotherhood of Carpenters and Joiners of America Issued for Convention to be held at St. Louis, Mo.,*

August 1, 1892, 27–30. Additional information appeared in *The Carpenter,* September 1886 and August 1890.

11. *The Carpenter,* May 1893.

12. Ibid., August 1896.

13. Ibid., August 1881, March 1888, and October 1890.

14. Ibid., October 1890.

15. Ibid., October 1893.

16. Thernstrom, *The Other Bostonians,* 230, Table 9.3.

17. Ulman, 64–66. According to detective Allan Pinkerton, "Printers are not all tramps, but, as stated, there is scarcely a printer who has not at some time been upon the road" (cited in Ulman, 64). See also Paul Fischer, "A Forgotten Gentry of the Fourth Estate," *Journalism Quarterly* (Spring 1965), 169.

18. *The Carpenter,* September 1883, November 1885, July 1885, March 1885, February 1884, December 1884, and November 1892.

19. Ibid., July 1882.

20. Ibid., August 1885, February 1889, February 1882, March 1882, December 1884, and February 1884.

21. *The Carpenter,* December 1881. According to Ulman, "Constitutions of national unions invariably required that local secretaries furnish the national secretaries with data concerning the number of travel cards issued and the 'condition of the trade.' " Some of these reports were then printed in the national journals (Ulman, 57).

22. Ibid., April 1886, and March 1887.

23. Ibid., June 1895.

24. For example, see Harvey S. Perloff, *Regions, Resources, and Economic Growth* (Baltimore: Johns Hopkins University Press, 1960).

25. *The Carpenter,* March 1890, April 1884, and May 1885. Other types of workers faced these same problems. See Ulman, 53–54.

26. Ibid., December 1885, April 1883, May 1883, and May 1893.

27. Ibid., December 1885.

28. Hobsbawm, 56–58. Because they paid a tramp allowance, British unions kept records of artisan travels which enabled Hobsbawm to measure the fluctuations in itinerancy.

29. *The Carpenter,* January 1885.

30. Thernstrom, *The Other Bostonians,* 229–32; Ulman, 66–67.

31. *The Carpenter,* July 1897.

32. Hobsbawm, 45. In the United States, the Molders' Union also noted the tendency of workers to travel in their younger days. An article in the *Iron Molders' Journal* in 1889 referred to "the traveling propensities of a large proportion of our

craft (that portion commonly dubbed tramps, with whom most of us are familiar, having belonged to that especial fraternity ourselves in earlier days) . . ." (cited in Ulman, 144).

33. Michael Katz argues that in Hamilton "people who had established families remained in the city more often than other groups of people" (Katz, 124). See also Clyde Griffin, "Workers Divided: The Effect of Class and Ethnic Differences in Poughkeepsie, New York, 1850–1880," in Thernstrom and Richard Sennett, eds., *Nineteenth-Century Cities: Essays in the New Urban History* (New Haven: Yale University Press, 1969), 61; Howard M. Gettleman, *Workingmen of Waltham: Mobility in American Urban Industrial Development, 1850–1890* (Baltimore: Johns Hopkins University Press, 1974), 38–39; and Jones.

34. For a fuller discussion, see Tygiel, 209–13.

35. In all likelihood the percentage figures for children born in California are too low. To simplify the sampling procedure, no more than five children were coded in any one family. Those chosen from the larger households were either those who were employed, or those who exhibited different birthplaces from the others. Many of the children who were born in California were therefore excluded, as were some born in other states. Since a vast majority of those who did appear in the sample were from California, it is safe to assume that most of those left out were also native to the state.

Children's birthplaces were also checked for two nonartisan groups of workers in San Francisco, teamsters and day laborers. The data indicate that these groups were no more mobile than were the carpenters during the childbearing years. In 1880, 77 percent of the laborers' children and 86 percent of the teamsters' offspring had been born in California; in 1900, the figures were 83 and 87 percent. Neither group showed a large number of families having two different birthplaces for their children. In 1880, both groups had a lower proportion of mobile families than did the carpenters, while in 1900, the figure for the laborers was only slightly higher. This would seem to indicate that while most studies show skilled workers as more persistent than semiskilled and unskilled, the difference arises not from married family men, but more probably among the single wage earners.

36. Frank Roney, *Frank Roney, Irish Rebel and California Labor Leader: An Autobiography,* Ira B. Cross, ed., (Berkeley: University of California Press, 1931), 311. It should be noted that Roney was a mechanic, not a carpenter.

37. *The Carpenter,* October 1889, March 1898, June 1906, and September 1906.

38. Stephan Thernstrom, "Urbanization, Migration, and Social Mobility in Late Nineteenth-Century America," in Barton J. Bernstein, ed., *Towards a New Past:*

Dissenting Essays in American History (New York: Vintage Books, 1968), 169 (emphasis added).

39. A study of transiency in the eighteenth century indicates that mobile families were smaller than average, which implies that the transients were younger married couples rather than those of a more advanced age (Jones).

40. Stephan Thernstrom, "Working Class Social Mobility in Industrial America," in Melvin Richter, ed., *Essays in Theory and History* (Cambridge: Harvard University Press, 1970), 225. See also Thernstrom, "Urbanization, Migration and Social Mobility" and *The Other Bostonians,* 231.

41. For a complete discussion of the role of itinerancy in the formation of national unions, see Ulman, 49–154.

42. Thernstrom, *The Other Bostonians,* 230, Table 9.3. One reason that skilled workers might have had higher persistence levels than nonskilled might be related to age. For example, the average age of San Francisco carpenters in both 1880 and 1900 was higher than that of either teamsters or laborers and the gap increased over the two decades. See Tygiel, 182.

43. See David Brody, *Steelworkers in America: The Non-Union Era* (New York: Harper & Row, 1960) and Ray Ginger, "Labor in a Massachusetts Cotton Mill," *Business History Review* 28 (1954), 67–91. See also Herbert Gutman, "Work, Culture, and Society in Industrializing America, 1815–1919," *American Historical Review* 78 (June 1973), 531–87.

44. Joan Scott, *The Glassworkers of Carmaux* (Cambridge: Harvard University Press, 1974).

45. See Christie, 19–28, 79–90; Tygiel, 101–27. Swinton cited in Christie, 44.

46. See William Haber, *Industrial Relations in the Building Industry* (Cambridge: Harvard University Press, 1930) and Frederick L. Ryan, *Industrial Relations in the San Francisco Building Trades* (Normal: University of Oklahoma Press, 1935).

47. *The Carpenter,* November 1882 and August 1885.

48. Ibid., January 1887 and October 1884.

49. Ibid., August 1881.

50. For the origins of the United Brotherhood of Carpenters and Joiners, see Christie, 37–40, and Gabriel Edmonston, "The Genesis of the Brotherhood of Carpenters," *The Carpenter,* October 1904.

51. A complete discussion of the evolution of the travel card in American unions can be found in Ulman, 49–154. Some unions experimented with the system of traveling loans similar to that described by Hobsbawm for England (41). According to Ulman, however, "the national traveling-loan system was not overly successful. Rates of repayment were low; moreover, the induced mobility was not always salutary from the viewpoint of the national union . . ." (58). In general, unions in the United States never developed the elaborate tramping system that prevailed in England.

52. *The Carpenter,* October 1883.

53. *Constitution of the United Brotherhood of Carpenters and Joiners, 1881,* Article X.

54. *The Carpenter,* January 1886, February 1886, and November 1885.

55. For examples of these complaints and inquiries by local secretaries, see ibid., January 1886, February 1884, and December 1886.

56. Ibid., February 1886.

57. *Constitution of the United Brotherhood of Carpenters and Joiners, 1886,* Article XVII. For the experiences of other unions utilizing the two-card system, see Ulman, 97.

58. *Constitution of the United Brotherhood of Carpenters and Joiners, 1888,* Articles XVII and XIX.

59. Ulman, 151–52.

60. *The Carpenter,* May 1884 and January 1888.

61. Hobsbawm, 67.

62. *The Carpenter,* October 1884, May 1882, and May 1888. This was true among other workers as well. According to an item in the *Iron Molders' Journal* in 1889, "[through] the traveling propensities of a large proportion of our craft . . . the seeds of unionism were scattered broadcast over the continent." (Cited in Ulman, 144.)

63. Cited in *The Carpenter,* February 1886.

64. *The Carpenter,* July 1885.

65. Ibid., August 1883.

66. Ibid., April 1888.

67. Ibid., April 1882, and October 1884.

68. See Christie, especially chapters 5–11.

69. For a discussion of these matters, see Ulman, 108–54.

70. *Constitution of the United Brotherhood of Carpenters and Joiners, 1891,* Section 113; *1903,* Section 114; *1893,* Section 113.

71. Ibid., *1895,* Section 113; *The Carpenter,* October 1893.

72. *Constitution of the United Brotherhood of Carpenters and Joiners, 1895,* Section 113.

73. Ibid., Section 115; this proviso was actually instituted in November 1896, according to *The Carpenter* of that month.

74. *The Carpenter,* August 1890.

75. Ulman, 116–17. This was upheld in an 1887 decision that had prohibited the collection of differences in initiation fees. See *The Carpenter*, September 1887.

76. *Constitution of the United Brotherhood of Carpenter and Joiners, 1907*, Section 134.

77. *The Carpenter*, September 1896, May 1881, June 1890, and August 1896.

78. Ibid., June 1896. Other unions debated the desirability of tramping artisans as well. See, for example, the continuing debate on this issue in the *Iron Molders' Journal* in the 1880s and 1890s.

Patricia A. Cooper

The "Traveling Fraternity": Union Cigar Makers
and Geographic Mobility, 1900–1919

As a lifelong observer of the Cigar Makers' International Union of America (CMIU) remarked, "The cigar maker is a wanderer."[1] The description was simple but accurate. John R. Ograin, who learned cigar making in Salt Lake City in 1904, estimated that "99 percent, more or less" of the cigar makers in this AFL craft union traveled at some time during their working years.[2] In any given year in the early twentieth century, one-third or more of the members of the various locals nationwide left their home base to travel and work elsewhere.[3] Herman Baust, a cigar maker in New Haven, Connecticut, during the 1910s, recalled that there were "cigar factories all over the country, and [cigar makers] would travel. They were great travelers. They'd work so long in a factory, then off they'd be." So central was geographic mobility to the CMIU that members nicknamed their organization the "traveling fraternity."[4]

Although in the past many scholars have viewed mobility exclusively in economic terms—workers moved only because they had to—and have also associated it with working class instability and fragmentation, the case of union cigar makers suggests a different picture.[5] Their mobility constituted a vital craft custom and an indispensable element of work culture. By work culture I mean the system of traditions, beliefs, and accepted behaviors of workers in a particular occupation or workplace and the meaning and function of these patterns. Work culture expresses the system of ideas and practices through which workers adjust, modify, mediate and resist the limits of their situation on the job. Cigar makers had a rich craft culture in the early twentieth century, one which stressed values of mutuality, collective action, pride, and respectability and operated to assert workers' sense of dignity and "manhood" before employers.[6]

Union cigar makers' mobility was part of the body of cigar makers' traditions, but at the same time, mobility helped to sustain their occupational culture on a national level. Work rules and ethical codes cut across ethnic[7] and geographic lines and were common to all. The tradition of travel was transmitted to every newcomer to the union and served as a rite of initiation, part of the process of becoming an insider within the fraternity. The cigar makers had created over the years a coherent, well-organized system to support and maintain this craft custom. It daily reinforced a sense of community and interdependence among workers. Rather than allowing geographic mobility to undermine their union, cigar makers used it to their advantage as a way of asserting control over their working lives.

Cigar makers' work culture survived to enter the twentieth century largely because changes in the structure of the industry and the work process had threatened, but had not yet fully undermined, union cigar makers' sources of strength. The introduction of the wooden shaping mold and a division of the labor process in the 1870s had provided manufacturers with the means to cut wages and reduce their dependence on skilled workers. In the early twentieth century, the system of divided labor, called team work, continued to expand, particularly in the second decade, as the number and size of large, antiunion firms, hiring women exclusively, increased.

Yet as Andrew Dawson and others have warned, skilled workers did not unilaterally suffer deskilling at the same time and in the same way. A look at specific occupations reveals a considerable degree of diversity and unevenness.[8] The cigar industry remained competitive and decentralized, and while several mechanical tools had been introduced which further simplified the labor process, technology had not yet advanced to the point of permitting mass production. The American Tobacco Company launched an intensive drive between 1901 and 1904 to monopolize cigar making as it had the rest of the tobacco industry, but James Duke was never able to gain control of more than 16 percent of production, in part because he needed the efficiency of mechanization.

The absence of machinery, along with a public prejudice in favor of hand-made goods, provided union cigar makers with a niche in the higher grade cigar market (cigars priced at ten cents and up made using imported tobaccos), which allowed them a degree of security. Gradually they held less and less influence in production of the expanding cheaper brands, where nonunion women increasingly were employed.[9] Union membership continued to grow in the twentieth century, although more slowly than before, from about 34,000 in 1900 to 40,000 in 1919—somewhere between 30 and 40 percent of all cigar makers in the country.[10]

Union cigar makers continued to work by hand, using only a cutting knife, a work board, and often the wooden shaping mold. Union rules frequently prohibited the team system. Thus, despite evolution in the industry, union cigar makers had been able to hold their own in the early twentieth century. Their skills were still needed and jobs were plentiful enough that travelers had a reasonable expectation of finding work. As one member explained it, "There was so much abundance of jobs that you didn't have to be afraid. You quit and come back in a couple of weeks."[11]

Cigar makers were certainly not the only skilled workers to be so mobile—carpenters, hatters, and printers had strong traditions of mobility and nearly every AFL craft union at some point issued traveling cards and assisted traveling members.[12] These customs were doubtless rooted in the long association of craft work and travel in Europe. On the continent, the seventeenth- and eighteenth-century French craft workers' convention of a *tour de France,* the German *Wanderflicht,* and customs of journeyman travel in Poland, Bohemia, Hungary and elsewhere all required travel for completion of craft training. Expanding preliminary research by Eric Hobsbawm, R. A. Leeson in *Travelling Brothers* has recently traced craft travel in England over six centuries, firmly linking thirteenth-century guilds with eighteenth- and nineteenth-century trade unions. Skilled craftsmen's mobility acted not only as a means of securing employment, but as a final stage of learning, a tradition passed from generation to generation.[13]

Just when and how the cigar makers' traveling custom in the United States originated remains a mystery because of fragmentary evidence. It is possible that German cigar makers practiced customs of journeyman travel and thus carried such traditions with them when they migrated to the United States before and after the Civil War. In any case, cigar makers in the United States were certainly traveling in the 1860s, for reciprocity among locals with regard to traveling members was a major concern of the newly formed National Cigar Makers' Union in 1864. Travelers could undercut wages in local areas and thus, throughout the 1870s and 1880s, members of the CMIU debated ways to control the problem. They experimented with several travel assistance programs during the following years and finally settled on a permanent plan of loans to members in 1880.[14]

The most obvious explanation of cigar makers' geographic mobility is that of basic economic necessity. Loss of a job due to local business downturns or strikes frequently prompted members to search for work elsewhere. The union's benefit package provided members who lost their jobs with three dollars a week, and strikers with five dollars a week. But such payments fell far short of regular wages ranging as high as thirty dollars a week. Many members therefore took to the road. By contrast, during periods of national economic distress, such as the depression of the 1890s and the recessions of 1907–9 and 1914–15, cigar makers stayed home. Rather than borrowing money to travel, cigar makers accepted the union's out-of-work benefit, since they recognized the futility of traveling when economic conditions were poor everywhere.[15]

A number of cigar makers doubtless were forced to travel because of personal factors. Certainly some were alcoholics, since drinking and socializing after work in saloons were so much a part of the everyday patterns of union cigar makers. Those with tuberculosis, a major health problem for cigar makers, migrated west to regain health in many cases. Those whose workmanship was poor were also included in the ranks of drifters. Within the trade, however, travelers generally had reputations for being some of the best craftsmen. Frank Shea, a stockboy and later foreman in the prosperous R. G. Sullivan factory in Manchester, New Hampshire, defended the skills of the travelers, noting that "to knock around the country you had to be a pretty good cigar maker." Raymond

Steber, a manufacturer in Warren, Pennsylvania, in business with his father, observed that "a lot of those fellows, those tourists, they'd worked in a million different factories and they were really experts."[16]

Travel as an economic decision should also be viewed in broader, cultural terms, as a group strategy to help cigar makers negotiate the limits of their position within the production process which made them so acutely vulnerable to shifts in the economy and the demands and power of employers. Cigar makers required manufacturers to spread the available work rather than lay off members if orders were slack. When the trade was "dull," young single members would "do as the large percentage of single men do under the system, 'go on the road,' which at certain times of the year is not taken as a 'pleasure trip,' and will willingly go rather than break his obligation to the union. . . ." Thus cigar makers could use the traveling system to avoid draining union benefit funds, prevent mass suspensions or scabbing in hard times by circulating the unemployed, and relieve pressure in any one locale.[17]

The reasons and impact of the traveling system extend beyond the bounds of necessity. A complex mix of motives sparked the various journeys. Consider, for example, William Theisen. In 1915, temporarily laid off from his job in Denver, he left and took another in Livingston, Montana, where he had heard about plenty of openings. After he had worked there a few months, two fellow workers who were planning to hobo to Seattle, Washington, by jumping aboard freight trains west coaxed him to join them. The trip to Seattle and back took about two weeks, as they worked making cigars occasionally along the way. When he returned, he paid his fare back to Denver and assumed his former job. His unemployment had initially forced him to leave Denver, but he had continued to travel for unrelated reasons.[18]

Travel must be understood in the context of a matrix of values and traditions embedded in cigar makers' occupational culture. In order to set their own work pace and combine work with leisure during the day, cigar makers demanded a piece rate system of payment—about fifteen to thirty dollars per thousand cigars. With each man responsible for his own production, he could control his time, choosing, within certain limits, when he wanted to work and when he would rather be elsewhere.

"When you're working piecework," John Ograin observed, "your time is your own," and cigar makers moved in and out of the factory freely during the eight-hour day. Raymond Steber in Warren remembered with annoyance that occasionally in the afternoon one might stand up calling, " 'Well, who wants to get drunk?' . . . and the whole crowd of them would put away their tools and adjourn to the nearest saloon, which . . . was only a few doors away . . . and we were shut down for the day."[19]

The work culture of the cigar makers stressed the diverging interests of boss and cigar makers. Members could be fined for "being on too intimate terms with the proprietor" or ostracized from the work group for being a "sucker," someone who did "things for the boss that wasn't called for."[20] Cigar makers used various means of asserting their interests in the workplace, including shop strikes—unofficial walkouts lasting only a few hours, but long enough to express collective displeasure. While recognizing the realities of manufacturers' power over them as wage earners and the limitations this placed on them, cigar makers believed that each member had the freedom to reject conditions which compromised manhood.[21]

The friendships formed in the cigar shop made strong bonds. "You have to have gone through it to know what it was all about," José Santana explained. "Developing from day to day, for years and years, it was a brotherhood . . . cigar makers' union was more like a brotherhood. Friendship and brotherhood." Since cigar making was a noiseless and sedentary trade, the hours spent at work were filled with endless conversation. After work the congenial atmosphere of the shop floor migrated to a nearby tavern. On weekends, picnics and playing baseball brought the cigar makers together again.[22]

The traveling tradition thus was a rite of passage, a cultural obligation of every newcomer to the union fraternity. This was especially true of hoboing. Most traveling was not hoboing, but everyone was expected to try this form of travel at least once. "I don't know why we did," remarked Ograin, "but you had to take a hobo trip. If you didn't hobo—why they used to say, 'All right. You're through with your apprenticeship. Now go out and learn the trade.' " Ograin tried to hobo since it was the "fashion," but when his experiment left him "ditched" north of Salt Lake City, minus his belongings, he resolved that his first hobo trip would be his last. Thereafter he traveled and worked in Denver, St. Louis, and Chicago, but he always paid his fare.[23]

Travel generally, and hoboing in particular, materialized from peer pressure and braggadocio, products of the masculine nature of the work culture. William Theisen had been reluctant to hobo, for example, but the two cigar makers he met in Livingston " 'mashed' it in so much they'd make you think that you're chicken or something," so he had finally given in. In shop conversation, travelers bragged about how many times they had traveled across the country, how many factories they had worked in, how they had escaped some threatening predicament, how their cigar making talents had enabled them to get jobs anywhere, or how far they had hoboed in one stretch. These workplace conversations encouraged others to try their skill on the road in order to test their proficiency and to gain admission to the cultural world of shop floor talk.[24]

The system of traveling itself provided cigar makers with a strong inducement to travel. By taking a break from the monotony and routine of work, cigar makers could have a role in shaping working life and making it more satisfying. Many cigar makers traveled out of curiosity. José Santana remembered listening to a cigar maker "talk all day about 'Frisco" and he decided to go there for himself to see what the city was like. Their traveling system allowed cigar makers to exercise individual choice and encouraged variation. They traveled for many reasons: a "pleasure trip," "adventure," "to escape the winter cold," and "itchings to be on the move."[25]

Cigar makers regarded their traveling as an assertion of their independence from employers and their right to move for any reason. Like the flexible hours they kept during the day, travel signified their freedom to control their own time. Travel additionally permitted cigar makers to distance themselves from the demands of any one workplace. Herman Baust remembered that many travelers he met had become very particular about shop conditions. "If they came in the shop, and something didn't suit them, the tobacco wasn't right, they'd go right out."[26]

The operation of the traveling system offers more clues about the system's impact on the cigar makers, both individually and collectively, and on the industry as a whole. Over the years, rank and file members, using their rights of initiative within the union governing apparatus, altered and modified the traveling system. They enforced a code of discipline to keep it running smoothly for the benefit of the group as a whole rather than the individuals within it.

Although cigar makers traveled at all stages of their lives, it is likely that a majority at any given time were young and single. José Santana, who traveled throughout the Unites States and Canada from 1909 to 1917, noted that he had been so mobile because "a man before he gets to the stage of raising a family, he needs to know about life." Thus, while travel and life cycle were clearly related, all members, whether traveling or not, had some connection to the system through their own experiences and through contact with newcomers. Although by custom, economic hard times usually sent the most mobile on the road first, the system stood open for anyone who needed or wanted to use it. A contingent of cigar makers became virtually addicted to constant movement and traveled throughout their lives regardless of other obligations or ties. Each month *Cigar Makers' Official Journal* (CMOJ), the union's own publication founded in 1875, carried notices from wives and children seeking to track down neglectful husbands or fathers. Such requests as "Anyone knowing the whereabouts of Fred Doxey will please notify his wife, Josie Doxey, 30 Darthmouth Street, Boston, Massachusetts," and "The children of Frank Meyer (40438) desire to know the whereabouts of their father, as they are in need" appeared monthly.[27]

A cigar maker who wanted to travel requested a traveling card from his local secretary, which proved his membership in good standing, and left for whatever destination he desired. He could also take out a travel loan of up to eight dollars. The exact amount, based on the train fare to the nearest local in whatever direction he wished to proceed, averaged around four dollars. He could accumulate a total debt of twenty dollars, but then his card was considered "full," and he could not borrow on it again until the debt had been reduced. Once he began working, 10 percent of his weekly earnings were taken to repay the loan.[28]

There were no set paths or routes, such as in the old guild systems.

Decisions on destination could be based partly on the general knowledge cigar makers accumulated about wages and conditions elsewhere through working and listening in a union shop. More current information was available through CMOJ, which was delivered to factories in the middle of each month. Each issue contained a "State of Trade" column grouping locals under headings of "Good," "Fair," and "Dull," and locals experiencing poor conditions or enforcing boycotts or strikes placed warnings in the journal. Information on local conditions also came from friends who wrote letters from distant points and newcomers to a factory who related their previous experiences. Union rules forbade a cigar maker from writing to factories or union secretaries to ask for a job because writing ahead for a specific job put a cigar maker ahead of his traveling colleagues, a violation of union principle stressing the interests of the collective group.[29]

Upon arriving at any union town, a cigar maker could expect to find familiar patterns and a warm welcome, even if he knew no one there. The traveler might first look for the union secretary by stopping at a union factory, union headquarters (if the local were big enough to support one), or, after work, at a local tavern. Secretaries dispensed travel loans to those who wanted to continue their journeys and provided information on housing and jobs to those who planned to stay and work. In some locals the traveler might receive a "meal ticket" for a free dinner and a "boarding house order," a guarantee to a rooming house keeper that the cigar maker had a job and would be able to meet his obligations. Enough cigar makers failed to pay board bills before leaving town to make this a matter of concern. Often a local covered the debt in order to preserve good relations with the boarding house and then attempted to track down the guilty party for reimbursement.[30]

Travelers who wanted to work deposited their travel cards with the secretary, who provided them with a list of job openings or sent them to see a foreman. Once he was hired, a cigar maker began working for a day to prove his skill. Soon the shop collector approached to make sure his membership was in order. In smaller union factories, cigar makers could get work even if no jobs were open. Travelers were given an "accommodation job": they could work for a day or an afternoon and make enough to move on.[31]

The traveling system built cigar makers' confidence and pride in themselves and their union because members knew they could head in any direction, find a job, and depend on fellow unionists for support and assistance. The union locals provided private loans to individuals in addition to travel loans, but cigar makers did not always have to go into debt. If his travel loan card were full, he might give his card to the shop collector, who passed the hat among the cigar makers in the shop, saying "This fellow needs a hand." Workers gave a nickel, dime, or whatever they had. To eliminate the necessity of repeated hat-passing, some locals contributed to a "tramp stake" or "tourist fund" which automatically gave out $1.50. Cigar makers regarded themselves as very generous—Herman Baust remembered that he was "always giving something." John Ograin recalled arriving at a factory in Eugene, Oregon early one morning and meeting several cigar makers before the factory opened. When one learned that Ograin had not yet eaten, he tossed "a quarter into my hand for breakfast. I really believe we had the most fraternal-minded group in the whole country."[32]

Cigar makers' work culture strongly condemned abuse of the traveling system, and members tried several ways of controlling it. For example, since some nonunion cigar makers joined the CMIU only when they wanted to travel, several locals refused to accept cards less than six months old except for apprentices who had just "finished their time." Those with loans were careful to avoid any misunderstanding with regard to repayment. John Fischer chose to keep in touch with the secretary of Local 162 of Green Bay, Wisconsin, concerning the money he had borrowed from the local. Writing from Cairo, Illinois, he thanked the local for the loan and explained that "I have just gone to work here and will pay up as soon as I can. I worked a little in Memphis, Tenn. Had to move. I am feeling somewhat better as it is getting a little cooler. Thanking the boys of Local 162, Green Bay Wisc. I am Yours Truly."[33]

CMOJ was particularly useful in enforcing rules governing travel. The journal carried notices from locals asking members to pay travel or private loans. If general calls for payment did not achieve results, the wayward cigar maker could have his name printed in the journal, an ignominious fate to be scrupulously avoided by those who valued their reputations as union men. To prevent such dishonor, some asked patience in letters to the union journal and promised to pay as soon as possible. Still, each issue included names of many who had hoped to escape specific notice for their misdeeds. Fred Doxey, mentioned above, was wanted not only by his wife. In May 1905, CMOJ contained the following: "Will Fred Doxey please send the three weeks' board to Mrs. Wigley that he owes her, and oblige Susan Wigley, Newport, R.I.?" Another notice read cryptically: "Chas. Rudy is wanted by Union 35. He knows what for." CMOJ also provided a vehicle for locals to warn each other about frauds or "an ungrateful traveler who don't deserve any help."[34]

Cigar makers used CMOJ to facilitate a "much boasted" communication system, providing a way for members to keep in touch with each other and with relatives. Local unions accepted mail for members, and letters not delivered were listed in the "Letter Box" column. Cigar makers could thus learn where mail was being held and send for it. After a month, any unclaimed letters, and there were few, were returned to the Post Office. The "Bureau of Information" column printed names of cigar makers who wanted to hear from cigar making friends. "Richard Bonnelli . . . Los Angeles, Cal., would like to hear from Chas. Ehrieke, formerly of Meriden, Conn. for old-time sake." Parents, sisters, brothers and wives used CMOJ to locate a relative or transmit news. "Nellie Rule would like to hear from her brother John, and let him know that his brother Michael died July 10, 1906." Or; "Fred Stroud, send address home at once. May seriously ill and mother almost frantic." Many notices included such phrases as, "When last heard from he was in Montana."[35]

The traveling system also worked as a resource in cigar makers' daily shop floor struggle with manufacturers. They could use it to regulate, in some measure, the size and distribution of the labor force. Threats of strikes had to be taken seriously because cigar makers had the machinery to remove members physically and reduce the chance for undercutting or scabbing during strikes or layoffs. Further, after the strike ended, weeks passed before word spread that it had been settled and enough workers reappeared to return production to normal, a serious risk for the relatively small, local market union manufacturer. Employers had learned to accept the traveling tradition because they depended on it to provide them with enough workers to fill their cigar making benches. Raymond Steber in Warren, Pennsylvania, admitted that there was little he could have done about the travelers, whom he called "tourists." "I suppose maybe we could have fired all the tourists and not hired any. Well, then we'd have been out of business for labor." The extent and frequency of mobility in the midst of generally high employment levels and relative prosperity in the trade intensified a condition of relative labor shortage. As long as union manufacturers wanted the delicate skills that the union monopolized, cigar makers could use their control over the distribution of needed workers and the apparent labor shortage as a resource.[36]

Travel meant that cigar makers could directly compare varying Bills of Prices, the cigar makers' wage agreement, and the different factory conditions and employer policies in various cities and use this information in formulating their own demands. Fresh arrivals would "tell you where they'd come from, how things were over there and over here," James Durso, a cigar maker in New Haven, Connecticut, recounted. If present conditions were less favorable than past ones, noted Frank Shea, who worked as a stockboy in Manchester, New Hampshire, the travelers called attention to the difference so that their presence sparked shop strikes. Raymond Stebler blamed all of his labor troubles on travelers, and complained that "we had many 'hobo' cigar makers. . . . They liked nothing better than turmoil, would . . . make ridiculous demands and go on strike at the drop of a hat." It is perhaps not surprising that tramping cigar makers in the nineteenth century had been the original organizers of the CMIU before such jobs were systematized in the 1880s. When the collective power of the cigar makers could not match that of manufacturers in trade matters, cigar makers could leave conditions which they interpreted personally as compromising dignity and self-respect.[37]

But the first two decades of the twentieth century proved to be the end of the craft work stage of cigar factory production, where craft customs, such as the cigar makers' celebrated mobility, flourished. During these transitional years, small union manufacturers with limited local and regional markets believed they needed union labor to produce the goods that consumers wanted. An ominous turn of events in August 1919 foreshadowed a change in these assumptions and in the configuration of the entire industry. In the midst of a strike in Boston, union cigar makers learned that Waitt and Bond Company, long a mainstay of the union, had opened two new plants in Newark, New Jersey, employing nonunion women operating new automatic cigar making machines. The American Machine and Foundry Company, formerly a subsidiary of the American Tobacco Company and part of the trust's initial plan in 1900 to take over the cigar industry using machinery, had finally succeeded in perfecting a cigar making device which could use relatively unskilled labor.[38]

The new machinery spread in the 1920s, but several other factors operated at the same time to affect both the union and the industry. Postwar cigar consumption levels dropped precipitously as consumers increasingly turned to cheaper cigarettes. Smokers became less concerned about quality and thus more interested in the least expensive cigars. Only the cheapest cigars could compete with cigarettes, yet in most cases they could not be produced cheaply enough to insure a profit without mechanization. The use of the cigar machine stimulated the concentration and consolidation of the industry as many smaller firms were either bought up or forced out of business. The largest firms alone could afford to lease the expensive machinery, and these were nonunion. With national markets and the cheaper products the public seemed to want, these corporations, run by managers, not family businessmen, did not feel they needed union labor to sell their goods. Manufacturers' conscious policy of relocating firms away from traditional areas of union strength to such nonunion, lower wage regions as New Jersey, Pennsylvania, and Florida also damaged the union's position. Cigar makers' craft traditions made them slow to even consider organizing the new machine operators. Prohibition removed a major retail outlet for union products, the saloon, further eroding the union's position. Membership fell from 40,000 in 1919 to 15,000 in 1933.[39]

Throughout the 1920s the number of union travelers declined, and no jobs awaited them. While some union companies such as Waitt and Bond had switched to machines, others had drastically cut back production or gone out of business, unable to compete. Since the handmade trade held no future, fewer young men entered it. As the population of union cigar makers aged, the number of travelers similarly dwindled. Layoffs forced many to abandon cigar making—William Theisen started working in a furniture store in 1924—and others, such as José Santana, turned to opening their own small shops as a strategy for continuing to work in the trade. In 1928 the members of the CMIU consented to dropping the travel loan, and the formal traveling system supported by the CMIU came to an end. The union recorded thousands of dollars of outstanding loans. "We decided to wipe out the debt," Ograin sighed. "We had about a quarter of a million dollars coming for traveling loans, but what the heck [was] the use of carrying it on the books? Most of them were dead."[40]

The traveling system never revived, although patterns of mobility among union cigar makers emerged again during the Depression, when many cigar makers moved looking desperately for any kind of work. By the 1930s nearly 80 percent of U.S. cigars were machine-made. One hand manufacturer in Connecticut who employed ten to fifteen men during the late 1930s remembered scores of cigar makers coming to the factory begging for jobs and sleeping nearby in vacant buildings alongside the railroad tracks. Tampa cigar makers in 1937, who had by then joined the CMIU, gathered what funds they could and paid local residents with cars to drive them to New York City, where relief checks were larger and the chance of a day's work outside the trade seemed more of a possibility. A tiny band of union cigar makers was on the move again, but this time it was a matter of sheer survival in a dying industry.[41]

The cigar makers' traveling system served their interests well into the early twentieth century. They used it to combine work and leisure, to alter the work environment, and to advance their collective interests vis-à-vis manufacturers. Through it they created a remarkably efficient informal communication network relaying information among hundreds of cities and towns all over the country. The frequent arrival of newcomers connected distant locals, served as a steady source of information and news from the outside world, and militated against the narrow concerns and isolation of one factory or shop. The mixing of people and experiences linked those who stayed with those who moved and helped to hold together a national occupational culture. The cigar makers had created a coherent, well-organized system to support and maintain this craft custom, a system which daily reinforced values of interdependence and community, freedom and independence. But cigar makers' craft work culture was a product of a transient and very specific set of conditions. When the industry began changing rapidly after 1919, that work culture and with it the cigar makers' tradition of mobility disappeared. In 1974, the 2,000 cigar makers left in the CMIU, most of whom operated automatic cigar making machines, voted to end the union's 110-year history and merge with the Retail, Wholesale and Department Store Union of America.

Notes

The author wishes to thank Susan Porter Benson, Cynthia Harrison, Barbara Melosh, William Pretzer, and Donald Ritchie for their comments on earlier drafts of this essay.

1. A. M. Simons, "A Label and Lives—The Story of the Cigar Makers," *Pearson's Magazine,* January 1917, 70.

2. John R. Ograin, letter to author, 29 September1979. John Ograin was born in Salt Lake City in 1889 and learned the trade of cigar making when he was fifteen. He moved to Chicago in 1917 and was elected vice-president of the CMIU in 1928. He is one of over fifty cigar makers, managers, and manufacturers I have interviewed since 1976 in connection with my study of workers in the cigar industry between 1900 and 1940. This essay draws on interviews with eleven people, all of whom were in some way associated with union cigar factories in the years before 1920. Except for some conversations with José Santana, all of these interviews are tape-recorded and in my possession.

3. It is impossible to determine precisely the volume of travel each year in the union. The CMIU published only yearly total loan amounts, not numbers of individual loans. Gauging turnover for one city using the 1900 census and city directories is not fruitful because the intervals are too long to capture the mobility of those workers who spent only a few weeks in one place. Any estimate is thus somewhat impressionistic. By dividing yearly travel amounts by eight dollars, the maximum amount of any loan, to reach a rough approximation of the number of loans granted, one reaches an estimate of 25–35 percent between 1900 and 1916. Most took less than that amount and many did not borrow at all. What lends further credence to the estimate is the attention given to traveling in the union's

monthly journal and the magnitude suggested by those interviewed. Considering other studies' findings on levels of geographic mobility in the general population, this rate is not surprising or exceptional.

4. Interview, Herman Baust, 24 March 1977, North Haven, Connecticut; *Cigar Makers' International Union Diamond Jubilee,* 26–28 July 1939 (Washington, D.C., 1939), 11. References to the "traveling fraternity" are scattered throughout the *Cigar Makers' Official Journal* (hereafter cited as CMOJ). From my reading of the journal and my interviews, it appears that during the 1870s and into the 1880s, the term referred primarily to those members who were traveling. By the early twentieth century, however, it was more commonly used to refer to the union as a whole.

5. Charles Stephenson has recently pointed out the problem with interpreting working class mobility in this way. See Charles Stephenson, "A Gathering of Strangers? Mobility, Social Structure, and Political Participation in the Formation of Nineteenth-Century American Workingclass Culture," in Milton Cantor, ed., *American Workingclass Culture: Explorations in American Labor and Social History* (Westport, Conn.: Greenwood Press, 1979), 32, 40. Nearly every craft union in the American Federation of Labor issued traveling cards and gave some assistance to traveling members. Lloyd Ulman has outlined these programs, but provided only a limited economic interpretation of them. See Lloyd Ulman, *The Rise of the National Trade Union: The Development and Significance of Its Structure, Governing Institutions, and Economic Policies* (Cambridge, Mass.: Harvard University Press, 1955), 53–54.

6. My definition of work culture is drawn from my dissertation, "From Hand Craft to Mass Production: Men, Women and Work Culture in American Cigar Factories, 1900–1919" (University of Maryland, 1981), to be published by the University of Illinois Press. My ideas about the concept have been influenced by the work of many scholars, including Barbara Melosh, *The Physician's Hand: Work Culture and Conflict in American Nursing* (Philadelphia: Temple University Press, 1982); Susan Porter Benson, "The 'Clerking Sisterhood': Rationalization and Work Culture of Saleswomen in American Department Stores, 1890–1960," *Radical America* 12 (March–April 1978), 41–55; David A. Bensman, "Artisan Culture, Business Union: American Hat Finishers in the Nineteenth Century" (Ph.D. dissertation, Columbia University, 1977); Bryan Palmer, "Most Uncommon Common Men: Craft and Culture in Historical Perspective," *Labour/Le Travailleur* 1 (1976), 5–31; Herbert Gutman, *Work Culture and Society in Industrializing America: Essays in American Working-Class and Social History* (New York: Random House, 1977); and David Montgomery, *Workers' Control in America: Studies in the History of Work, Technology and Labor Struggles* (Cambridge, Mass.: Harvard University Press, 1979).

7. Germans continued to dominate the union in the early twentieth century as they had in the nineteenth, but members represented a wide spectrum of ethnic groups including Bohemians, Belgians, Dutch, Poles, Irish, British, Scandinavians, and German and Russian Jews. There were some Cubans in the union as well.

8. Andrew Dawson, "The Paradox of Dynamic Technological Change and the Labor Aristocracy in the United States, 1880–1914," *Labor History* 20 (Summer 1979), 325–51.

9. For a general survey of these conditions see Willis Baer, *The Economic Development of the Cigar Manufacturing Industry in the United States* (Lancaster, Pa.: n.p., 1933), 99–107; Meyer Jacobstein, *The Tobacco Industry in the United States* (New York: Columbia University Press, 1907), 11, 87–88, 146–47; Lucy Windsor Killough, *The Tobacco Products Industry in New York and Its Environs* (New York: Regional Plan of New York, 1924), 20–24; Wilmoth D. Evans, *Mechanization and Productivity of Labor in the Cigar Manufacturing Industry,* in U.S. Department of Labor, Bureau of Labor, Bureau of Labor Statistics, Bulletin 660 (Washington, D.C., 1938), 54–55; U.S. Bureau of Labor, *Eleventh Special Report of the Commissioner of Labor. Regulation and Restriction of Output* (Washington, D.C., 1904), 573, 577, 583; U.S. Bureau of Corporations, *Report of the Commissioner of Corporations in the Tobacco Industry,* pt. 1, *Position of the Tobacco Combination in the Industry* (Washington, D.C., 1909), 423–27; CMOJ, April 1920, 2–4, and September 1912, 12–16.

10. Census figures group together all tobacco workers, thus making it difficult to distinguish cigar makers from other workers. The CMIU collected its own records and printed them in CMOJ, September 1901, 8; September 1912, 14–15; and April 1920, 3. The 1910 *Census of Occupations* broke down tobacco occupations, and these figures roughly correspond with union data for 1912. See U.S. Department of Commerce, Bureau of the Census, *Thirteenth Census of the United States,* 1910, vol. 4, *Population, Occupational Statistics,* 396.

11. Interview with José Santana 13 August 1976, Chicago, Illinois. José Santana was born in Mayaguez, Puerto Rico in 1890 and came to the mainland in 1909. A third section of the U.S. cigar industry was the Clear Havana industry. These cigars, modeled after their Cuban counterparts, were made in Tampa and Key West, Florida, by Cuban and Spanish workmen using centuries-old methods of handwork on hundreds of intricate styles and shapes. These were the country's most expensive cigars, costing fifteen to twenty-five cents and up. Several union factories made Clear Havana cigars—particularly those in Denver, Chicago, New York City, and San Francisco.

12. Concerning these skilled workers see Bensman, "Artisan Culture, Business Union," 97–104; William Pretzer, " 'Love of Grog and Desperate Passion for Clean Shirts': The Tramp Printer in Nineteenth-Century America," paper read at the

Organization of American Historians convention, Detroit, Michigan, April 1981; Jules Tygiel's essay in this book. These tradesmen were all less mobile in the twentieth century than in the nineteenth century.

13. Peter Bourke, *Popular Culture in Early Modern Europe* (New York: Harper & Row, 1978), 36–40; William James Ashley, *Surveys, Historic and Economic,* reprint (New York: A. M. Kelley, 1966), 251–57; Georges Renard, *Guilds in the Middle Ages,* reprint (New York: A. M. Kelley, 1968 [1918]), 13, 70; George Clune, *The Medieval Guild System* (Dublin: Browne and Nolan, Ltd., 1943), 179; Sidney Webb and Beatrice Webb, *History of Trade Unionism,* reprint (Clifton, New Jersey: A. M. Kelley, 1973 [1920]), 25, 444–51; Helga Grebing, *The History of the German Labour Movement: A Survey* (London: Wolff, 1969), 26, 29; Joan Scott, *Glassworkers of Carmaux: French Craftsmen and Political Action in a Nineteenth-Century City* (Cambridge, Mass.: Harvard University Press, 1974), 46–52; Eric Hobsbawm, "The Tramping Artisan," in *Labouring Men: Studies in the History of Labour* (London: Weidenfeld and Nicolson, 1964), 34–63; R. A. Leeson, *Travelling Brothers: The Six Centuries' Road from Craft Fellowship to Trade Unionism* (London: G. Allen & Unwin, 1979).

14. CMOJ, October 1980, 6–7 and July 1910, 2–3; Marie H. Hourwich, "Cigar Makers' Union History, 1851–1879," Research Files, Box 22, David Saposs Papers, State Historical Society of Wisconsin (hereafter cited as SHSW), Madison, Wisc.: Ulman, *National Trade Union,* 51, 58; James B. Kennedy, *Beneficiary Features of American Trade Unions* (Baltimore: Johns Hopkins University Press, 1908), 594–95. See also CMOJ, December 1876, 2; March 1872, 2; April 1877, 2.

15. *Constitution of the Cigar Makers' International Union of America,* 1896, 1912, 1916, 1917, 1919, Section 79, Series V, Box 2, Cigar Makers' International Union of America Collection, McKeldin Library, University of Maryland, College Park, Maryland; "By-Laws of the Cigar Makers' Union No. 192 of Manchester, N.H.," Manchester Public Library, Manchester, N.H.,; Interview, Santana, January 11, 1976, by telephone; CMOJ, June 1910, 4 and April 1920, 4.

16. CMOJ, December 1915, 39; September 1902, 5; April 1903, 3; Interview, Baust, 24 March 1977; Interview, T. Frank Shea, 26 June 1979, Manchester, New Hampshire; Interview, Raymond W. Steber, 24 July 1978, Warren, Pennsylvania. T. Frank Shea worked for the R. G. Sullivan factory in Manchester, New Hampshire from 1909, when he was seventeen, to 1961, first as a stockboy and later as a foreman. Raymond Steber and his father ran a union factory in Warren, Pennsylvania, until 1914 when, angered by disruptive strikes, they moved the factory to Reading. The notion that travelers were expert workmen was not confined to cigar making alone. See Paul Fisher, "A Forgotten Gentry of the Fourth Estate," *Journalism Quarterly* 33 (1956), 167–75.

17. CMOJ, March 1906, 6 and June 1906, 11; Interview, Santana, 11 January 1976, by telephone.

18. Interview, William Theisen, 17 August 1979, Denver, Colorado. William Theisen began learning cigar making in Denver in 1912. His father was a laborer born in Germany and his mother was a homemaker born in the United States.

19. Interview, Santana, 18 November 1979, by telephone; "Bill of Prices," for Baltimore, Cincinnati, Chicago, Philadelphia and New York, U.S. Department of Labor Library, Washington, D.C.; "Bill of Prices" for Milwaukee and Philadelphia, SHSW; "Bill of Prices," for Manchester, New Hampshire; "Bill of Prices," for Boston, Boston Public Library, Boston, Mass.; David A. McCabe, *The Standard Rate in American Trade Unions* (Baltimore: Johns Hopkins Press, 1912), 53, 55; CMOJ, May 1904, 5; Interview, Ograin, 17 May 1980; Interview, Steber, 24 July 1978; Steber to author, 15 June 1978.

20. Minutes of Local 208, Kalamazoo, Michigan, 8 July 1907, Western Michigan University, Kalamazoo, Michigan; CMOJ, September 1904, 8; Interview, Ograin, 17 May 1980. ("By-Laws" for several of the locals including Chicago, Kalamazoo, Boston, and Detroit at SHSW and Department of Labor libraries include rules on propriety with regard to associating with manufacturers.)

21. Algie Simons, "A Label and Lives," 73; Interview, Theisen, 17 August 1979; Interview, Steber, 24 July 1978; Interview, Baust, 24 March 1977; Interview, T. Frank Shea 26 June 1979; *Tobacco Leaf,* 24 June 1903; 6. In his CMOJ editorials, CMIU President George W. Perkins frequently admonished members for striking so hastily. See for example, CMOJ, September 1903, 8; June 1903, 8; and March 1909, 8. For a discussion of the term "manhood" see David Montgomery, "Workers' Control of Machine Production in the Nineteenth Century," in his *Workers' Control in America,* 9–31.

22. Interview, James Durso, 24 March 1977; Interview, Baust, 24 March 1977; Interview, Santana, 20 May 1979, 13 August 1976, and 22 July 1979, by telephone; Interview, T. Frank Shea, 26 June 1979; "By-Laws," Local 192, 10; CMOJ, May 1906, 4; August 1906, 2; October 1906, 3; November 1906, 4; August 1905; 10; and December 1902, 11; Norman Eliason, "The Language of the Buckeye," *American Speech* 12 (1937), 270–74. James Durso was born in New York City of Italian parents who moved to New Haven when he was six. His father was a bricklayer, but he became a cigar maker because a childhood injury weakened one arm. He began working in the early 1920s.

23. Interview, Ograin, 11 August 1976; Ograin to author, 29 September 1979; Interview, Ograin, 2 August 1977; Interview, Leon Rogiers, 27 June 1979, Manchester, New Hampshire; Interview, Theisen, 17 August 1979. Leon Rogiers learned the trade in Belgium and emigrated to the United States in about 1909 or 1910 as a teenager.

24. *Cigar Makers' Diamond Jubilee*, 10; CMOJ, October 1904, 7; March 1906, 5; and June 1906, 11; Interview, Santana, 28 May 1979, by telephone; "Gold Star Buckeye," typescript, 1937, Papers of the Works Progress Administration, New Hampshire Federal Writer's Project, Manchester City Library, Manchester, New Hampshire; Interview, Margaret Kehm, 25 July 1978, Warren, Pennsylvania; Interview, Leon Rogiers, 27 June 1979. Margaret Kehm learned to strip tobacco in a cigar factory in Warren, Pennsylvania.

25. Interview, Santana.

26. Interview, Baust, 24 March 1977; *Cigar Makers' Union Diamond Jubilee*, 10.

27. Interview, Santana, 18 November 1979, by telephone; Interview, Kehm, 25 July 1978; CMOJ, February 1914, 26; January 1900, 14; March 1911, 10; April 1908, 6; June 1910, 7; February 1909, 14; and September 1913, 13. Margaret and George Kehm traveled and worked together for five years before settling in Warren, and raising a family. Ograin noted that cases of traveling couples were not altogether rare.

28. *Cigar Makers' Constitution*, Section 16; Jacobstein, *Tobacco Industry*, 90, 148–50; Interview, Ograin, 17 May 1980; *Cigar Makers' Union Diamond Jubilee*, 11.

29. CMOJ, February 1900, 12; July 1901, 7; February 1902, 4; and October 1914, 3; Interview, Santana, 18 May 1979; *Cigar Makers' Constitution*, Section 16. Prohibitions against writing ahead were included in union by-laws as well. These were not always strictly obeyed, however, according to many of the cigar makers I interviewed.

30. *Cigar Makers' Constitution*, Section 113; Lloyd Ulman, *National Trade Union*, 79–84; CMOJ, October 1906, 9; May 1910, 7; January 1908, 4; June 1900, 3; and July 1903, 1; "List of Secretaries," each issue; Interview, Steber, 24 July 1978, Warren, Pennsylvania; Interview, Santana, 6 July 1977; Interview, Theisen, 17 August 1979; Interview, Julius Sodekson, 29 June 1979, Hebrew Rehabilitation Center, Roslindale, Mass. Sodekson worked as a cigar packer in Boston during the years before World War I. Raymond Steber estimated that half his cigar makers were travelers. Cigar makers apparently came into contact with tramps and hoboes when they themselves hoboed. Theisen, for example, made use of the hobo "jungle," the tramp camping grounds outside of town, along the railroad tracks, on two occasions.

31. Interview, T. Frank Shea, 26 June 1979; Interview, Santana, 24 February 1980, by telephone; Norman Eliason, "The Language of the Buckeye," *American Speech* 12 (1937), 270–74; Interview, Ograin, 17 May 1980; CMOJ, September 1909, 3.

32. *Cigar Makers' Union Diamond Jubilee*, 11; Interview, Durso, 24 March 1977;

Interview, Baust, 24 March 1977; "By-Laws," Local 192, Manchester, New Hampshire, 13; CMOJ, August 1907, 6; Interview, Ograin, 19 May 1979.

33. *Cigar Makers' Union Diamond Jubilee,* 11; Interview, Ograin, 19 May 1979; CMOJ, December 1915, 39 and September 1902, 3; Fischer to Jules Babeau, 25 September 1919, Cigar Makers' Local 162, Green Bay Wisconsin Collection, SHSW.

34. CMOJ, April 1903, 5; January 1904, 5; June 1904, 13; January 1908, 4–5; February 1915, 30; March 1917, 22; June 1910, 7; and May 1905, 16; Interview, Ograin, 17 May 1980; *Cigar Makers' Constitution,* Sections 109 and 111.

35. CMOJ, February 1900, 7; April 1903, 5; December 1906, 20; December 1907, 13; June 1910, 7; and January 1916, 31.

36. Interview, Steber, 24 July 1978; Interview, Santana, 16 September 1978; *Tobacco,* 2 February 1900, 7; 23 November 1900, 7; *Tobacco Leaf,* 26 November 1902, 6; 17 June 1903, 11; 29 November 1905, 10, 48; 7 February 1906, 6; 24 January 1906, 4; 6 February 1907, 26; and 14 September 1911, 11. Cigar makers had their own ratio of cigar makers to population: "We used to figure that one cigar maker for every 1,000 population" (Interview, Ograin, 17 May 1980).

37. Interview, Durso, 24 March 1978; Samuel Gompers, *Seventy Years of Life and Labor: An Autobiography,* Vol. 1 (New York: A. M. Kelley, 1967 [1925]), 177; Charles Stephenson, "A Gathering of Strangers?", 48, 49.

38. U.S. Bureau of Corporations, *Report,* pt. 1, 87; CMOJ, August 1919, 2; *Tobacco,* 14 August 1919, 5.

39. General sources concerning these developments are Baer, *Cigar Manufacturing Industry,* 216; J. H. Korson, "The Technological Development of the Cigar Manufacturing Industry: A Study in Social Change," (Ph.D. dissertation, Yale University, 1937); Interview, Ograin, 8 July 1977. Evidence in the trade press suggests that manufacturers consciously used machinery as a way of acquiring a new, less militant labor force.

40. Daniel B. Creamer and Gladys V. Swackhamer, *Cigar Makers—After the Lay-Off: A Case Study of the Effects of Mechanization on Employment of Hand Cigar Makers* (Philadelphia: Works Progress Administration, 1937); Interview, Ograin, 8 July 1977.

41. Interview, John Uhl, 24 March 1977, North Haven, Conn.; Ethnic Studies—Alabama/Nevada, 41–44, Ybor City-Material-Florida, Section 2, typescript, Works Progress Administration, Federal Writers Project Files, Archive of Folksong, Library of Congress, Washington, D.C.

Part III: Perspectives on the Industrial Tramps

Michael Davis

Forced to Tramp: The Perspective
of the Labor Press, 1870–1900

In 1901 the *American Federationist* asked Terence V. Powderly, the former Grand Master of the Knights of Labor, to describe his most "thrill-
ing experience" during his years as the senior statesman of the American
labor movement. Surprisingly, Powderly recalled neither his accomplishments as the mayor of Scranton, Pennsylvania, nor his achievements as the
leader of the country's largest labor organization of the 1880s. Instead he
remembered back almost thirty years to his "painful experience as a
tramp":

One morning in 1874 I stood where the waters of Lake Erie narrow down and
quicken into the Niagara River at Buffalo. I had tramped the ties of the Canada
Southern . . . from Windsor, Ontario to Buffalo, N.Y., a distance of two hundred
and fifty miles, on foot.

The panic of 1873 still held the floor, and refusing to yield it, I thought that
perhaps Canada might afford better opportunities for employment than the
United States. I applied at every machine shop, great and small, along the line of
that railway, and was thrilled along the entire tramp by the positive way in which a
negative answer could be given to a request for employment. Unsuccessful, footsore, heart-sick and hungry, I stood looking from the dock into the water.

Out of employment and money, through no fault of mine, I was reminded of the
lines:

"Now is the winter of our discontent,
Out of work and the divil the cent"[1]

Undoubtedly many of Powderly's readers were stirred to recollect
their own tramping days and "winters of discontent." While estimating

the numbers of wandering jobless is difficult, contemporary accounts clearly emphasized the "vast" and unprecedented magnitude of the tramping armies. On 25 September 1875, the *National Labor Tribune* claimed that "two millions of men are wandering about in idleness," while the *Workingman's Advocate* of 6 March 1875 had said that "every store and house is visited [by tramps] from three to six times per day." A generation later, during the Panic of 1893, the *Journal of the Knights of Labor* (JKL) for 26 December 1893 noted in an angry Christmas editorial, "Three million men and women are tramping from door to door this day, within less than a week of the celebration of the birth of the First Great Socialist. . . ." Even if these estimates were wildly exaggerated (as Carroll D. Wright asserted in his pioneering and controversial study of joblessness),[2] they did reflect the labor press's concern with a problem—forced tramping— which periodically threatened to engulf large sections of the working class. A recent study extrapolates from jailhouse lodging statistics to suggest that as many as a fifth of American workers in the late nineteenth century passed the night (at one time or another in their lives) as indigent and homeless "guests" of a local police department—as boarded "tramps" by official reckoning.[3]

"Tramping," then, was a bitterly remembered, and all too frequently experienced chapter of the collective biography of American labor in the Gilded Age. At the same time, however, tramping wore a Janus-like mask: what the labor press saw as the tragedy of the involuntary unemployed appeared in the eyes of many "reformers" and representatives of the propertied classes as the mark of Cain. While the *National Labor Tribune* (NLT) for 25 September 1875, for instance, maintained that "society is a criminal and the tramps are its victims," the highly esteemed charity reformer, Professor Francis Wayland of Yale, charged that tramps constituted a "dangerous class" who were "at war with all social institutions."[4] At the same time that the labor press fought for ameliorative public action to remove the causes of "enforced idleness," much of the daily press was demanding the physical suppression of tramps. The *Chicago Tribune* even advocated that tramps should be killed off by poisoning handouts with strychnine.[5]

"Rendering the Subject Complex"

This study, based mainly on a selective survey of the late nineteenth-century labor press, engages briefly the major treatments by the press of the issues posed by tramping as well as experiential descriptions by tramps themselves. In 1885, near the zenith of the growth of the Knights of Labor, there were at least 400 labor newspapers and even a national "Associated Labor Press." This study has systematically examined the four most influential newspapers within the most relevant periods of cyclical economic downturns and mass unemployment. *The Workingman's Advocate*, Chicago, was recognized as the "foremost labor voice of the country" until its cessation in 1879.[6] Originally founded as the official newspaper of the National Labor Union, it was edited during its last decade by Andrew S. Cameron, one of the most important midwestern labor leaders of the nineteenth century. *(National) Labor Tribune*, Pittsburgh, "the largest Circulation of any Class Paper in the United States" (from masthead), was edited successively by John M. Davis and Thomas A. Armstrong. It was first the organ of the Amalgamated Iron and Steel Workers, later being officially sponsored by the Knights of Labor. *John Swinton's Paper*, New York, although short-lived, had a powerful national influence and expressed a generally more radical social viewpoint than the *National Labor Tribune*. *Journal of United Labor* (after 1888, *Journal of Knights of Labor*), Philadelphia and Washington, D.C., was the Knights' national newspaper, and in the mid-eighties circulated in a membership of nearly three-quarters of a million. It continued to be published until 1918.

Between 1873 and 1894, the labor press acquired a more coherent understanding of the ideological function of the "tramp menace" in the conflict between labor and capital. In the seventies there had been considerable confusion within the labor press on how to react to the emergence of the tramp scare. Initially the press insisted on differentiating between the involuntary unemployed and what was conceded to be the stratum of "professional tramps." Thus a "wandering mechanic" writing to the *National Labor Tribune* (4 September 1875) attempted to differentiate tramps "by necessity" like himself from the smaller number of tramps "by choice" and "by profession." Similarly the *Iron Molders' Journal* (September 1875) contrasted "our tramp . . . the honest, hard-fisted mechanic or laborer" to the "bummer, the periodical inmate of our work-houses and county jails, the politician out of power, or the fugitive from justice . . . we have these classes at all times, good or bad." Meanwhile, out West, the *Workingman's Advocate* (30 December 1876) tried to disentangle the class of "honest and industrious men" on the tramp from the "scamps who are prowling about the country, refusing to work, but neglecting no opportunity to steal. . . ."

By the eighties, however, labor journalists and trade unionists began to see the futility or irrelevance of attempting to draw hard and fast boundaries between "honest" and "dishonest" tramps; for, in fact, antitramp legislation was criminalizing the indigent unemployed without distinction. Indeed, in John Swinton's opinion (JSP, 6 December 1885) the "tramp" was simply the "creation of villainous class legislation," a phantom created by juridical stigmatization. For the *Journal of United Labor* (JUL), alternatively, it was the class press itself which was primarily responsible for confecting this illusory category. After noting that in the preceding generation "no workingman considered himself degraded by being '*on the tramp,*'" the *Journal* continued, "These men ['Jay Gould and his class'] have continually persisted in associating the word tramp with the words vagabond, idler, thief, and, in order not to be stingy in their synonyms, they have thrown the word loafer into the bargain. *This has been so successfully done by the press that tramp now stands as an incontrovertible term, and a complete equivalent for all the others. They have thus rendered the subject complex . . .*" (JUL, December 1883, 604, my emphasis).

Increasingly also from the early eighties the labor movement emphasized the connection between tramp scares and the downturns of the business cycle. Thus for Samuel Gompers, testifying before the Blaine committee in 1883, the most irrefutable evidence of the true nature of the tramp problem was the fact that with the return of "prosperity" in 1880 complaints against tramps had been "reduced almost to a minimum." In Gompers's view the overwhelming majority of "tramps" were simply "honest-intentioned workingmen" whom "the employing class have made superfluous," a fraction of whom "may have become demoralized" and turned into alcoholics or vagrants by circumstances over which they had no control.[7] By 1893 the equation between cyclical unemployment and mass tramping (and, hence, the "tramp problem") had become so broadly accepted within the labor movement that the *Journal of the Knights of Labor* could wonder what kind of "out kilter" mentality believed that the problem could be solved by "punishing and persecuting these tramps?" "One would think that it wouldn't require a very high order of intellect to enable men to understand that the remedy must be found in reforming the industrial system that makes financial panics and wholesale enforced idleness inevitable" (JKL, 2 November 1893).

Some historians, most notably Paul T. Ringenbach,[8] have advanced the thesis that the relationship between tramping and the political economy was only gradually revealed by arduous social investigation conducted in the half-century between 1880 and 1920. Asserting that the attitudes of the charity reform movement and academic social science were indicative of an underlying "public consensus," Ringenbach has maintained that the macroeconomic roots of unemployment were only gradually "discovered" as philanthropy evolved into modern social work armed with more adequate social statistics and theoretical models. In fact, as the labor press abundantly reveals, there was public disagreement over the interpretation of these phenomena from the very beginning. Charity reformers and their wealthy patrons deployed their putative "scientific" studies to defend an ideology of individual culpability against the critique of trade unionists, populists, and socialists who already indicted social-structural causes, if not capitalism per se. The labor press and various radical movements vigorously challenged the charity movement's construction of a unitary social stratum of "tramps" as a "dangerous class" prowling the outskirts of "decent society."

Thus the figure of the tramp which played such a lurid and central role in middle-class perceptions of unemployment and social disorder was the least innocent or consensually objective of categories. The social diffusion of the charity reform movement's conception of the tramp, abetted by the great newspaper barons of the day, became a cornerstone of bourgeois efforts to criminalize unemployment, maintain a passive reserve army of labor, and incite a fear of radicalism. Consequently, definitions of tramping and tramps became the pivots of a sustained ideological class struggle between labor and the left on one side, and the alliance of business-academia-charity on the other. At the same time, the problem of forced tramping provoked internal debates within the labor movement that exposed the tensions between the older ideology of "productivism" (with its repudiation of social stratification in general) and newer stands of "class struggle" politics, whether Marxist or anarchist.

By bracketing the category "tramp" and exposing the false conflation of involuntary transiency and criminality which the concept implied, the labor press helped clear the way for a direct confrontation of ideologies. The critique of the so-called tramp problem was an integral and by no means unimportant part of the elaboration of the labor movement's own alternative theory of American industrial society. Indeed, the letters of tramps to the labor press reveal a far more accurate and profound understanding of the political economy of late nineteenth-century capitalism than do the treatises of some of the most famous contemporary academics and social scientists.

"Was It for This We Fought?"

The earliest mention of tramps which I have been able to locate occurs in the *National Labor Tribune* on 24 January 1874—just a few months after the collapse of Jay Cooke and Company started the Wall Street Panic of 1873.[9] In a letter titled "Hard Times," a correspondent writes about conditions in the small coal mining towns of Larimer and Irwin, Pennsylvania, where over half the local pits had been shut down. In desperation the unemployed miners "went to the river to work," but not finding enough work there they were "being turned into unwilling tramps" and forced to leave the area. There is no further mention of tramps until the fall of the same year, when an editorial (NLT, 24 November 1876) urged readers to treat tramps "kindly" for "they have left homes as warm and cheery as yours to wander out alone in the cold world."

By the winter of 1875 general distress in the country had reached an alarming level, and starvation amongst the working class was widely reported. New York City had suspended outdoor relief in the aftermath of the Tweed Ring scandals, and private soup kitchens in every large city were overwhelmed with hungry people. In an angry editorial, the NLT (13 January 1875) announced that the "army of Labor" had been cast out by unemployment into a "Judean wilderness of oppression and want. . . . Thousands and tens of thousands of men are wandering listlessly, hopelessly, in search of work. Footsore, heart-sick, shivering in the bleak winds of a severe winter, they roam to and fro. . . . Where it will end Providence only knows. Was it for this we travelled the seas for a land of Liberty? Was it for this we fought?"

Time and again the labor press compared the tramping "armies" of the unemployed with Lincoln's Grand Army which had saved the Republic, reminding its leaders that the tramps of today had "once tramped at Gettysburg . . . where their present defamers would not dare to tramp." (NLT, 23 December 1876). Many letters appeared in the labor press from disillusioned and embittered Union veterans who had been forced on the tramp. One such wanderer, writing to a New York paper in the fall of 1875, claimed that most tramps were really "superior men of generous impulses" who had been first to enlist in defense of their country, only to return to be "spurned by stock-jobbers and shoddy government contractors."[10] An editorial in the NLT (17 August 1875) warned industrialists that tramps had "hearts as courageous as have ever swept rebellion from a battlefield and . . . they will yet rise and overturn the monied aristocracy that has erected itself on their degradation and poverty."

A year later another editorial took up the Civil War motif again. Recalling the sacrifices of the working classes in assuring the victory of the Union, the NLT (27 May 1876) looked at the new "Army of Tramps" which was also calling men away from homes and breaking up families:

What an ocean of misery . . . four million idle men? . . . How many of this vast army are kind fathers, who have homes behind them, a wife and children full of grief and dread, are pinched with hunger? What are the thoughts of children when they see father gone, mother in distress? . . . What anguish fills the hearts of wives when they see the broken home circle? . . . Homes are broken, desolate, hearts are crushed. . . . Who shall disband this vast army? Who shall say to the forlorn traveler a thousand miles from home, in hunger and idleness, " Arise, ye son of Labor, return to your home, where plenty awaits you!?"

A decade later, during the recession of 1882–85, many war veterans were forced on the tramp for a second time. One "old soldier on the tramp," writing from Indiana to *John Swinton's Paper* (26 July 1885), claimed that he had "never saw it as bad as it is now." Although he was an "able-bodied machinist" there was no work available, and at least 800 to 1,000 men were jobless in his home town. Swearing that he would never again come to the rescue "of such a Government that allows its soldiers to starve," he proposed to "rig me up some kind of an outfit, take to the country, and forage."

The large number of veterans among the transient unemployed un-doubtedly gave trampdom its peculiar "military" form of organization—the well-organized tramp camp, traveling in regular bands, and the as-sumption of "ranks" by tramp leaders—which observers noted from the mid-seventies onward. Forced out on the roadways and hounded every-where by authorities, the tramps created a veritable science of survival and movement. Without underestimating the diversity of their individual itineraries or the combinations of modes of transport which might be employed on a single trek, tramps tended to follow one of two patterns: In the densely populated eastern states, unemployed workers were as likely to walk (to "tramp" in the most literal sense) from town to town and from meal to meal as they were to hop a freight. In the prairie and western states, on the other hand, the unemployed had no alternative but to master the difficult and very dangerous art of riding "the blinds and rods."[11] While an entire genre of American adventure stories has been built around the exploits of the railroad tramp or hobo, less attention has been paid to the sometimes equally herculean exploits of the eastern tramp relying only on his dependable "shanks mare." Powderly's 500-mile walk into Canada was not so exceptional when compared to Walter Wyckoff's famous account of an eighteen-month "experiment in reality" as a drifting laborer. Wyckoff gives vivid descriptions of the twenty- and thirty-mile-a-day stints which were considered a "fair day's walk." Starting in the summer of 1891, he ultimately tramped 2,500 miles of road between Connecticut and California.[12]

While the unemployed might start out tramping in short orbits around home towns, they were often led to gamble on the supposed better job prospects further west. Western employers, in turn, purposely sought to create advantageous surpluses of labor by luring tramps from the East with false advertisements.[13] In response, most labor newspapers developed an institution called the "Don't Come Here" (or "Stay Away") column to warn the transient unemployed away from areas where strikes were in progress or where joblessness was already acute.[14]

"Don't Come Here," begged Virginia City miners in the spring of 1875, there are "three thousand unemployed on the Comstock" (NLT, 22 May 1875). "Steer clear of this place and give us a chance," asked workmen "from the Lone Star state" in 1884 (NLT, 7 June 1884). "Interested parties may crack up British Columbia to the skies, but at the present time there are too many miners here," warned a correspondent from faraway Vancouver Island (NLT, 19 April 1884). The *Journal of United Labor* reported in March 1884 that hundreds of workers were being lured to Duluth by employers although there was actually a "depression" there. The year before, *John Swinton's Paper* (4 November 1883) had reprinted a story from the *San Francisco Opinion* entitled "Five Thousand Tramps": "There are no less than 5,000 men walking our streets who, a few years ago were rich and have not today a place to lay their heads. They look poverty-stricken, ready to commit suicide, and know not whither to turn. The railway has ruined the country and mine manipulators the city."

By the mid-eighties the dream of a western frontier of opportunity had distinctly soured. A trade unionist in the Dakotas implored his eastern comrades, "In the name of Humanity, I beg of you . . . do not send any young men out West. There are already too, too many for anything in the Far West. . . . 'Go West' young man does not suit the close of the year 1885. . ." (JSP, 6 December 1885). In another letter during the same period, a correspondent of John Swinton's pitying the "advance guard of tramps" which had just arrived from the East, observed that "the man without capital has no place anymore in the West. The West is running to big things and Queen Anne houses" (JSP, 24 May 1885). This perception that the western labor markets were becoming saturated with job seekers from the East was dramatically reinforced by the fact that the Panic of 1893 struck first in the western mining states, creating a spontaneous mass movement eastward of thousands of desperate western laborers—a reverse migration from the once promised land which rudely awoke America to the end of the frontier and provided the impetus for Coxey's Army.

"The World Is a Desert to Us"

The labor press also recorded with poignancy the tramps' desperate struggles for sheer survival. Winter was a season of trial and torment for the homeless strata of society, and normally tramps had to accept the hospitality of almshouses and jail lodgings—even if conditions there only slightly improved on the Black Hole of Calcutta. During the famous hard freeze of 1885, however, tens of thousands of tramps were caught out in the open in the Midwest and Canada. Kansas and Missouri had been especially hard hit by recession: JSP reported that the streets of Kansas City (Kansas) "are thronged with idle laborers," while in St. Louis "at least 15,000 out-of-work, and in Carondelet mills are silent—many workmen who were buying homes have abandoned them to seek work elsewhere" (JSP, 18 January 1885). Meanwhile up in Canada, "thousands upon thousands of idle workmen are walking the highways of the Dominion" (ibid.). Many of these jobless bands were encamped along roads and rail lines where the severe early frosts hit, and Swinton's paper captured the pathos of a situation where camp fires were "the best thing going for a great many squads of Missourians who go a-gypsying in December, though they are not gypsies and all had once thought that they had a chance of becoming President of the United States . . ." (4 January 1885).

Another great peril of protracted tramping was the loss of all moorings to home and family. An anonymous letter to the NLT in the fall of 1877 (10 November) entitled "A Tale of a Tramp" contains a poignant description of the desolate aloneness experienced by the unemployed on the tramp:

I am a vagrant and a vagabond. One year ago I was an industrious, respectable head of a family. My family are now a thousand miles away, scattered and broken up. They and I hardly hope to meet again. The world is a desert to us. I have no friend. I have no roof to live under, no table to eat at, no clothes to distinguish me from thieves. Yet I am not a thief. I have nothing. I am welcomed by no human being; and I am at the mercy of the lowest; yet I do not feel as if I could honestly take a pair of shoes or a coat without the owner's consent. What has brought me to this?

Although the hard times exiled many other fathers from their families, the typical tramp was likely a "lost son." Carrol D. Wright stressed the disproportionate share of young workers in unemployment, while all the surveys of homeless men and tramps conducted in the period point to a high percentage of single men, with further indications that the average age declined in depression years.[15] Frequently private and public relief was restricted to family heads, and some industries seem to have had informal seniority systems providing for the laying off of single men during depression periods, with the remaining work redistributed among married men.

"I wish I was a married man," wrote a young miner in 1882 from a small mining village near Braidwood, Illinois. "If I was I could get work anywhere and be in the full enjoyment of all the rights and privileges of American citizenship." Noting that the "panic times are coming on us again," the single miner explained that the Braidwood operators were "again beginning to proscribe young men." Mine superintendents first laid off the single men, then "crowded" the married men "three into each place, where they cannot possibly do more than the work of two." The mine owners' motive in sharing the work out among the family men was hardly altruistic, since married men were all company householders and "something must be done to get the rents." Furthermore, the layoff of the single men created "a diversion of feelings among the men" which eroded solidarity and defused militancy. The younger miners abandoned any hope of being rehired after hundreds of desperate, tramping miners from even harder hit areas inundated Braidwood. Listing the "manufacturing of tramps out of our young men" as one of four major grievances, the writer emphasized that "the men of Braidwood must do something very soon to save them-

selves from themselves. . . . the necessity of organization is becoming every day more apparent" (NLT, 11 August 1882).

A different kind of employer "divide and rule" strategy manufactured tramps out of the young mule-spinners of Massachusetts in the 1870s. In an interview conducted by the Bureau of Statistics of Labor, a veteran mule-spinner bitterly attacked the segmented labor system in the mills that prevented apprentices from graduating into the ranks of journeymen: "I find that, during my twelve years' service as a mule-spinner, I have observed that boys who work in the mule-room are not allowed to follow up spinning as an occupation. As soon as they are competent, or arrive at the age of 18 or 20 years, they are, as a general rule, discharged. . . ."[16]

The precarious job security of the single male worker, however, was frequently superior to that of his working sisters. Relief officers and charity officials regularly cajoled unemployed single women to enter domestic service—supposedly a reliable source of employment even in bad times. Sources like the 1895 Massachusetts Board's *Report on the Unemployed* graphically show, however, that many proud working women preferred slow starvation on a pittance to what they regarded as the degradation and quasi slavery of the household servant's life. Whether out of desperation, the bold assertion of independence, or for other motives, jobless women occasionally went on the tramp in spite of the severe social sanctions and purported dangers. The labor press viewed the woman tramp through sympathetic but unwaveringly patriarchal eyes as a shocking symbol of capitalism's deprecation of working-class family life. On 30 September 1876 the *NLT* registered the sensation caused by a woman tramp from New York who applied to the mayor of Altoona, Pennsylvania for relief: "Ought not we men to blush for shame at such a sight? Are we not able to keep our wives and sisters at home? Does it not bring the blush of shame to our cheeks to know that a woman finds it necessary to take to the road for bread?"

Nine years later *John Swinton's Paper* (22 February 1885) reprinted an account of a local working class, including some 600 young women, forced en masse upon the tramp. In the Willimantic River Valley of Connecticut, fifteen local firms—woolen mills and stove factories—locked out over 3,000 operatives. In the absence of union relief funds or sympathetic local charity, the jobless factory hands were left with no alternative to starvation except to beg in the surrounding countryside for food and casual work.

In the severity of the Winter young girls have tramped from place to place in search of work, have begged shelter and food, slept in outhouses and barns, and are today the victims of hunger and exposure. Wholly defenseless, they are thrown into temptation and the lowest forms of vagrancy. The males tramp out farther in the state and become desperate and vicious, while the old people and infants remain in the villages starving by inches.

Cases of women tramps like the unemployed Willimantic operatives forced recognition of trampdom's distaff dimension, and some town jails began to set aside separate cells for female tramp lodgers. Yet the female tramp remained an unusual sight, and the *Journal of the Knights of Labor* in 1893 (28 December) could still record the "gallant" astonishment of California train crews to the sight of groups of unemployed women riding the rails:

It appears that a number of women have taken to the road as tramps and are traveling toward California. They are said to be honest women, who are in search of employment. There are three of them who are said to be headed for Sacramento, having traveled together from Portland. They were without means and starvation stared them in the face if they remained in the Oregon metropolis during the winter. It was a decidedly bold thing for women to do, but these three maidens determined to get to California in regulation tramp fashion. . . . None of the train crew interfered with the women. At various stations the girls went about and begged food. At one place, it is reported, a tramp insulted one of the women, when the three sailed in together and gave him a trouncing that he will remember for many and many a day.[17]

The Tramping Artisan in America

Was tramping in the United States ever formally organized by the trade unions themselves, as in the famous British case described by Hobsbawm and Leeson?[18] Here the labor press and contemporary documentation provide insight into signal differences in the formation of American and British trade unionism, and their respective ability to regulate the pulsations of the reserve army of labor. In Britain organized tramping played an integral role in the constitution of early trade unionism. Until its slow breakdown between 1850 and 1914, the craft union tramp system in the British Isles (and there is solid evidence of its extension to Ireland as well) provided skilled workers with an ingenious method of giving relief to members, reducing competition in labor markets, passing communications between branches, and organizing new localities—all without need of a centralized union bureaucracy. The system was impressively well organized through networks of craftsmen's pubs, while the traveling journeymen on the road—whom Leeson explains were commonly called "tramps" from the late eighteenth century onward—easily distinguished themselves from "true vagabonds and vagrants" by their proud possession of ornate tramping passports or "blanks."[19] Although the geographical fixity of new mechanical occupations and the mass unemployment of the late 1840s finally swamped the tramping system, it was admirably successful in allowing the seedlings of trade unionism to survive the repressive era of the Combination Acts (1800–1830).

In the United States the most highly organized tramping system, and the closest analogue to the British model, appears to have been that of the iron molders. In testimony before the Massachusetts house in 1895, a local molders' official described the operation of his union's tramping system while at the same time noting its relative novelty:

Q. Is there any out-of-work benefit in your organization?

A. No, sir; but we give meals to men belonging to the union on the road. We [North Adams, Massachusetts lodge] have averaged three meals a week. To anyone coming along late at night, we give a supper and a bed and a breakfast. . . .

Q. Are those fellows tramping?

A. Yes, sir.

Q. Are they ever regarded as tramps by the public authorities?

A. It is very rarely they get themselves in trouble like that. . . . As a rule, when a man travels like that he travels with his card in his pocket, and he knows that at whatever foundry he strikes he is regarded as a white man.

Q. Are there any other organizations that furnish meals and lodgings?

A. I do not know of any.[20]

Although this example shows the existence of "tramping artisans" in the organized, British sense at various times in the late nineteenth century, systematic tramping was far rarer and more episodic on this side of the Atlantic—a difference undoubtedly related to the more discontinuous history of American trade unionism and the severity of the repression it faced.

The weakness of American trade unions vis-à-vis their British cousins also implied that if the tramping system was undeveloped, so too was its more modern alternative: the stationary out-of-work benefits which were one of the hallmarks of English "New Model Unionism" in the fifties and sixties. During the great depression of the seventies, trade union relief in the United States was almost not existent, and workers, to avoid the workhouse or the road, were forced to "double up" families in cramped and fetid conditions.[21] When hard times again hit in the eighties, John Swinton (JSP, 19 April 1885) sadly reported that, despite a "great debate" over the necessity of adopting the British system of trade union unemployment insurance, only four New York unions had actually succeeded in establishing an out-of-work benefit: the German Typographers, a local of the Furniture Workers, and two locals of British-based unions (the Amalgamated Engineers and the Amalgamated Carpenters). Despite Foner's claim that the nineties "saw the first widespread contribution to unemployment relief by trade unions,"[22] there is little evidence of any decisive improvement. Indeed, in Massachusetts the legislative investigating body found that only the Cigar Makers were integrated into a national system of union insurance. Other unions—the Textile Workers, Printers, Boston Plasterers, Machinists, Painters, and Garment Workers—relied upon special subscriptions or fund-raising events to provide token sums of money and/or food to their jobless members. A few unions, including Boston's Central Labor Union, undertook public fund-raising appeals for the relief of local workers in general.[23] Still the Massachusetts report came to the conclusion that "as the out-of-work benefit proper has been adopted in but few trades in Massachusetts, it formed the minor portion of the relief afforded by the organizations. . . . In most trades in which the out-of-work benefit has been adopted it is a local rather than a general custom. It necessitates heavy dues, and most organizations are unwilling to impose these."[24]

All Species of Tramps . . .

In general, therefore, the confused and anarchic apparatus of public, private and trade union relief failed to ensure the immediate needs of large sections of the unemployed working class. In the face of such general "trampification," the dividing line between the proud craft "tramp" and the general "vagabond," which still persisted in Britain through late Victorian times, was scarcely meaningful in the United States. At the same time—as the contemporary labor press vividly chronicles—certain crafts and occupations, both skilled and unskilled, were particularly plagued by the problem of forced tramping. Mining seems to have been a special case in point. The relief and unemployment problems of the industrial city were magnified in the small mining camp. Frequently the entire employment of a mining town collapsed with the shutting down of a pit. Miners living in company housing had little security of tenure, and the truck system encouraged indebtedness and made it difficult for miners to accumulate savings for subsistence in hard times. Relief, public or private, was not nearly so likely to be available in an isolated mining village, and often there was no philanthropic local middle class to provide emergency charity. Furthermore, the effects of periodic slumps were reinforced by other factors (blacklisting, immigration, long-term trends towards wage reduction, and the rapid geographical expansion of industry) that made tramping a familiar problem to the nineteenth-century miner.

For instance, in 1868, Bethel, Pennsylvania, had been a "prosperous village and every one was employed that wanted to work." By 1876, however, the pit payroll fell to less than 10 percent of its previous level, and the annual income of the miners was under $200. After the miners had sold their houses and most of their personal belongings to buy food, a desperate group tried their luck in the coal fields of Clay County, Indiana. There they discovered a situation "even worse" than their own, and were not able to find enough work to pay their fares home. "So they had to return on foot and beg their way, and thus, of course, become the much dreaded and despised tramps of the day" (NLT, 1 December 1877).

The unemployed miner on the tramp became such a familiar sight in the seventies that his exploits were sometimes caricatured in the labor press. One such "tall story" described the adventures of a boisterous Illinois miner who tramped into Ohio searching for work, only to be arrested for the attempted murder of a mine superintendent after weeks of frustrated waiting at the ill-famed Boanerges colliery in Stark County. The most astonishing aspect of the tale, however, is the description of mining equipment supposedly carried on the tramp by this "humble son of subterranean toil":

My working tools consist of thirteen picks, each nine pounds weight, besides the "smasher," which I use when cars are plenty; it weighs twenty-two pounds, and has a handle seven feet long. My sledgehammer is ninety pounds weight, and I have four wedges each two and a half feet in length. I usually use a horse-rake for cleaning the coals. . . . Times becoming rather slack in the prairie state, I longed to come East, and bidding my widowed mother a fond adieu, started on foot for the great State of Ohio. All my picks were shoved down behind my back, inside of my coat . . . I carried my sledge over my left shoulder, and the wedges in my coat pockets, and after many day's wandering I landed footsore and weary at the State capital of Ohio . . . [NLT, 19 August 1876].

Even highly paid and qualified craftsmen were sometimes forced to tramp. In his autobiography, James J. Davis left a graphic account of tramping iron puddlers during the early nineties. Like the Braidwood miners, Pittsburgh puddlers dealt with a trade recession by sharing out work among married men while the single men were forced to join "the crowds of idle men roaming from mill to mill." Davis's peregrinations carried him through the iron industry of Pennsylvania and Ohio until "deciding that the North held no openings," he tramped down to Birmingham, Alabama. According to Davis the goal of the tramping puddler was not just a job, but a furnace of his own. Furnaces were traditionally passed from father to son, and in an age of increasing technological encroachment upon the elite and arduous art of puddling, many younger puddlers tramped quixotically in the search of a furnace where they could be "a real boss puddler."[25]

Thus both unemployment and the desire to retrieve disappearing craft prerogatives drove the puddlers to tramp.

Among the less skilled, it is not surprising that a large number of involuntary tramps came from the ranks of occupations characterized by transiency and unreliable employment. It is important, however, to avoid reducing this category—as writers on the "hobo" have tended to do—solely to the western seasonal laborer in agriculture, lumber, construction, and mining. An equally significant group of unskilled and semiskilled workers who contributed to the population of trampdom were the "floating strata" of manufacturing industry.

In his famous analysis of the "different forms of the relative surplus-population" of industrial society, Marx distinguished a "floating surplus-population" of operatives who constituted the immediately available "reserve army" of production. He attributed the existence of these "floating strata" both to the effects of the accumulation process in general and to the division of labor between children and adults (and between the sexes) in particular.

In the automatic factories, as in all the great workshops, where machinery enters as a factor, or where only the modern division of labour is carried out, large numbers of boys are employed up to the age of maturity. When this term is once reached, only a very small number continue to find employment in the same branches of industry, whilst the majority are regularly discharged. This majority forms an element of the floating surplus-populations, growing with the extension of these branches of industry. . . . That the natural increase of the number of labourers does not satisfy the requirements of the accumulation of capital, and yet all the time is in excess of them, is a contradiction inherent to the movement of capital itself. It wants larger numbers of youthful laborers, a smaller number of adults.[26]

In his well-known study of working-class social mobility in nineteenth-century Newburyport, Massachusetts, Stephan Thernstrom has shown the importance of this floating stratum in the workforce of a typical New England factory town. During the depression of 1857, a thousand laborers were forced to leave Newburyport, while during the "recovery" year of 1879 some 1,120 "tramps"—235 of whom called themselves mill operatives—sought police lodging in the city (presumably looking for jobs).[27] Thernstrom also partially corroborates Marx's idea that a disjuncture between youth and adult employment markets contributed to the creation of this surplus workforce.

Adult laborers employed in Newburyport in 1850 had somewhat greater prospects for occupational advance than those who arrived after 1850. In the case of sons of these men, however, the trend was in the opposite direction. Some four fifths of the laborers' sons who entered the labor market during the 1850's found semiskilled positions; while the shrinking of semiskilled opportunities after 1860 forced some of these youths back into unskilled jobs. . . . [28]

The young Massachusetts mule-spinners described earlier also fit into this category of floating labor and periodic tramps. So too do the large numbers of jobless shoemakers carrying their toolboxes who were often seen applying for a night's shelter at wayfarers' lodges or police stations in New England during the nineties. In Haverhill, T. T. Pomeroy of the Central Labor Union testified before the special Massachusetts Board on the Unemployed regarding the plight of the tramp shoemaker:

We keep a sort of employment bureau, and last year [1893] we harbored in our quarters anywhere from a few to 40 or 50 at a time. I am pretty familiar with the trade and with the men, and that crowd were shoemakers. I have been with them a good deal every night, and have heard them talk, and I know lots of them that were regarded as skilled laborers,—perhaps not the most efficient, but men who were fairly comfortable, pleasant companions, rather easy going and perhaps careless, fair hands in ordinary conditions,—who became tramps in the last year.[29]

The other category of unskilled and semiskilled labor, whose profile has been described in studies of the hobo, might be called (after Marx) the "nomad proletariat." Like the floating strata of manufacturing industry, the outdoor gang laborer was frequently metamorphized into a tramp by seasonal fluctuations in employment as well as by recession periods. Allsop has suggested a lineage of continuity between the canal navvy of the 1840s, the tramping railroad laborer of the 1880s, and the "gandy dancing" hobo worker of the First World War period. "The shock-trooper of the American expansion, the man with bed-roll on back who free-lanced beyond the community redoubts, building the canals and roads and rights-of-way, spiking rails, felling timber, drilling oil, digging mines, fencing prairie, harvesting wheat, was the hobo."[30]

The category of "nomad proletariat" avoids various confusions inherent in the term "hobo" (which had become increasingly common in the usage of the 1890s) and is also preferable because it includes the tens of thousands of transient outdoor laborers employed east of the Mississippi on railroad gangs and other major construction. In the Newburyport tramp statistics of 1879 which Thernstrom quotes, there are 381 listed as laborers.[31] The Massachusetts localities which reported occupational status of tramps housed/jailed in the survey taken by the 1895 commission all agreed (without providing specific data) that laborers were the most common category of "shovel bums": ". . . they are men who perhaps will work three or four months at contract work, on the sewers and on the roads. In the summer time they spend their money just as quick as they get it, and they will go around taking in all the cities and towns. As a rule they go among themselves. That gang of men always talk of what good bosses such and such men are, and what bad bosses such and such men are."[32]

Finally, in a special class altogether, were workers of various skills and occupations who had been forced to tramp as a result of employer victimization. As Clarence Bonnett has pointed out, "Blacklisting of strikers was quite general in the period 1873–76" as powerful employer associations emerged to combat trade unionism.[33] Later, in the 1880s, with the rise of the Knights of Labor and the widespread adoption of boycotting as an auxiliary tactic to the strike, employer resistance and organization redoubled with the widespread exchange of blacklists. One of the most famous examples of a worker branded by the blacklist and forced on the tramp was Powderly himself. As a young man Powderly had been appointed president of the Pennsylvania branch of the National Labor Congress by Richard Trevellick, who years later in John Swinton's Paper described the consequences:

Years ago I, as President of the National Labor Congress, appointed a young blacksmith as president of the organization in his state. He was a competent, industrious, honest and sober mechanic: but when his appointment became known he was discharged. . . . After vainly searching for work in the vicinity of his home, he went on foot 40 miles; he there got work, but his name and position in the Congress was learned and he was again put on the road. For months, footsore, weary and hungry, he tramped over 500 miles and no work for him. Was that a boycott? That youth was T. V. Powderly.[34]

The Struggle against Tramp Laws

Of all the grievances and complaints cited in the late nineteenth-century labor press, it would seem that few things were felt more universally noxious by organized working people than the criminalization of unemployment. Vagrancy and antitramp legislation created a profound gulf between middle-class and working-class opinion in the Gilded Age. The 1877 conference of the Boards of Public Charities at Saratoga Springs established broad agreement between businessmen, academics, and charity officials concerning the proper solution to the "tramp problem." Shaken by the recent rioting of workers and the unemployed (the "Great Rebellion of 1877"), which Professor Francis Wayland of Yale had blamed on the "great standing army of professional tramps,"[35] assembled luminaries of social science and charity administration gave hearty endorsement to the model of "scientific charity" pioneered by the Charity Organization Society in Britain. Its strategy for reducing "sin" was two-pronged. First it proposed to reduce the level of relief provided to the jobless masses by eliminating "indiscriminate charity" in the form of soup kitchens, free lodgings, municipal relief work, and houseless poor asylums to weed out the "undeserving poor."[36] Secondly, in accordance with the Victorian liberal idée fixe of the "dangerous classes," the COS advocated the repression of the "residuum" of "degenerate" paupers and tramps.

Ironically, the leadership of former "radicals" in Republican state legislatures reproduced some of the most onerous features of the southern black codes in their legislation against tramps. As the charity reform movement gained a national hegemony by the early eighties,[37] draconian antitramp laws began to appear in state after state. The new tramp laws were incomparably more harsh than the traditional vagrancy legislation which they superseded. Connecticut, for example, had had a tramp act since 1727; variously amended over the next century and a half, it gave local magistrates the discretion to sentence "all vagabonds and vagrants" (together with runaways, drunks, prostitutes, and others) to the house of correction for a maximum of forty days. The law which replaced it put a five-dollar bounty on the head of "every tramp" (an entirely new legal category) and increased the maximum punishment to three years in the state prison for tramps in possession of any "dangerous weapon."[38] Similarly, Ohio's justifiably notorious tramp act had a clause which mandated three years' imprisonment for the "offenses" of kindling a fire on the highway or entering a yard uninvited.[39] Tramp legislation literally attempted (as Engels put it) to *outlaw* a section of the working class.[40] The Ohio supreme court's review of an appeal against tramp law conviction illustrates the novel juridical categories involved in the legislation of antitramp laws.

Speaking of the class, the genus tramp, in this country, is a public enemy. He is numerous and he is dangerous. He is a nomad, a wanderer on the face of the earth, with his hand against every honest man, women and child in so far as they do not, promptly and fully, supply his demands. He is a thief, a robber, often a murderer, and always a nuisance. . . . So numerous has the class become that the members may be said to overrun the improved parts of the country. . . . It will not be understood that there may not be differences in tramps. There may be. Some may be less worthless and vicious than others; but all pirates were not alike brutal and bloody. . . . The whole system has become so gross an abuse as to require the strong hand of the law for its suppression. . . . Why not this law? Is there not sufficient difference between the condition . . . of a pauper in his own country, and the same character abroad, and between the situation of the people of the country where the pauper resides and those of distinct neighborhoods, to warrant a legal distinction? . . . In short, tramping makes a different character of the same person. And why may they not, when thus grouped, be regarded as a class? . . . The objection that the act prescribes a cruel and unusual punishment we think not well taken. Imprisonment at hard labor is neither cruel or unusual.[41]

It is not surprising that the contemporary labor movement frequently saw analogies between the crusade to outlaw the tramp and earlier "class" legislation on the status of vagabonds and slaves. For instance, a Pennsylvania trade unionist, J. E. Emerson of Beaver Falls, wrote a letter to the NLT (1 December 1877) comparing his state's newly enacted antitramp law—

which made it "a crime to be out of employment and money at the same time"—with Tudor legislation against vagabondage. He also sardonically discerned the shadow of Henry VII (who was purported to have executed 72,000 vagabonds) in the bloodthirsty proposals of the *Chicago Tribune* to exterminate tramps en masse.[42]

There is, however, an interesting difference in the editorial reaction of the most prominent labor papers to the implications of tramp legislation—indeed, a difference that can be taken as an index of divergent ideological development within the labor movement. For the NLT, which still clung to a "productivist" ideology which distinguished between producers and nonproducers but not between classes, the central iniquity of the antitramp laws was that they "aim to knock down the personal privileges of a part of the population and set up and define classes." On 13 March 1883 the paper wrote, "The tendency of law makers of late has been to obey the demands of those who would grind the face of the poor, give the unfortunate never a chance to recover, and prefer that labor should be confined to a class by itself without prospect or ambition toward betterment . . . as seen in conspiracy laws—come out in bold relief in the tramp enactment." For the JSP, on the other hand, which was far more expressive of socialist and radical currents within the New York labor movement, "the atrocious tramp bill now before the New York legislature . . . was the very climax of capitalist deviltry" (26 March 1885). John Swinton (a correspondent of Marx) goes on:

The Journal of Commerce says "The penitentiary is the only institution that holds any promise for the conversion of the tramp from the error of his ways." But suppose the error of the tramp's ways is his inability to find work, on account of the state of things brought about by capitalism? In that case, it seems to us, the guilty parties who ought to be sent to the penitentiary are those who, through their mastery of the industrial forces, are responsible for this social racket."

But whether they interpreted this "class legislation" as meaning the creation of classes or, conversely, as the product of class rule, the ranks of labor were united in their belief that the antitramp acts, by criminalizing unemployment, would perforce turn the unemployed into criminals. An early article in the *Workingmen's Advocate* (6 March 1875), for example, blames industrial overproduction for creating tramps, and goes on to observe that "the very attempt to stop men from seeking employment, would compel resistance, or more likely the resort to theft. It would at once metamorphose an army of 'tramps' into an army of thieves." A writer to the NLT (4 September 1875), after asserting that the overwhelming majority of tramps are honest workmen, vowed that "if outlawed" the starving mechanics would fight back. One laborer, responding to a *Chicago Times* editorial against "vagabonds," asked, "How long can we subsist on [our] 'character as honest workingmen'?"[43] Another wondered what happened to the rights of workingmen to travel and seek employment as they so please (NLT, 12 January 1878). The drastic proscriptions on the individual freedom of the worker embodied in the tramp legislation forced the working-class movement to recognize a contradiction between the rights of person and those of property. A tramping Civil War veteran, writing to the NLT (10 November 1877), averred that although he had always stood by law and order, "the right to live honestly is more sacred than the right to hold 'property.'" Skilled craftsmen like the Molders, who formerly had had little sympathy for the "idle," now endorsed the right of the unemployed to survive by whatever means necessary:

The man who is willing to work and can not get it to do, is neither a pauper nor a criminal; . . . he would be a coward to see his family suffer with hunger, and . . . would be a suicide to starve, when food could be had for the taking of it, and the man or men who would send a fellow-man to prison under such circumstances should purchase a rope and go and hang themselves as a disgrace to the earth they pollute with their presences.[44]

Finally, the tramp laws encountered the organized resistance of labor organizations. In 1878, for instance, there were demonstrations in New York against the proposed tramp law, while four years later in Pittsburgh 25,000 marched for repeal of the Pennsylvania act (NLT, 24 June 1882). The Preamble and Principles of the Knights of Labor condemned tramp legislation and more generally fought for the "abrogation of all laws that do not bear equally upon capitalists and laborers." Moreover, John Swinton on 17 January 1886, proposed that tramps should organize themselves to march on Washington: "Before you 'Go West, Young Man,' take a turn toward Washington. . . . . Camping places can always be found in the shadow of the White House, or the Capitol, or the Treasury Department, or the monument! Your member of the Congress, ay, even the Millionaire Senator, will vote any relief that may be needed for their own safety." Eight years later Swinton's half-serious proposal became Coxey's famous army. The flight eastwards of thousands of jobless western miners and railroad laborers in the late fall of 1893 and winter 1894 had already assumed a semimilitary organization when it became a "petition in boots." Quite apart from the eccentric views of General Coxey himself or of his various subalterns in the Grand Army of the Unemployed, the great political significance of the demonstration was its massive popularity, seen in the hundreds of thousands of populists, farmers, and fellow workers who turned out to cheer on the detachments of the army in its march on Washington. The "tramp" became the hero of the hour to the sympathetic Americans whose views had never been reflected outside of the labor press.

Notes

1. Terence V. Powderly, "My Painful Experience as a Tramp," *American Federationist* 8, no. 9 (September 1901), 332. An early version of Powderly's vicissitudes as a tramp was included in his inaugural speech as vice-president of the Irish Land League in Buffalo, 1881 (quoted in *John Swinton's Paper*, 30 May 1886).

2. Carroll D. Wright, Massachusetts Bureau of Statistics of Labor, *Tenth Annual Report* (1879), 3–13. But see also Swinton's critique of Wright's *First Annual Report* of the National Labor Bureau (*JSP*, 13 June 1886).

3. Eric H. Monkkonen, *Police in Urban America, 1860–1920* (New York: Cambridge University Press, 1981).

4. Paul T. Ringenbach, *Tramps and Reformers, 1873–1916: The Discovery of Unemployment in New York,* (Westport, Conn.: Greenwood Press, 1973), 14.

5. Quoted in NLT, 1 December 1877.

6. Frank L. Mott, *A History of American Magazines*, vol. 2, 1865–1885 (Cambridge, Mass.: Harvard University Press, 1957), 299. Years examined include, for *The Workingman's Advocate,* 1865–79; for the *National Labor Tribune,* 1873–77 and 1882–86; for *John Swinton's Paper,* 1882–86; and for the *Journal of United Labor,* 1882–86 and 1892–94.

7. The tramp laws also spurred some craft unions to introduce special traveling benefits so that unemployed members would not have to tramp in search of work. "The laws of the State of New York, passed during the panic, made poverty a crime, and the man who went from one place to another in quest of work was often punished and sent to prison as a 'tramp.' Our union at that time introduced a traveling benefit, so that the members of our craft were saved from the operation of that law, and could go in search of work with sufficient means to carry them from place to place." (Samuel Gompers, testimony before Blair committee, 1883, in *Report of the Committee of the Senate upon the Relations between Labor and Capitol* [sic] *and Testimony Taken by the Committee,* vol. I (Washington, 1885). See also Ringenbach, *Tramps and Reformers:* "As the impact of the depression of 1882–1886 lessened, unemployment figures dropped, and public interest in tramps declined as well. . . . Between 1889 and 1893, the tramp was little discussed; apparently he was not considered a problem. . . . During the panic of 1893 the appearance of countless job seekers on the city streets again revived concern over the tramp problem" (p. 36). See also Austin Lewis, *The Rise of the American Proletarian,* (Chicago: C. H. Kerr, 1907), 120.

8. Ringenbach, *Tramps and Reformers.*

9. "Who heard of a tramp ten, five, or even three years ago? *No One!*" (NLT, 17 August 1875). Although I have found no evidence of the usage of the term "tramp" applied to the wandering unemployed during the recession of 1867–68, the record unemployment levels of these years (50,000 in New York City, 25,000 in Chicago) anticipated the fate of labor in subsequent decades. "Police reported that for the first time in their experience, 'American mechanics' nightly sought shelter in station houses—by the dozens and with their families." David Montgomery, *Beyond Equality: Labor and the Radical Republicans, 1862–1872,* (New York: Knopf, 1967), 263.

10. Quoted in NLT, 4 September 1875. The author of the letter provided the following sketch of his recent odyssey as a tramp. "Twelve months ago, left penniless by misfortune, I started from New York in search of employment. I am a mechanic, and am regarded as competent in my business. During this year I have traversed seventeen States and obtained in that time six weeks' work. I have faced starvation; been months at a time without a bed; the thermometer was 30 below zero last winter I slept in the woods, and while honestly seeking employment I have been two and three days without food. When, in God's name, I asked for something to keep soul and body together, I have been repulsed as a 'tramp and vagabond' by those who thanked God for his Mercies and Praised charities."

11. An 1868 article in *Harpers* described train-riding harvest hands in Minnesota;

for a discussion of the origins of the venerable science of catching a fast freight, see Kenneth Allsop, *Hard Travelling: The Hobo and His History* (New York: New American Library, 1967), 331–32.

12. Walter Wyckoff, *The Workers: An Experiment in Reality* (New York: Scribner's, 1898).

13. According to JSP (1 March 1885), a bogus ad in a New York paper for camel-drivers in Egypt drew throngs of desperate applicants. Similarly Foner relates how in February 1878 the newspapers carried the story that the S.S. *Metropolis* had sunk on its way to South America with a boatload of laborers from the United States. "One hour after the news that the ship had gone down had arrived in Philadelphia," the *New York Tribune* reported, "the office of Messieurs Collins was besieged by hundreds of hunger-bitten, decent men, begging for the places of the drowned laborers." Phillip S. Foner, *History of the Labor Movement in the United States*, Vol. I (New York: International, 1947), 444.

14. In 1884 the Patterson Local Assembly 1288 of the Knights of Labor proposed the establishment of an open column in the national paper listing employment conditions in different regions and trades so that workers would not be falsely induced to tramp. See JUL, March 1884, 658–59.

15. Carroll D. Wright, Massachusetts Bureau of Statistics of Labor, *Tenth Annual Report*.

16. Ibid., 137.

17. Although the JKL attributes this story to the *San Francisco Examiner*, the original version was published by the *Sacramento Bee* on 1 November 1893. The *Bee* version noted that California was currently "overrun with tramps," most of whom had come from mining camps in the Rockies.

18. Eric Hobsbawm, "The Tramping Artisan" (1951) in *Laboring Men* (New York: Basic Books, 1965), 34–63. R. A. Leeson, *Travelling Brothers: Six Centuries Road from Craft Fellowship to Trade Unionism* (London: Allen and Unwin, 1980).

19. Leeson, *Travelling Brothers*, 190–92.

20. *Report of the Massachusetts Board to Investigate the Subject of the Unemployed*, 13 March 1895, House Document Number 50, part 2, "The Unemployed: Way-farers," 54. Feder describes this 850-page report as offering "the most significant data on relief measures of the nineties, and so far as I know . . . the only state study of unemployment relief in any depression before 1929 covering so wide a field." Leah H. Feder, *Unemployment Relief in Periods of Depression: A Study of Measures Adopted in Certain American Cities, 1857 through 1922* (New York: Russell Sage Foundation, 1936), 87. See also the articles by Tygiel and Cooper in this book.

21. See Feder, *Unemployment Relief*, 40. The WA (20 March 1875) describes a

workingmen's "secret political society," the "United Sons of Industry," which was organized in Grand Rapids, Michigan to help destitute workers and to provide a reading room for the unemployed.

22. Foner, *History of the Labor Movement,* 236.

23. *Report of the Massachusetts Board,* 76.

24. Ibid.

25. James J. Davis, *The Iron Puddler: My Life in the Rolling Mills and What Came of It* (Indianapolis: Bobbs, Merrill, 1922), 114–21.

26. Karl Marx, *Capital,* Vol. 1 (Harmondsworth: Penguin, 1976), 794–95.

27. Stephan Thernstrom, *Poverty and Progress: Social Mobility in a Nineteenth Century City* (Cambridge, Mass.: Harvard University Press, 1964), 134.

28. Ibid., 113–14.

29. *Report of the Massachusetts Board,* Ibid.

30. Allsop, *Hard Travelling,* 1.

31. Thernstrom, *Poverty and Progress,* 134.

32. *Report of the Massachusetts Board.* The witness, a "Detective" who claimed to have traveled all over the country disguised as a tramp, makes the following distinctions: "There are three grades of tramps on the road. There are what they call the town bums, shovel bums and hobos. The town bums . . . most commonly tramp among themselves, and when you get in with them, the topic of conversation is, 'Well, have you struck many good chewing towns on the line of this road? Are there many hot stops, etc. . . . The general hobos, —— fools they think they are,—they are not going to kill themselves for a dollar and a half a day, not by a long shot. . . . And they are dangerous,—I must admit they are dangerous. They will go into a town, and if they find boys that have no parents, no one to look after them . . . those boys are taken with them, and there is a squad of the hobos always together. They never go one by one, they will go eight or ten in a squad. . . . They teach those boys to steal and beg and do anything they want to" (86–87).

33. Clarence Bonnett, *History of Employers Associations in the United States* (New York: Vantage, 1956), 114.

34. From a speech by "Captain" Richard Trevellick, quoted in JSP, 30 May 1886. Perhaps the most massive category of blacklisted, tramping trade unionists were the railroad "boomers". As Allsop has explained, these were a virtual caste of blacklisted brakemen and firemen who free-lanced under assumed names wherever work could be found. Between jobs they tramped the rails with the connivance of sympathetic train crews who left them alone as long as they could show a union card. After the defeat of the great American Railway Union strike in 1894, the number of "boomers" was drastically multiplied. "If a man had been prominent in the 1894 Pullman strike, the letter of reference with which the General Managers

Association had in law to furnish him was likely to be (although this was not discovered for nearly a year after the strike) on a sheet of paper with the watermark of a broken-neck crane. Rank and file strikers, or men shifting ground for other reasons, got a reference bearing the watermark with the cranes and head erect and were eligible for consideration up the line; but if the head drooped—no job" (Allsop, 156–57).

35. See Ringenbach, *Tramps and Reformers,* 14.

36. The reform of charity and relief administration excluded entire categories of the unemployed from organized aid. In New York, for instance, the Association for Improving the Condition of the Poor, after adopting a system of registration in the summer of 1877, dropped some 2,000 names from its rolls. Similarly, the Indianapolis Committee on Benevolence of the Common Council refused to establish a much needed soup house because it was "impossible to discriminate between worthy and unworthy poor." And in Chicago, although some concessions were made after tens of thousands of workers were mobilized by the "Socio-Political Association" against the cuts in aid, still 60 percent of the relief applicants were rejected as "not deserving relief" and "single able-bodied men" were not even considered (See Feder, *Unemployment Relief,* 47, 51–53, 57). Thus, by excluding single men from relief, it would seem that "scientific charity" ensured the expanded reproduction of the very "tramps" which it had set out to suppress.

37. "Nearly all the States of our Union have imported the English plan, and theory of official charity, without much scrutiny, and with all their defects." (D. O. Kellog, "The Pauper Question," *Atlantic Monthly,* May 1883, quoted in Samuel Leavitt, "The Tramps and the Law," *Forum* 2 [October 1886], 190).

38. Connecticut Bureau of Labor Statistics, *Third Annual Report* (Hartford 1887), 140–42. This report contains an interesting conjecture about the relationship between war and vagrancy: "Wars have been followed by acts referring to 'tramps.' Our armies have been made up of volunteers. War deranges the habits of the citizen soldier. He sometimes finds it difficult to fall back into his old habits of industry. War deranges all business relations, and produces abnormal conditions that make beggary common. Tramp laws appeared in 1727 and 1879. The first after the war against the French in Canada. This act was amended in 1769 after the French and Indian war, and again added to in 1821. The second act appeared after the war of the Rebellion" (223).

39. See Leavitt, "Tramps and the Law," 147.

40. "Laws are necessary only because there are persons in existence who own nothing. . . . This is directly expressed in but few laws, as, for instance, those against vagabonds and tramps, in which the proletariat as such is outlawed. . . ." Frederich Engels, "The Condition of the Working Class in England," in Karl Marx and Friedrich Engels, *Collected Works*, Vol. 4 (New York: International Publishers, 1975), 567.

41. *State* v. *Hogan*, 63 Ohio (1900), 215–18. "Statutes intended to suppress the tramp nuisance have been enacted by a number of the states of the union, notably Vermont, New Hampshire, Massachusetts, Rhode Island, Pennsylvania, Indiana, Iowa, and Wisconsin. These statutes are like that of Ohio so far as classification is concerned, and nearly all prescribe a like punishment" (219). Leavitt claimed that Pennsylvania antitramp legislation of 1876 "furnished the groundwork for most of our tramp laws, as far as they diverge from those of England. . . . Vagrants are now for the first time called tramps" (196).

42. The populist governor of Kansas, Lorenzo D. Lewelling, made the same analogy again in 1893 in his famous "Tramp Circular," which repealed his state's antitramp act of 1889. "Drawing the analogy between conditions in Elizabethan England, pre-revolutionary France, and America in the 1890s, Lewelling held that each of these societies underwent precisely the same formative experience. Men were uprooted from independent positions and transformed into surplus labor—into so-called tramps and vagabonds." See Norman Pollack, *The Populist Response to Industrial America: Midwestern Populist Thought* (Cambridge, Mass.: Harvard University Press, 1962), 33.

43. Quoted in Herbert Gutman, "The Tompkins Square 'Riot' in New York City," *Labor History* 6, no. 7 (Winter 1965), 69.

44. Quoted in WA, 15 January 1876.

Lynn Weiner

Sisters of the Road:
Women Transients and Tramps

I n 1903, the problem of the woman tramp in the United States was
brought up at the National Conference of Charities and Correction.
"In speaking of tramps, I noticed that they left out the tramp woman and
girl altogether," complained Mrs. O. L. Amigh, of Geneva, Illinois. "From
my childhood up, I have seen tramp women and girls, and they are the
greatest menace to the community of any class of people who tramp. They
may not be quite as numerous as men and boys, but it does not take so
many of them to do a great deal of harm."[1]

By the turn of the century, the line between the male transient worker
and the female tramp was very thin, and of the two the female tramp
posed a far greater threat to social order. Until the Depression of the
1930s, welfare agencies could not easily reach her, while her style of life
placed her far beyond the limits of acceptable behavior. Especially before
the 1930s, the female tramps who chose to defy sex role conventions
symbolized a criticism of cultural mores as great as any other presented by
women of that time.

But female tramps were only one segment of the population of transient women in the late nineteenth and early twentieth centuries. Because
the transient labor force was differentiated by sex, society labeled the
male transient workers who moved in and out of manual and agricultural
employment as hoboes and tramps, while it considered women transient
workers, who toiled mainly in cities, to be the more respectable "women
adrift."[2]

This distinction reflected the difference between the two major
groups of women transients. The first group consisted of women self-

identified as tramps and hoboes who took to the road for adventure or work; they were seen as wholly beyond the pale of respectable behavior and unredeemable by social reform. The second group, comprised of women who migrated to and within cities to find work and housing, were seen as socially salvagable, for they were but one step outside the boundaries of the acceptable female role; many were only working until marriage would reestablish their domestic identity. It was only when the two groups threatened to merge during the economic crisis of the 1930s that women tramps became labeled as a problem group subject to social policy.

This essay examines the history of women transients and tramps from the late nineteenth century through the 1930s in the United States. In this era, widely shared values about sex roles prevailed to render the transient woman a marginal place in an already marginal culture.

Women self-identified as tramps were barely visible, drawing sporadic attention as "road sisters" at best and "hay bags" at worst.[3] When they were noticed, it was with the recognition that they defied all contemporary standards of work and virtue. "Show me a lady hobo," one male hobo argued, "and I'll show you an angular-bodied, flint-eyed, masculine-minded travesty upon her sex."[4] Ben Reitman, anarchist and self-styled "King of the Hoboes," suggested that the woman tramp represented a most radical challenge to the social order. "What happens when women cut their apron strings, turn their backs on home, lose their respect for authority, and become satisfied that they can get a living and take care of themselves anywhere in the world and feel they are the equal of men. . . . Will these wandering women help bring on a social revolution [?]"[5] Women labeled as tramps symbolized extreme deviance from "woman's place" in American society—a place characterized by dependency, domesticity, submission, and the other prescribed female virtues.[6] By tramping, they abandoned all claims to the privileges and constraints conferred upon their more conventional sisters.

Male tramps emblemized sharply different values about a man's role in society. The ideas of freedom and independence which were anathema for women were idealized for men, and accounts of trampdom often exalted the wanderlust of the tramping male. "Jack the Hobo," for one, reflected liberated and rugged individualism to an admiring *Atlantic Monthly* writer in 1907.[7] While this respect for transiency was tempered with a healthy fear of the consequences of rootlessness, still it was a respect rarely accorded the woman on the road.

The investigations and first-person accounts of the tramping life which proliferated in the late nineteenth and early twentieth centuries usually ignored women. J. J. McCook's "tramp census" of 1893, for example, found no women at all. As late as 1920 one tramp's diary recorded no meetings with women on the road.[8] Those women who do emerge in the male accounts of trampdom were famous miscreants and colorful oddities. Boston Mary, Creole Helen, and Peg-leg Annie were among the archtypical beggers, thieves and fortune-tellers preserved for history by contemporary writers.[9]

Even these tramping women were held in low esteem within the subculture of the tramp. Male tramps, one writer suggested in 1911, "deprecate the admission of women to their ranks. . . . [Women] have no standing on the road, and at best are only *tolerated*. . . ."[10] Another tramp declared that in twenty-five years on the road he had never met a woman who was a true hobo, motivated by a combination of wanderlust and independence. Rather, the women he had come across were lowly criminals and vagrants.[11]

We know very little about the true history of women who tramped. The highest estimates of the female tramp population were made during the 1930s, when some studies suggested that as many as one in ten persons on the road were women and girls.[12] Prior to this time, the proportion of women among tramps was probably much lower. Bertha Thompson, known as "Boxcar Bertha," stated that in her childhood in the 1910s women hoboes "were still few enough in those days to cause a little stir. . . ." Ethel Lynn, who tramped across the country in 1908, reported that farmers, railroad men, and male hoboes alike were astonished to find a woman on the road.[13] Another observer noted in 1911 that while women had become visible among the hobo class, still "there seems little danger of individual tendencies developing into a popular movement."[14]

It is likely that an examination of welfare records might yield useful data about the population of tramping women in this period. Poorhouses and police station lodgings accommodated thousands of women who found themselves in cities with no place to sleep. In New York City in 1874, for instance, two out of five police station lodgers—some 12,000 persons—were women who turned to the stations as a last resort for shelter.[15]

Many of these women, however, were not tramps in any sense of the word, but were the local homeless and destitute women known as "bag ladies" in the later twentieth century. It is necessary to carefully define the parameters of tramp identity. Generally it is the unattached transient male who traveled by foot or by boxcar from job to job and city to city who was labeled a tramp or a hobo. For women, we have seen, the group identified as transient included urban self-supporting workers; it might also include unmarried mothers with children, aged and destitute widows, itinerant workers, and the urban poor. For the purposes of this discussion we will emphasize one group—the single, unmarried, and generally young women who left their homes either to seek employment in the cities or adventure on the road.

Sources for the history of the woman tramp are rare. Two autobiographies of women tramps, however, provide rich evidence for the study of women on the road. Although both record travels undertaken in the 1920s, they offer evidence of practices of women tramps in earlier times as well.

In *Sister of the Road: The Autobiography of Boxcar Bertha,* Bertha Thompson recounted her adventures as a tramp in the years after World War I. The daughter of anarchists, she rode the boxcars and hitchhiked across the country, occasionally finding employment as a clerical worker, domestic servant, or prostitute. She recorded her encounters with other women who, like her, chose the freedom and adventure of the tramping life to the restraints of conventional domesticity. Among these women were Dorothy Mack, an itinerant saleswoman, Leg-and-a-half Peggy, a tramping prostitute, and Lizzie Davis, self-styled "Queen of the Hoboes" and itinerant clerical worker, panhandler, and shoplifter.

Thompson described the movements and gatherings of these women. For many of them, Chicago became a major center in the early 1920s. "They came in bronzed from hitch-hiking, in khaki. They came in ragged in men's overalls, having ridden freights, decking mail trains, riding the reefers, or riding the blinds on passenger trains. They came in driving their own dilapidated Fords or in the rattling side-cars of men hoboes' motorcycles. A few of them even had bicycles. They were from the west, south, east and north, even from Canada." Some of these women, Thompson added, traveled by stowing away on boats or even on airplanes, and some had their fares paid by charity organization societies, where charity workers thought they were sending the women home.[16]

Within large cities there were known gathering places for women tramps. In Chicago, they gravitated to the near north side, an area bristling with cheap rooming and boarding houses. Of "Red Martha" Biegler's boarding house there, for example, Thompson wrote that, "When any of us hobo girls were broke or hungry, we always knew where we could get a meal and a bed, and no questions asked."[17]

Thompson observed that the social services for these women did not match those available to men. Men tramps had an easier time finding food and lodging in cities, mostly at missionary societies and in flophouses. But at the same time, Thompson portrayed a kind of subculture of female trampdom, complete with organizations such as the Women Itinerants' Hobo Union, and women hobo conventions, like the one held in Webster Hall in New York City in 1932.[18]

Barbara Starke [pseud.], the author of *Touch and Go: The Story of a Girl's Escape,* provides another firsthand account of female trampdon. Starke told of her life as a "rebel girl hobo" in the mid-1920s. She left her New England family to "cut all the ties that bound me; clothes would not matter nor possessions hamper. I would start from the bottom up and erect my own scale of values."[19] Dressed in corduroy knickers, she traveled to and from the West Coast, now and then working in an office, sleeping in hay stacks, and taking a lover. Her adventures ended as she entered the "net" of the conventional domestic and work life she had fled. Her description of her new job in New York City portrayed a room "sectioned off by filing cases, with a brick wall outside the window, and a dozen stenographers clicking at their desks in the artifical lights"—a sharp contrast indeed to the open fields of her travels.[20]

Both of these works must be taken critically. Like the publications of their male counterparts, these accounts of the tramping life are vulnerable to charges of exaggeration and poetic license. But still they are valuable as social history for their descriptions of the motivations and practices of women on the road in the early twentieth century. Moreover, they provide evidence that at least some of the women self-identified as tramps chose that life not because of a desperate search for employment, but because of an equally desperate need to escape the confines of the conventional female role of the era.

These documents and others allow us to construct the outlines of the characteristics of the small population of women tramps who wandered the roads. Women tramps appear to have shared patterns of dress, work, and sexual behavior which set them apart from other members of the female labor force.

Many women tramps differed most visibly from other women by the way they dressed. Many of them dressed in men's clothing, and in fact some chose to "pass" as men, which may account for their invisibility to such observers as J. J. McCook. Both Boxcar Bertha Thompson and Barbara Starke were among the women who wore pants, knickers, and other apparel associated in that era with masculinity.

Women practiced cross-dressing for two reasons. First, it allowed ease of work and travel in an era when women's clothing prohibited movement. Women in skirts could not as easily "ride the rails" nor could they as comfortably work at manual or agricultural labor. Second, a woman dressed as a man might avoid detection by fellow travelers and railroad guards who might harass or sexually molest her. Several accounts of tramp life describe chilling rape scenes of the lone woman discovered in a boxcar or hobo jungle.[21]

Some women who dressed as men unwittingly broke local laws. Anna Hedstrom, for one, was a transient laborer charged in 1893 in St. Paul, Minnesota with the crime of "dressing as a man." Hedstrom, garbed in "rough working clothes" including a flannel shirt, heavy shoes, and a slouch hat, denied knowledge of the law and expressed her desire to avoid traditional woman's work. "She disliked housework and furthermore was able to earn more money as a man," she told the court. She also declared her intention to move on and find work in a lumber camp. Her case was dismissed with the provision that she dress in women's clothing.[22]

Another characteristic of women on the road—one which they shared with men—was their habit of moving in and out of the labor force. Several accounts reported that women tramps worked for a while, took to the road, and then found employment again. Bertha Thompson described this pattern among the women she met during her travels:

Many worked from time to time. Some were typists, some file clerks, and carried with them recommendations from the companies they had worked for. I knew one that first summer who was a graduate nurse. The only thing she carried with her on the road was a conservative looking dress which she could put on when she went to register for a job. She'd stay on the case, or a couple of cases, and then she'd pack the good dress away and go out on the road in trousers, hitch-hiking.[23]

Like men tramps, many women tramps saw employment as only an occasional need, and chose not to become enmeshed in a regular job routine. Hence their identity as tramps was fluid, fluctuating with the patterns of their work and travels.

The tramping nurse reveals another characteristic of women tramps— their propensity to hitchhike. By the 1920s, when the dominant mode of travel for men tramps was still the boxcar, for women it may have been easier to solicit rides from motorists. Bertha Thompson reported that the women she met traveled more often by car than by train. She described listening to the women hoboes of her childhood tell of hitchhiking and of taking "wild and exciting rides with strangers across the long stretches of prairies." Barbara Starke noted that women could more easily hitch rides than could men, stating that "sometimes there are advantages to being born a girl; perhaps it was even better to be a girl, once away from the restrictions accorded a female."[24] This practice of hitchhiking, too, may have contributed to the relative invisibility of women tramps, for they were less likely to run afoul of either railroad police or the men tramps who traveled by boxcar. Prior to the availability of the automobile, women tramps probably traveled as men did—by boxcar, by foot, by bicycle, and by paid transportation.

Perhaps the most threatening characteristic of these wandering women was the nature of their sexual lives. The respectability and social status of women in this era was very tightly tied to domestic virtues and to family life. The women who lived outside the family lost their claim to this respectability. Indeed, if one of the fears about men tramps was that they would destroy or steal property, the major fear about women tramps was that they would turn to prostitution or in other ways exhibit immoral sexual behavior. For women, moreover, the term "tramp" came to denote not a transient worker, as it did for men, but rather a sexual outcaste. Frank Laubach, in his study of vagrancy published in 1916, observed that the "female kind of vagrant" was a prostitute.[25] And Josiah Flynt, in his 1893 *Tramping with Tramps,* argued that women would "take to the streets" rather than to the road, finding in prostitution the same escape from societal requirements found by men in the identity of hobo.[26]

While most accounts of women tramps do not confirm that they were usually prostitutes [although to be sure some were; Bertha Thompson, for one, worked for a short time in a brothel], it is clear that these women as a group did practice freer sexual habits than did the majority of women in their era. Some women tramps traded their sexual availability for protection. Maggie, a woman interviewed by Thompson in the 1920s, "accepted the fact that it was easier for a woman to get along on the road if she was not too particular and she frankly considered her body as her working capital."[27] Other women tramps self-consciously sought sexual freedom, such as those like Barbara Starke, who defied social mores by taking and abandoning lovers freely. Most shocking to some observers, perhaps, was the small group of "lady lovers" on the road—the lesbians who tended to travel together and who occasionally grouped in communal lodgings in the cities.[28]

Some women tramps traded their domestic skills along with their bodies for male protection. Even while creating their own subculture, some women played roles which reflected prevailing sexual expectations. Several reports observed that in the "hobo jungles," which were transient settlements on the side of railroad junctions, women took on typical domestic tasks. They cooked the food which men gathered, and also washed and repaired men's clothing.[29] In short, they bartered domestic tasks for protection and support, much like their counterparts in more conventional society.

In general, however, women tramps defied most expectations about the female social role. Away from the family and outside of any domestic influences, they lived lives of freedom unknown to most women of the period. Their invisibility stemmed not only from their relatively small numbers, but also from their defiance of widely shared sex role prescriptions.

When reformers and the public did take note of their existence, it was with distaste. The Committee on Vagrancy of the Conference of Charities in New York City, for example, maintained in 1916 that the "unhappy creature" which was a homeless woman faced more degradation than did a male hobo, for "unless a woman is a confirmed drunkard, she can usually find some home where at least her board will be gladly given in return for her services. . . ." The committee warned against the establishment of shelters for women tramps like those which existed for men, arguing that such shelters would only encourage immorality.[30] Frank Laubach summed up the response to the woman tramp, arguing that "Society will not tolerate in females the same kind of vagrancy that it will tolerate in men."[31] Woman's adherence to domesticity was too central to the health of the social order.

Society would, however, tolerate a different kind of transiency in women—that of the young woman living on her own and working in large cities. We have considered thus far the evidence describing women labeled—by themselves and by others—as tramps. But these women represented only a small proportion of transient women. Far more numerous were the single, unattached women who migrated to large cities to seek work and housing in the late nineteenth and early twentieth centuries. By 1900, nearly a third of all urban women workers—some 400,000—constituted a floating labor supply. They toiled in offices, stores, factories, and private homes.[32] They were not considered to be tramps or hoboes, but to be "women adrift"—a label in common use at the turn of the century. In short, while economic and social forces pushed thousands of single men into the identity of "tramp," similar forces also pushed most transient women not into the tramping life but into the urban labor force. If the road represented freedom from the constraints of the industrial work culture for men, work in turn to some degree represented freedom for women who had traditionally been bound to the home.

The woman transient was drawn to the city by rapidly expanding employment opportunities and driven there by the constriction of opportunities in rural America. The female labor market required a flexible supply of transients, for where men were needed for agricultural and manual labor, women were increasingly required for clerical, sales, and manufacturing occupations. By 1900 over 111,000 urban women worked in offices, over 65,000 worked in stores, and over 19,000 worked in textile mills.[33]

These jobs, often seasonal, depended upon the rhythms of the business cycle. Sales work, for example, required more labor in December for the holiday trade and less in the slack seasons. One investigator wrote of saleswork in 1912 that "there would seem to be evidence . . . that the occupation of saleswoman is regarded in the main as unskilled, that positions may be readily and indifferently filled by a new group of individuals, and that the number of positions may be considerably lessened or very greatly enlarged, according to the seasonal necessities without apparent harm to the industry."[34] Similarly, the push and pull of the business cycle drove employment in millinery work, waitressing, office work, and factory labor.[35] Hence women in these occupations were often forced to go from job to job within the city.

Domestic service was still the most common occupation for women in this era. Twenty-seven percent of urban women workers were servants in 1900, and nearly 80 percent of them were boarders and lodgers, most of them living with their employers in partial payment for their labor.[36] Surprisingly, many of these servants too were transients. For example, in Minnesota in the 1860s and 1870s, domestic servants often abandoned their jobs during harvest season, going to work for higher wages in the fields of the nearby countryside. They returned to their employers' homes only at the onset of winter.[37]

The female labor force, in short, was marked by the same mobility which marked the male labor force. But the female work experience was more likely to be urban, while jobs for men were more readily available outside of cities in harvest fields, on railroad lines, on road projects, and so on. Noting the high degree of transiency among working women in Toledo, Ohio, in the 1920s, one report stated that the "outstanding characteristic of this group of non-family working women was movement and change. They shifted in their work; they shifted in their places of living."[38] For the unskilled or semiskilled woman worker, transiency—from farm to city or from job to job within a city—was a fact of life.

While male tramps elicited the concern of reformers in this period, it was these urban women transients, and not women tramps, who were the subject of a parallel reform movement. Women tramps were so deviant their existence was unthinkable to many, and their numbers were relatively few. But young women transients in cities were seen as both numerous and reachable. Reformers hoped to reanchor them to the protections of domesticity. They feared that society was endangered by the population of young women living without the moral guidance of the family. Without some assurance that these women would adhere to domestic virtues, community respectability and purity were imperiled. As a result, a number of urban institutions, such as supervised boarding homes and supervised transient lodgings, were established for women in this period. It was not until a number of these transient women were forced on the road in the 1930s that public attention focused on women tramps as well.

In the late nineteenth century, reformers believed that the housing available to the poorly paid working woman posed a danger both to her health and to her morality. According to the U.S. Department of Labor in 1889, the districts which were the "ordinary homes of the poorer paid among the working girls in large cities" were marked by "narrow crowded streets, where drinking shops, gambling houses, and brothels abound."[39] Groups such as the Young Women's Christian Association set up both "permanent" and transient boarding houses to cast a net of respectability over these women adrift in the city.

The first travelers' aid organization had been founded in 1851, when the former mayor of St. Louis, Bryan Mullanphy, bequeathed over $300,000 for a "fund to furnish relief to all poor emigrants and travelers coming to

St. Louis on their way, bona fide, to settle in the West."[40] By the 1860s, travelers' aid work had narrowed to mean the moral protection of women and children traveling on their own.

Organizations such as the YWCA took up the work of travelers' aid, the Boston branch, for example, reporting in 1866 that

it is well known that many young women come to the city from homes in the country where they have enjoyed the blessings of parental affection and care and guardianship. . . . They generally come inexperienced, unacquainted with the difficulties which are before them, obliged to seek their homes where snares are spread on every side, with no kind hand to lead, or wise and judicious acquaintance to advise. It was felt that some agency should be devised that would *meet young women on their arrival in the city,* conduct them to proper homes, and counsel them.

By the next year, the Boston YWCA had housed some 250 transient women in its attempts to provide moral protection.[41]

The first travelers' aid work was generally to advertise referral services in railway depots. By the 1880s, travelers' aid workers, usually women, sat in terminals and way stations and distributed cards and religious tracts while supervising the passage of women through the city. Travelers' aid sponsors established women's hotels and transient homes in most large cities by the 1870s and 1880s. These lodgings typically aimed to "provide a temporary home under healthful influences" for women who could prove "good character" and who usually stayed in the establishments for a short amount of time, usually from two to four weeks.[42]

This transient housing met a real need for temporary residences for women. Nationally, by 1893, at least seventy-five transient homes had been founded by religious and reform groups, providing a capacity to accommodate, sometimes free of charge, nearly 4,000 women.[43] To some degree, these homes may have provided an alternative to the police station lodgings which had been so frequently used earlier in the century.

In 1912, the concept of travelers' aid reached the White House, when the Illinois Vice Commission visited President Woodrow Wilson to discuss the relationship between the employment of women and prostitution. Illinois Senator Niels Juul suggested that travelers' aid homes should expand under government sponsorship, arguing that "the government takes care of a pound of tobacco. It follows the commodity from Kentucky or Virginia across the state line, and even counts the number of cigars made out of that pound of tobacco. If the national government can devote so much time to a pound of tobacco . . . it can surely devote some time to the care of womanhood. . . ."[44] This attempt to elevate travelers' aid work from voluntary charity to state policy failed, however, and travelers' aid remained in the domain of reformers. In 1917, local travelers' aid workers united to form the National Travelers' Aid Society.[45]

The travelers' aid movement was altered—as were all welfare movements—by the Depression of the 1930s. At that time, travelers' aid began to focus on men as well as women travelers and became widely involved in social welfare work during the Depression. The governing principle of travelers' aid changed from moral protection to social casework, as the organization began to cooperate with the Federal Transient Program, which was established in 1933, to identify and bring the population of wandering men and women under the supervision of the government.[46]

This change in the travelers' aid movement illustrates the relationship between the woman tramp and the transient woman. As job opportunities for women became severely constricted, many white collar workers and other urban women workers were forced by unemployment to join the ranks of women tramps. Now women became visible on the road and as a homeless force in the cities, where they slept on park benches and in hotel lobbies or rode the subways all night. "We have had female hitchhikers and women transients before the depression," one investigator wrote, "but never so many as the present crisis has produced."[47]

Collection methods limited statistics about women on the road at this time. Welfare agencies gathered data, but typically women refused to participate in charitable institutions such as breadlines and shelters. Moreover, some unattached women claimed they were married or in other ways obscured their identities.[48] One study, however, surveyed the numbers of transient women in 800 cities in 1933, and found nearly 10,000 of them, nearly 2,000 living in hobo jungles. These women, furthermore, represented only about one-fifth of the women on the road throughout the country. Other studies, cited earlier, found that as many as one in ten tramping transients were female.[49]

Because this population of tramps now included young women who had been considered "respectable," they could no longer be ignored. Women and girls who tramped became the subjects of a proliferation of books and magazine articles, including Thomas Minehan's study of boy and girl tramps and articles like Walter Reckless's "Why Women Become Hoboes," published in the *American Mercury* in 1934.[50]

Most of these studies argued that economic conditions forced women on the road, and that they no longer chose the life of the tramp for ideological purposes. Boxcar Bertha Thompson noted that it was a "new order, certainly, from that of the old hard-boiled sister of the road who chose the road for adventure and freedom in living and loving!"[51] The woman tramp of the 1930s, unlike some of her counterparts in the earlier era, did not have the choice of a more conventional life.

The recognition of the new order of women tramps and transients led to local and federal government efforts to stem the tide of homelessness. Bertha Thompson urged the establishment of improved public services for women on the road, including the funding of wayside stations with libraries, bathing facilities, mailboxes, and employment, personal, and legal counselors.[52] The Federal Emergency Relief Administration and local charities did set up such services as work rooms, employment bureaus, shelters, work camps, and registration bureaus. As the government intervened in the world of tramp, too, the term "tramp" gradually gave way to the term "transient" to define the homeless person traveling on the road.[53]

The federal government soon shaped its policy regarding these transients. For the first time it aimed to protect society from vagrancy, to socialize transients and reclaim them from the life on the road. The government also provided care for the sick and aged among the transient population, and in general attempted to halt the "aimless wandering" brought on by the Depression, a wandering which in the case of women threatened to swell the ranks of those female tramps already associated with a radical rejection of dominant cultural values.[54]

The problem of women on the road faded as the Depression wore on.

The government claimed that its programs effectively diminished the numbers of unattached women on the road to about 1 percent of the tramp population by the mid-1930s.[55] Whatever the cause of this reduction, women tramps did seem to drop from sight again by the end of the Depression.

The female transient worker, like the male tramp, had played an important role in the labor force at the turn of the century, filling a critical need for labor in the burgeoning urban economy. The formation of such agencies as travelers' aid institutions attempted to reaffirm her relationship to traditional morality and domesticity, while bridging the distance between her actual and prescriptive social roles. By the end of the 1930s, the urban self-supporting woman was no longer considered to be a "transient" problem, while women tramps, once again reduced to an isolated group, disappeared from the cultural landscape.

Notes

1. "Minutes and Discussions," in *Proceedings of the National Conference of Charities and Correction* (1903), 517.
2. While the public saw male hoboes, tramps, and bums as one population, others drew fine distinctions between the three groups. Jack MacBeth, president of Chicago's Hobo College, suggested in 1935, "A hobo is a migratory worker, a tramp is a migratory nonworker, and a bum is a nonmigratory nonworker." See *Chicago Evening American*, 7 January 1935, clipping in the Ben Reitman papers, University of Illinois at Chicago, Supplement 2, File 62.
3. Godfrey Irwin, *American Tramp and Underworld Slang* (New York: Sears Publishing Co., Inc., n.d. but ca. 1930), 159; James Forbes, "The Tramp, or Caste in the Jungle," *Outlook*, 19 August 1911, 874.
4. Cliff Maxwell, "Lady Vagabonds," *Scribner's* 85 (March 1929), 292.
5. Ben Reitman, manuscript notes for Ben Reitman, ed., *Sister of the Road: the Autobiography of Box-Car Bertha*, Reitman Papers, File 39, 22. *Sister of the Road* was first published in 1937 by the Macauley Company; an edition was also issued in 1975 by Harper Colophon Books.
6. For a fuller discussion of the female role prescription, see Lynn Weiner, "From the Working Girl to the Working Mother: The Debate Over Women, Work, and Morality in the United States, 1820–1980," Ph.D. dissertation, Boston University, 1981.

7. "The Call of the Shirt," *Atlantic Monthly* (May 1907), 725–28.

8. J. J. McCook, "A Tramp Census and Its Revelations," *The Forum* (August 1893), 753–56; Hapgood Powers, *Journal* (Sept.–Nov. 1920), Hapgood Powers Papers, folder 3, box 1, Minnesota Historical Society, St. Paul, Minnesota.

9. Josiah Flynt Willard [Josiah Flynt], *Tramping with Tramps* (New York: The Century Company, 1901), 317–35; Samuel Milton Elam, "Lady Hoboes," *New Republic*, January 1930, 164–69; Forbes, 874; Maxwell, 288–92.

10. Forbes, 874.

11. Maxwell, 289.

12. For example, see Thomas Minehan, "Girls of the Road," *Independent Woman* 13 (October 1934), 316.

13. Reitman, *Sister of the Road*, 15; Ethel Lynn, *The Adventures of a Woman Hobo* (New York: George H. Doran Co., 1917).

14. Forbes, 870.

15. Leah Feder, *Unemployment Relief in Periods of Depression* (New York: Russell Sage Foundation, 1936), 64–65.

16. Reitman, *Sister of the Road*, 68–69.

17. Ibid., 60.

18. Ibid., 239–41.

19. Barbara Starke [pseud.], *Touch and Go: The Story of a Girl's Escape* (London: Jonathan Cape, 1931), 37. This work was published in the United States as *Born in Captivity: The Story of a Girl's Escape* (Indianapolis: Bobbs, Merrill, 1931).

20. Ibid., 271.

21. Ibid.; Reitman, *Sister of the Road*; Elam, 164; Forbes, 874.

22. The story of Anna Hedstrom is recounted in *Svenska Amerikanska Posten,* 17 October 1893, translated by A. Norbeck, WPA Annals Collection, file 2, Minnesota Historical Society. For another example of cross-dressing, involving a Swedish woman working as a farmhand, see *Minneapolis Tribune,* 11 June 1886.

23. Reitman, *Sister of the Road*, 70–71.

24. Ibid., 16; Starke, 224–25.

25. Frank C. Laubach, *Why There Are Vagrants: A Study Based upon an Examination of One Hundred Men* (New York: Columbia University Press, 1916), 71.

26. Flynt, 7.

27. Reitman, *Sister of the Road*, 39.

28. Ibid.: 66–70. Reitman, in his "Outcast Narratives," describes Eve, a tramping lesbian. See Outcast Narratives #61, Reitman papers, Supplement 2, file 9.

29. Reitman, *Sister of the Road*, 14; Minehan, p. 335.

30. "Report of Committee on Vagrancy of the Conference of Charities in New York City," *Charities Review* 5 (May 1896), 341–55.

31. Laubach, 71.

32. U.S. Department of Commerce, Bureau of the Census, *Statistics of Women at Work* (Washington, D.C.: Government Printing Office, 1912), Table 26, 198–200. These data are for twenty-seven cities surveyed in 1900. For a fuller discussion of the history of "women adrift" see Weiner, part I.

33. Bureau of the Census, *Women at Work*, Table 27, pp. 208–9.

34. Elizabeth Beardsley Butler, *Saleswomen in Mercantile Stores* (New York: Charities Publication Committee, 1912), 87.

35. See, for example, Mary Van Kleek, *A Seasonal Industry: A Study of the Millinery Trade in New York* (New York: Russell Sage Foundation, 1917), 72–73. Van Kleek found that milliners were in demand through the fall and winter and faced their slow season from May through August.

36. Bureau of the Census, *Women at Work*, Table 26. See also David M. Katzman, *Seven Days a Week: Women and Domestic Service in Industrializing America* (New York: Oxford University Press, 1978).

37. *St. Paul Daily Pioneer*, 1 August 1868; *Minneapolis Tribune*, 18 August 1878.

38. Information Bureau on Women's Work, *The Floating World* (Toledo, Ohio: Information Bureau on Women's Work, 1927), 31.

39. U.S. Department of Labor, Commissioner of Labor, *Fourth Annual Report: Working Women in Large Cities* (Washington, D.C.: Government Printing Office, 1889), 31.

40. National Travelers' Aid Association, "100-Year Travelers' Aid Calendar," n.d., typewritten, Travelers' Aid Association of America Records, Box 2, University of Minnesota, Social Welfare History Archives, Minneapolis, Minnesota. This collection will hereafter be cited as TA records. See also Bertha McCall, "Historical Resume of Bryan Mullanphy Fund," 1949, typewritten, TA records, Box 2.

41. Quoted in "Early History of Selected Travelers' Aid Societies," n.d., typewritten, TA Records, 4–6.

42. Weiner, 72–75.

43. Calculated from U.S. Department of Labor, *Boarding Clubs and Homes for Working Women*, by Mary S. Ferguson, Department of Labor Bulletin No. 15 (Washington, D.C.: Government Printing Office, 1898), Tables II and III, 187–90.

44. Thomas H. Russell, *The Girl's Fight for a Living: How to Protect the Working Woman from Dangers Due to Low Wages* (Chicago: M. A. Donahue & Co., 1913), 146.

45. TA, "100-Year Calendar," 2.

46. See "Women and Girls," in *Service to Transients: A Monthly Exchange of Experience Among Travelers' Aid Societies*, Bulletin No. 1 (July 1933), 5, TA Records.

47. Walter Reckless, "Why Women Become Hoboes," *American Mercury* 31 (February 1934), 180.

48. Ibid., 175; Marlise Johnston, "The Woman Out of Work," *Review of Reviews* 87 (February 1933), 30–32.

49. See *The Nation* (9 August 1933), 143, for a summary of this study by the U.S. Women's Bureau.

50. Minehan, *Boy and Girl Tramps in America* (New York: Farrar and Rinehart, Inc., 1934); Reckless, 175–80. See also Darragh Aldrich, *Girl Going Nowhere* (New York: H. C. Kinsey & Co., Inc., 1939).

51. Reitman, *Sister of the Road,* pp. 254–55.

52. Ibid., 240–41.

53. Ellen Potter, "Transient and Homeless Persons," *Social Work Yearbook 1935* (New York: Russell Sage Foundation, 1935).

54. Ellery Reed, *Federal Transient Program: An Evaluative Survey, May to July 1934* (New York: The Committee on Care of Transient and Homeless, 1934), 32–33.

55. Ibid.

Eric H. Monkkonen

Regional Dimensions
of Tramping, North
and South, 1880–1910

In order to develop a firmly based dimensional image of the tramps'
world in the late nineteenth century, we must establish a conceptual
map bounding their travels. Such a description is, to be sure, little more
than two-dimensional, and it can not capture the whole mental world of
those tramps moving through it. But in order to construct our composite
picture of tramping, the two-dimensional world is essential, even though
limited. After all, real origins and vague, shifting destinations, laced together by the streams of tramping workers, defined the geographical
possibilities and limitations for the late nineteenth-century tramp. The
tramps' knowledge of far-flung geographic and economic regions depended on information which included travel routes, and information
which did not include routes was in essence not information. Without
access, without knowledge, the tramp network could not have existed,
much less flourished. Of course, we cannot recover all of the information
available to tramps. But remaining impressionistic and quantitative evidence can contribute to the description and analysis of late nineteenth-
century tramp travel patterns. What tramps did will serve us as a conservative behavioral sketch of what they knew.

At the time no one tried to grasp or estimate the patterns of tramp
travel with any accuracy or systematic approach.[1] As a result, our understanding of late nineteenth-century tramping is most limited concerning
one of its basic features—the actual travel patterns of tramps. Regional
influences—attraction, repulsion, cultural, economic—formed an interrelated aspect of tramp travel patterns. Through the media of region and
transport such diverse factors as communications links, craft skills, railroad

policies, and differing work cultures affected everything from destinations to modes of travel to trip success. A reconstitution of the fragmentary evidence suggests that region and transport combined to determine all of the others. Rail access constituted the primary determinant of tramp travel patterns. When further influenced by regionally distributed differences, it made an elemental building block of the tramp world.

Astute observers of late nineteenth-century tramps often typologized the individuals who tramped. These typologies substituted for a larger causal analysis of tramping. The typological descriptions of who tramped provided the basis for inferring individual reasons for tramping. Followed by generalizations based on such overviews, one could substitute the aggregation of individual reasons and motivations for a causal analysis. Each step in this chain of analysis is impeccable, but the chain does not address the original causal questions. For example, the (imagined) discovery that all tramps were drunks does not lead to the necessary conclusion that the tramping system exists because of drunkenness. Not only did this method of thought lead to a false analysis of tramping, but because it focused attention on a causal problem, it allowed for the creation of some incorrect notions of tramp travel patterns. Thus observers created an analysis which impeded critical, elemental description. As a consequence, the appealing if incorrect notion that tramps survived the brutal northern winters by heading south could be propounded without close examination.

Late-nineteenth-century observers made some important if incomplete observations suggesting regional differences in the kinds of people who tramped. Typically, the literature portrayed western tramps as hale and hearty outdoorsmen, while those from the Northeast were more often shown as the defectives of industrial society. Southern tramps shared neither stereotype. Within the larger world of tramps, images of two contrasting kinds of southern tramps coexisted: the embittered, alienated nihilists and the socially inadequate. In his unpublished autobiography Dr. Ben Reitman of Chicago described his tramping exercises north and south, sketching unusually perceptive vignettes of tramp "types" he had encountered and befriended.[2]

Reitman met "New Orleans Slim," "a lanky, cranky, malarial old hobo" and his eighteen-year-old son, "Louisiana Blue," who dressed in blue denim and "certainly sang the blues" in a jungle near Lima, Ohio, in about 1889. Slim had almost all of the characteristics to be expected from the commonly portrayed embittered southern tramp. Claiming to be a Confederate veteran, Slim railed against the government and "everybody and everything." He matched in critical vehemence, if not programmatic solutions, "any agitators" Reitman heard later in his life. Slim's previous travel experience throughout the South, a place "held in terror by all northern tramps," impressed Reitman and the other tramps. They thought Slim and his son had tramped the South successfully because he was a Civil War veteran. Tramps in the North had often claimed to be Yankee veterans during the depression of the 1870s.[3] But in their case, only the maimed had earned a modest amount of sympathy, and one must question the value of being a Confederate vet in the South.

A black teenager from Tennessee named Johnson, whom Reitman had encountered twice in about 1895, contrasted sharply with the embittered "Louisiana Slim." Reitman spoke to him first in a Des Moines, Iowa railroad yard. Dressed in rags, Johnson had poked his head out of a boxcar and confusedly asked Reitman where he was. Johnson's ignorance, his soleless shoes, and his inability to feed himself all astounded Reitman. Ignorant tramps did not get far or survive long. He tried to help Johnson learn basic survival skills, showing him how to beg, where to get food, and telling him his plan to find and rob a Jewish clothing merchant was foolish. Later, Johnson actually did walk into a clothing store in Omaha, where police arrested him before he could even get into any clothes to steal. He and Reitman met again in jail. The pathetic inability of this "gloomy, inoffensive chap" combined with his naively stereotyped view of the world and the world's racial prejudice to spell a less than rosy future for him.

Johnson's plight suggests that becoming a tramp in the late-nineteenth-century South differed dramatically from the North or West. There, the ways of the road could be easily picked up, and tramp traditions had passed from person to person. And only those who chose to do so traveled alone.[4] One other black, a Mississippian, shared a cell with Reitman in the Omaha jail. Reitman mentions him very briefly, typing him as lazy and religious. Yet this man, who traveled under the moniker "Chitlins," probably came closer to representing southern trampdom. He had begun his work history on a large farm as a porter, later moving north to St. Louis to become a waiter. Defined in comparative language, he was a wandering semiskilled laborer who had worked his way north. He had followed an established river route and urban migration pattern. We would like to know more about this more typical southern tramp, but unfortunately, Reitman tells us little else about him.

Several regional and social characteristics of late nineteenth-century tramps may be examined with existing quantitative data. These characteristics indicate circulation patterns, sketch social and demographic profiles of the tramps, and imply regional origins. Though covering substantially more people than those found in literary sources, these samples contain unknown biases. The data include the list of tramps kept by the Fifth Precinct police station in Washington, D.C., published information in the 1880 and 1890 censuses relating to the police, "tramp censuses" made by the social reformer J. J. McCook, and an extensive police lodgers record from Red Wing, Minnesota. These data allow us privileged glimpses of the birthplace, destination, home, age, gender, race, ethnicity, occupation, and simple numerical quantity of late nineteenth-century tramps. The data are fragmentary in that they come from limited locations and arbitrary points in time. But their reconstitution allows the opportunity to make tentative generalizations which modify the even more idiosyncratic literary perceptions of late nineteenth-century tramps.

The perceptual geography of trampdom created by popular eastern writers on tramps plotted a vaguely triangular shape with Boston at the apex, Washington, D.C., at the bottom and an unclearly defined West as the third point. The firmly fixed notion that tramps wintered in the South created an abrupt deviation from the smooth triangle of this literary mental map. This perception triggers an interesting set of empirical and theoretical questions. Did tramps really winter in the South? Was this just a rationale employed by popular writers to assuage disturbing humanitarian questions about winter survival of indigents? Did tramps generally belong to the urban industrial North? Were there regionally closed circulation patterns and nested hierarchies? Or did most tramps, in fact flow through the large triangle implied in the literature?

Because the sources for examining the nature of trampdom are limited to urban places, the most systematic and quantitative aspect of this examination must be restricted to cities. This does not mean there were no rural tramps or farm laborers. But the best and most systematic information about tramping comes from an urban bureaucracy, the police. While occasionally they arrested tramps for vagrancy, police more often had a supportive relationship with tramps. They lodged them overnight on station house floors or in special lodging rooms, and sometimes provided breakfast, all for no cost or fear of arrests. Cities with formally organized police forces, however small, provide a base for careful, comparative observations. The marginal and unintentional nature of sources on tramping reflect their subjects' social status.

These sources allow us to critically and systematically amend the literary and idiosyncratic notions concerning tramp character, and they provide significant supplemental evidence. The descriptions of tramps by those who actually tramped themselves have a much greater ring of truth than do the perceptions of local police reporters, their companions in the local judiciary, and magazine writers. The almost jocular tendency to stereotype tramps clearly put cultural blinders on many who dealt with them. This may be best observed in tramp registers, ostensibly simple factual lists. For instance, the registers listing tramps who lodged overnight in Red Wing, Minnesota, note that virtually all were intemperate, unskilled laborers during the years between 1890 and 1920. Similarly, the McCook tramp censuses claimed to count an astonishingly high proportion of intemperate tramps. In such cases we should read the notation "intemperate" as the ideology of the person making the record. The hurried notations of busy police desk clerks answering McCook's queries reflect in no way an informed evaluation. The example of the Fifth Precinct register of Washington, D.C., makes clear that when actually asked for their occupation, tramps gave specific answers. Thus, in the case of temperateness, and sometimes the case of occupation, tramp registers merely confirm the cultural biases against tramps as unskilled and intemperate wanderers.

Other perceptions of tramps may be challenged with quantitative evidence. Such is the instance with the cynical, elite notion that tramps cared for themselves in the winter by vacationing in the South. For example, a Washington, D.C., judge conjured up the image of tramps heading to Florida for a lazy winter spent eating oranges and sunbathing. He professed surprise that one of several tramps he was sentencing carried soap and salt.[5] The fiction of tramps spending leisurely winters in the South helped distance and remove compassion and understanding, as did the belief that tramps liked to tramp and that they ate well with their "fastidious tastes." Reitman's expressed fear of tramping in the South should raise our suspicions concerning the accuracy of the judge's point of view. On the face of it, this assertion had no easy test: Reitman the tramp asserted fear of the South, while more commonly, newspaper editors assumed tramps flocked south.

The seasonal variation in the number of overnight lodgings given to tramps by the police shows that lodgings increased in the winter, both in the North and in the South. This empirical observation supports neither side, for it simply implies that in bad weather tramps needed shelter more often, no matter what the region. Another feasible test of the assertion that northern tramps wintered in the South derives from an analysis of the Fifth Precinct, Washington, D.C., police station lodging record. During the early 1890s the station recorded administering 1,003 overnight lodgings to 841 individual tramps. This record gives systematic if selective insight into the kinds of people who tramped and who had to ask for free lodging at the police station. Furthermore, because the record lists the places where the tramps originated, we can discover the direction of travel taken by these people during various seasons. If tramps did winter in the South, then the peak in winter lodgings should have been composed of persons whose trips originated in the North. On the other hand, the spring and summer should have seen an influx of tramps whose trips originated in the South, heading back north again. Table 1 shows that indeed a slightly higher proportion of tramps from the North passed through the station house in the cold months of November through February than did tramps from the South, with the opposite in the warm months, March through October. While the differences are statistically significant, the determination of any substantive import is quite difficult, as

Table 1: Seasonality of Overnight Lodgings, Tramps

Trip Origin	Cold (Oct.–Feb.)	Warm (Mar.–Sept.)	Total
North	88.2%	11.8%	100%
	(323)	(44)	(367)
South	80.5%	19.5%	100%
	(500)	(119)	(619)

Source: Register of Lodgers, Fifth Precinct, 1891–95, Record Group 351, Records of the Government of the District of Columbia, National Archives and Records Service, Washington, D.C.

Note: This list comprises but a fragment of all lodgers in Washington police stations; when compared with the total number given out by the police, the Fifth Precinct list accounts for the following: (1891–92) 5.44 percent, (1892–93) 8.31 percent, (1894–95) 2.07 percent. Source for comparison numbers: the *Annual Reports* of the Washington police.

a vast majority of all tramps, from both the North and South, spent winter nights in the station house.

One might say, crudely, that in the cold months the southern warmth attracted the 8 percent greater proportion of all northern tramps as compared to southern tramps. Even this must be qualified, as 60 percent of the total tramps were from the South, if we include Maryland, or 30 percent of the tramps were from the South, if we exclude Maryland. And, unfortunately, no clerks recorded the destinations of these people. In any case, the results give strong support to neither set of perceptions. Proportionally more northerners headed south in the winter than did southerners head north. But more to the point, tramps clearly moved in *both* directions in the winter, moves which involved staying overnight in places like police stations.[6] While it must have been relatively easy as well as comforting for the middle class to persuade itself that all homeless wanderers were flocking South, the evidence hardly supports such a notion. Most of the homeless of the North spent their winters in northern cities.[7]

If the South was not filled with northern tramps escaping the cold, then the tramps who did occupy southern jail lodgings must have been southern in origin.[8] Did the South as a region support fewer tramps than other regions? Certainly, given the larger argument of this book conceptualizing the late nineteenth-century tramp as an artifact and facilitator of industrial expansion, one would predict that the South as a region would have required fewer tramps. To see if tramping did vary in magnitude between different regions of the United States, an accurate as possible idea of its extent must be established. In most cities the only free alternative to the outdoors was to be found in police station lodging. Occasionally the police supplemented a municipal lodging house (as in Louisville, the Wayfarer's Rest), but these became more prominent urban organizations in the mid-1890s, postdating much of the period data examined here. The unadjusted annual lodgings given by the police cannot easily be used as an absolute measure of the numbers of indigent tramps. Most cities allowed a free stay of several nights, and tramps evaded any time limits by using different names and moving from one station house to another.

However, the annual number of lodgings per capita (of city population) can serve as a rough comparative index to the number of homeless people in various cities and towns. This tactic allows a regional comparison and remains sensitive to the measurement dilemma. Table 2 presents annual police lodgings per capita for four major regions. These cities have been paired to maximize similarities in location, size, and function. The years selected for comparison correspond exactly for each pair, a critical consideration since annual levels in tramping fluctuated with the national unemployment rates.

Table 2 shows that southern cities clearly had the lowest level of tramping, northern cities the highest. The range within the South alone was also large. Thus, although we can accurately speak of the lesser amount of southern tramping, we should not make the mistake of then conceiving of the South as an homogeneous entity. Between the regions the range of police care for tramps varied considerably, with southern cities showing far less exertion, in their tradition of more modest urban services. Northeastern cities were most consistent in their levels of tramp care, while the numbers of tramps aided in the South varied a great deal. This, of course, makes generalization difficult, for the consistency and range of services affect the measurement of the number of the homeless

Table 2: Comparative Police Lodging Rates (per 1,000 urban population)

City Pair: Years for Comparison	South	North
New Orleans/Cleveland: 1891–3	3.5	5.9
Washington/Newark: 1873–86	54.6	141.7
Louisville/Detroit: 1870, 1871, 1873, 1876	29.7	48.8
Richmond/New Haven: 1874–88	13.5	50.0

Source: Data compiled from annual police reports for each city each year.

Note: Cities paired on basis of similar size and location, with data for comparable year as available. City size ranking in 1880: New Orleans (10), Cleveland (11), Washington (14), Newark (15), Louisville (16), Detroit (18), Richmond (25), and New Haven (26). Using data from the 1890 census volume, *Social Statistics of Cities* (Washington: G.P.O., 1895) gives the following comparable values: Northeast = 35.5 (n = 99); South = 21.9 (n = 23); Midwest = 31.8 (n = 87); West = 51.3 (n = 17). Respective standard deviations = 3.4; 7.8; 4.9; 37.3.

needy. We can only crudely rank the regions, then, with the North having the most tramps, the South the fewest.[9]

The data limitations will not allow an estimation of the relative contribution of various regionally independent factors. That is, it may have been that nonregionally determined influences led to an appearance of regional differences in tramping. But they can be briefly discussed. First, the local level of police service combined with the concurrent existence of municipal lodging houses or other welfare services may have exerted an independent influence on the lodging rates. For instance, if the police only had room for fifteen lodgers, then an enormous number of tramps in need of lodging would not have upped the rates beyond this physical limit. The averaging of rates over several years, as in Table 2, helps capture the level of demand as well as possible. Presumably police with even limited resources would expand the space reserved for lodgers over a several-year period of time if drastically needed.

The location of each city within a larger urban network also exerted independent effects on the number of lodgers. Table 2 demonstrates this particularly for Newark, which acted more like New York City than like a smaller place. Further, railroad access to the cities and the city location in rail transfer networks also affected the number of tramps, as did the local availability of jobs. Cities without easy freight train access and without seasonably variable labor demands would have had few tramps. In spite of these frustrating measurement problems, it does clearly appear that the farther south a city, the fewer tramps it had—New Orleans police accomodated only 3.5 per 1,000 city population, while to the north St. Louis had 12.6 per 1,000, and even further north, Chicago had 28.1 per 1,000.

This suggestive if not definitive analysis can be refined further if we are willing to forego the advantages of stability and accuracy gained by averaging several years together. Cross-sectional data gathered by the Bureau of the Census for its 1890 volume on the *Social Statistics of Cities* contains a rich set of information on cities and their accommodation of tramps at police stations. The limitation to this data set must be made clear: there was no such thing as a typical year for tramps. The analysis here covers a year with its own peculiar limitations—1890, which had a relatively high level of employment. These data encompass 221 American cities in all regions. The analysis above can be respecified in the form of a multiple regression equation, estimating the relative independent contributions of railroads per capita, city size, police expenditures per capita, and region to the level of tramping, as measured by the number of police lodgers per capita in that single year. Region, in the equation in Table 3, has been included as a series of dummy variables for the four major regions in the United States. The advantage of using multiple regression here is twofold. First, the method estimates the magnitude of variation in lodgers per capita between cities—R^2. Second, given that the equation proves to be relatively powerful (that is, a substantively high R^2 and statistical significance), it estimates the contribution of each independent variable to the equation while holding the effects of the others constant. This means, for instance, a more careful determination of a city's regional attraction for tramps after taking into account the impact of other critical variables, like the number of trains and overall size.

Each independent variable has been included for a specific reason. The annual cost of the city police per capita captures any variation in the overnight lodging which came purely from the level of police service. This

Table 3: Regression of Police Station Lodgers, 1890

Lodgers =	9.91 +	6.53 T +	.0317 P$	−21.4 Dw	−5.4 DS	−.00004 P +	1.07 Dne
SEE =		.809	.005	10.58	9.27	.000	5.75
F =		65.28	7.09	4.10	.34	.061	.35

Adj. R² = .529 (N = 221)   F = 42.35

Average annual lodgers (1880–90) per 1,000; T = All trains per day per 1,000; P = City Population. P$ = Average annual cost for police (1880–90) per 1,000; Regional dummies for West (Dw), South (Ps) and Northeast (Dne). See Table 1. Note for mean values of lodgers for each region. Mean values by region for police expenditures and trains per day as follows:

Region	Northeast	South	Midwest	West
Daily trains per 1,000	2.7	1.0	2.1	5.7
Police expenditures per 1,000	$669	$795	$560	$1334

Source: *Social Statistics of Cities*, Eleventh Census, 1890 (Washington, 1895).

assumes that all else being equal, police departments with higher per capita budgets would have been able to accommodate more tramps. Another variable, had it been available, might better have captured related variation—some measure, for instance, of free lodging provided in each city by nonpolice organizations. The absolute size of each city, that is, population, has been included to capture the presumed attractiveness larger cities had for tramps. If larger places attracted more tramps simply because they had a greater number of jobs, we need search no further for an explanation for the small number of southern (but not western) tramps. The number of trains daily entering each city, per capita, measures the relative accessibility of each city to tramps. This variable's inclusion makes possible a more finely tuned estimate of region versus opportunity influences on a city's tramp population. A better measure would have been the daily number of noncommuter freight trains, for ratios of local commuter to long-distance trains often varied. Savannah, for instance, had ten commuter trains and twenty noncommuter trains daily, while for New

Orleans the figures were four and thirty-five. The latter figure captures the information most relevant, but sporadically missing information forced the usage of the daily number figure in the regression analysis. And finally, a dummy variable for each region of the United States—the Northeast, the South, the Midwest and the West—has been included. (A "dummy" variable is dichotomous, indicating only if an attribute is present or not.) If a region had an especially strong factor attracting or repelling tramps, the dummy variables should capture this, the other three variables accounting for the principle factors affecting urban attractiveness for tramps.

(One might well ask, what about local employment opportunities and levels of unemployment? In fact, the dependent variable here, lodgers per capita, might be the best measure of unemployment available for the nineteenth century. It seems reasonable to assume, in lieu of any other measure of this economic circumstance, that much of the unaccounted for variation in lodging did indeed come from local employment conditions. That is, we might use the variation unaccounted for by the equations as a measure of actual unemployment. However, the sign and meaning of this relationship is unclear. Temporary job opportunities associated with events like the Atlanta Exposition probably attracted many who stayed in police stations. It may well have been that the availability of local employment of a new, temporary nature increased rather than decreased the number of homeless job seekers.)[10]

Table 3 contains the results of the estimated equation. The coefficient in front of each variable shows what the actual value of a variable would have to be multiplied by to estimate the number of lodgers for an individual city. The sign shows whether this value would be added to or subtracted from the others to obtain the estimate. The standard error of estimate (SEE) indexes the quality of the coefficient—the smaller relative to the coeffecient, the better. For example, the trains per capita variable is strongly positive while the dummy variable for the South has no clear positive or negative sign. This shows the positive impact trains made on the number of tramps and the lack of influence made by southern location. The adjusted R^2 shows the proportion of variation in tramps per capita the complete model accounts for—about 53 percent—an amount both statistically and substantively significant. The variables appear in the equation in order of diminishing importance. Only the first three are of statistical or substantive significance, and in fact the inclusion of the subsequent variables slightly lowers the adjusted R^2 from the value at which it stands with only the first three variables included.

Several conclusions of importance emerge from the equations in Table 3. Most clearly, only one region—the West—had an effect on the level of tramping. Far fewer tramps than might have been expected appeared there. Earlier and more simply comprehended information had indicated that the South had an unusually low per capita number of tramps relative to the North. But the difference in the number of daily trains per capita, and to a lesser degree, the amount spent per capita on police service account for this regional variation. In other words, regional economic lag, nothing cultural, caused the small number of tramps. Ben Reitman's perception of the dangers of southern tramping were probably accurate and may well have reflected the kind of information which helped deter northern tramps from wintering in the South, but underlying causes, the lack of transportation and lower levels of local government spending, created the concrete conditions discouraging tramps.

The notion that different kinds of people tramped in different regions cannot be tested as carefully as one would wish with the available data. Only the data from Red Wing, Minnesota, have details on place of birth, but tramps passing through Red Wing were mainly local people. The Washington data allow some tentative inferences about northern and southern tramps. To define southern tramps I have separated out as southern all those tramps who listed states from Virginia south as their point of trip origin. Maryland, as a point of origin, creates a problem: had northerners, passing through and spending a few days in Baltimore, for instance, listed it as their point of origin? To deal with this definitional problem, I have used two separate definitions of northerners, both including and excluding those from Maryland. It must be understood that this definition of "southern" has its base in the person's self-defined point of origin and may conceal bias. After all, this analysis labels a person as a southerner on the basis of an answer given to a desk sergeant's query— "Where are you from?"[11]

Of the 619 overnight lodgings given out to people from Maryland or points further south, 19 were for women. Only one woman from the North stayed in the station house. Using the more rigorous definition, as in Table 4, still gives a disproportionate number of women from the South. As most nineteenth-century literature on tramps focused on men, this raises an interesting issue. Were there in fact few women tramps in the North, thus giving rise to the perception of tramping as being an all-male role, or were observers so blinded by stereotyping that they failed to see women tramps?[12] The New York City police had separate lodging rooms for men and women, which suggests that women may well have been exluded from police lodging in smaller cities where they could neither have been lodged with men nor housed separately. If so, then the small number of women tramps on the police lists may have resulted from inadequate police care, the Victorian perception of reality becoming a self-fulfilling prophecy.

My earlier study of the Columbus, Ohio poorhouse, located on the edge of the city, noted a greater proportion of women tramps (7.3 percent) than in the Washington police station.[13] Perhaps women on the tramp simply had to stay overnight in less convenient and less visible places than did men. Of the southern cities responding to J. J. McCook's 1893 survey, one, Savannah, claimed no women, while Norfolk, Newport, Kentucky, and Louisville claimed 4 percent, 0.5 percent, and 2 percent respectively. Let us speculate on the possibility that there were in fact more women in the southern tramp's world than in the North. The "push" to become a tramp—and "push" probably accounted for most of the reason to tramp—affected somewhat differently the poor of the South than it did the poor of the North. The conditions which forced people to leave their homes in search of work, while affecting proportionally the same southerners as northerners, affected the poorest of both genders in the South, forcing more southern women to tramp. If this was true, then the age, race, and occupations of the tramps should reflect it.

Table 4 displays the comparative proportions of southern tramps who were women, black, or foreign-born. It also shows the median ages for tramps from the two regions. Compared to tramps from the North, southern tramps were older, were proportionally more often blacks,

Table 4: Southern, Northern, and Ohio Tramps:
Demographic Characteristics

	South[a] (ratio to pop. at risk)[d]		North[b] (ratio to pop. at risk)		Ohio[c] (1860–85)
Median Age[e]	32	(.608)	29	(.829)	30.5
Percent Women	4.2%	(.085)	0.3%	(.006)	7.3%
Percent Black	28.4%	(.917)	6.3%	(2.85)	1.6%
Birthplace:					
U.S.	86.0%	(.334)	76.6%	(.986)	31.0%
Ireland	9.5%		6.0%		22.2%
Germany	1.8%		8.7%		24.1%

Source: Washington, D.C., lodgers data; Franklin County Ohio Infirmary.

Note: Chi-squared for women, blacks, native-born against north/south all at significance greater than .004.

(a) South here defined as D.C. and farther south; Maryland excluded because of the possibility that persons from the north passing through Baltimore claimed Maryland as trip origin. N = 285.

(b) North defined as Pennsylvania and north: Maryland excluded. N = 367.

(c) Persons listed as tramps staying in Franklin County, Ohio, poorhouse. N = 3,111. See Monkkonen, *Dangerous Class,* 160.

(d) Ratio obtained by dividing percent of tramps by percent of regional population. Black percentage urban only, native-born from 1900 rather than 1890. Underrepresentation less than 1, overrepresentation greater than 1.

(e) Median age of Louisville tramps at Wayfarer's Rest, 1891, 32 years old. McCook papers. Mean age of southern tramps, 35.2; northern tramps, 33.2.

were more native-born, and of the foreign-born, were more Irish and much less German. In itself this information has descriptive importance, but placed in the context of groups "at risk," there emerge several implications about the meaning of southern tramping in the context of the region. That is, the tramps may be examined for themselves and also to give insights on the society of their origin.

Southern tramps were slightly older than northern tramps, a difference which is heightened in the context of a relatively young southern society. A comparison of the two ratios shows that the tramps of the South were quite a bit older than we might have expected given the age of the sending population. Likewise, considering the populations at risk also heightens the difference between percentages of women north and south. Moreover, while as a body southern tramps had a greater proportion of black people in their ranks, blacks were slightly underrepresented compared to the sending southern society. In contrast, although making up only 6.3 percent of the northern tramps, black people were overrepresented compared to the black urban population of the North. The same distortion holds true, though much less dramatically, for native-born people, who composed a greater share of the southern tramps than northern tramps, but who should have had even a greater share in order to match the population at risk. Examined in the context of the south, southern tramps were disproportionately white, foreign-born, and old.

That black people should have been underrepresented indicates that the difficulty of black survival in a white-dominated world even extended to the lot of the tramp. The slender number of black tramps supplements the implications of several other articles in this book: the status of tramps may not have been quite as low as earlier presumed. Their marginal existence while traveling often depended on material wastage of the economy—food, shelter, transport—all of which on one level were "gifts" to tramps, "gifts" denied more to blacks than whites. Railroads supplied their transport, people the food, taxpayers the police lodging. It should be pointed out, parenthetically, that tramps and those who aided them paid the cost of maintaining the floating workforce. Ultimately, the employers of temporary labor and the larger economy benefited. In other words, as marginal and undesirable an existence as tramping may have been, it was an existence offering geographical mobility and marginal occupational opportunities which largely excluded blacks.

Actual tramps showed a surprising range of occupations according to the Washington, D.C., lists. About half the southerners were unskilled workers, while the other half claimed some sort of skilled occupational experience (47.4 percent listed skilled occupations). This contrasts with those from the North, of whom only 41 percent listed their occupations as unskilled. Southern tramps constituted a surprisingly skilled group, considering the region's essentially rural labor force. A handful of the southerners even claimed white collar or professional skills. Those most skilled constituted a statistically significant greater proportion of southern tramps than they did of northern tramps. Although the actual numbers are small, the specific occupational differences are revealing. Only two occupational categories had a majority of southerners, farmers and servants (twenty-one out of twenty-six and all five respectively). Solely northern occupations included mainly craft skills—those of tinners, molders, bricklayers, butchers and soldiers.[14]

As well as occupational category, regional origin affected travel distance and urban origins of the tramps staying in Washington. Few southern tramps had traveled very far. Only 9 percent came from further than 300 miles away, while over 75 percent of the northerners had come that far. Although the comparative proportions vary according to the definition of region employed, the basic difference persists—southern tramps did not travel as far as northern ones. And more of them came from smaller towns. Again, the exact differences vary by regional definition criteria, but in either case the differences are statistically and substantively significant. Only 6 percent of the northern tramps came from towns with populations under 5,000, as opposed to 25 percent of the southerners. Thus, for at least one-fourth of the southern tramps, the trip through Washington was an experience in urbanization as well as migration. Of course, in the 1890s the South was far more rural than the North. Eighty-nine percent of the region's population lived in places with less than 2,500 people, as opposed to only 41 percent of the northeastern United States. Even though the southern tramps were more rural than northern tramps, when compared with the South as a whole, they represent a uniquely urban subgroup, even though many were from small places.

The differences between southern and the more commonly and publicly scrutinized northeastern tramps suggest that the perception of tramping as a social problem could occur only in the context of highly self-conscious social change. Best exemplified in J. J. McCook's studies, this perception tied the vagaries of industrial employment to the regional social structure, a structure which included tramps. In the South, as a

Table 5: Southern and Northern Tramps:
Occupations, Trip Length, and Origins

Occupation	South[a]		North[b]	
Professional	3	4.56%	0	3.0%
White Collar	10		11	
Skilled	137		205	
Unskilled	135	47.4%	151	41.1%

(Chi-squared for unskilled versus all other not significant)

Trip Length			North (including Maryland)
501+ mi.	6	26	31
301–500 mi.	3	50	51
101–300 mi.	134	235	240
Less than 100 mi.	137	25	334

(Chi-squared for trip + or − 100 mi. all significant over .0001, except for North including Maryland)

Origin's Populations			
50,001+	137	262	526
5,001–50,000	57	47	71
Less than 5,000	67 (25.7%)	20 (6.1%)	42 (6.6%)

(Chi-square significant above .002 for all)

Source: Washington, D.C., lodgers data.

(a) South defined as in Table 4.

(b) North excludes Maryland.

contrast, tramping provoked the kind of amused reaction typified by a *Washington Post* article. The article, with detached irony, preferred to cast tramps as "humanity's protest against civilization," the "unsettlement of labor" deserving mention only as a lesser cause.[15] This journalistic reaction must be placed within the traditional vein of humorous editorial disdain, as tramps in the South also created fear and occasional violent attacks. Many were suspected of being barnburners, arsonists who struck at the very foundations of southern agriculture.[16] The fear of such criminals worked within the stereotypical essence of tramping—anonymity and mobility. This fear reflects the agricultural center of southern wealth and stability.

The element essential to tramping, movement, made them appear anonymous to the more rooted. Once made anonymous, they became eligible for treatment based on stereotypes. And in the pantheon of late nineteenth-century stereotypes, tramps emblemized two different major social threats. First, they challenged the Victorian ideology which attached value to order, stability, hard work, and the nuclear family. The tramps' very existence highlighted these values as cultural rather than universal. The continuous faceless presence of numerous people with unpredictable and unstable lives, unburdened with regular employment or family, provided a daily reminder of an ambiguous reality.

The very presence of tramps also posed a second threat to anyone possessing personal property, valuing public order, fearing that rootlessness caused crime, or reading a great inequality as democratic failure. Tramps caused such reactions, usually unconsciously. In a series of articles, Jack London dramatized his boyish adventures while traveling toward Washington with Coxey's Army of unemployed in 1893–94. He reveled in the fear and outrage caused by his particular band of misfits. His testimony may not be taken as representing the thinking or consciousness of most tramps with Coxey, but he showed extraordinary sensitivity to the mechanisms by which tramps provoked certain kinds of fear, moral indignation, and ideological contrasts. Probably London's enjoyment of this fear set him well apart from most tramps, especially those who were more deeply stigmatized. For most who tramped, the experience made up one component of their lives as urban industrial workers, not grist for the adventure writer's mill. For them, the threat of having to go on the tramp, to become an outcast, remained an integral part of their life possibilities.

In conclusion, we can see that although not nearly so dramatic as the literature suggests, there were minor north/south tramp differences.

Southern tramps came from a slightly higher echelon of their society than did northern tramps. While many of the southern tramps were black, blacks were underrepresented when compared to the whole South. A few more southern women tramped. Southern tramps were somewhat older. Skill levels resembled those of northern tramps. Fewer southerners tramped because there were fewer railroads and lower levels of urban service in the South. The pushes to tramp were probably the same North and South, but the South had fewer pulls. Few trains and few cities also meant less information about jobs, modes of travel, and destinations. That Johnson, the black teenager from Tennessee, should end up in jail in Omaha, ignorant of survival in a world of railroads, brakemen, handouts, big cities and temporary work, is characteristic of what might be expected of southern tramps.

These underlying reasons also account for the picture of the South which excludes that of the nineteenth-century scourge, the tramp. The image included a sense of extraordinary stability—the South was seen as a region which could resist the emergence of the tramp army roving the North. When massive urbanization and new transport forms did come to the South by the mid-twentieth century, the conditions and nature of tramping had changed nationally. In the 1930s the automobile made the tramps far less visible because they no longer had to congregate in public and could travel privately in disparate directions. Thus the South could urbanize and industrialize in the twentieth century without experiencing the painful vision of vast numbers of workers riding the rails, begging on the streets, sleeping in jails, and making demands on the police for social services. The image of the stable South could remain untarnished by Coxey's Army's embarrassing demands.

We are left, then, a tramp world where simple, obvious factors like trains and cities accounted for far more than did wanderlust or regional culture. The "roving army of the unemployed" did not rove, but followed fixed routes to rational destinations. Nor was it an army, except in the sense of a modern guerrilla force moving in very small groups, living off the people. Like the economy they helped build, a variety of tramps peopled the industrial landscape of the late nineteenth and early twentieth centuries, an important part of a historical moment both frightening and exciting in its dimensions.

Notes

I wish to thank the Academic Senate of the University of California, Los Angeles, for a grant supporting the research reported here. In addition, I wish to thank David Waterhouse for his research assistance.

1. The first empirical estimate of travel patterns appeared in a quite brilliant and perceptive set of papers published by the U.S. Department of Agriculture in the early 1920s. Based on a large sample of carefully conducted interviews in the wheat fields of the Midwest, the studies quite clearly show a limited range of east-west (not north-south) movements by the harvest workers, dispelling another myth, that harvesters followed the maturing wheat crop. The studies point out the basic reason for this: once they had moved from a city into a farming area, the sources of information for harvesters disappeared, and thus they were forced to head back east to, say, Chicago, rather than move north to another farming region. See U.S.D.A. Department Bulletin No. 1211, Don D. Lescohier, "Sources of Supply and Conditions of Employment of Harvest Labor in the Wheat Belt" (23 May 1924), 20, for map of travel patterns. See also Lescohier, Bulletin No. 1020, "Harvest Labor Problems in the Wheat Belt" (1922) and Bulletin No. 1230, "Conditions Affecting the Demand for Harvest Labor in the Wheat Belt" (1924).

2. Ben L. Reitman papers, Manuscript Collection, University of Illinois at Chicago Circle. As opposed to other tramp narratives of the late nineteenth century, Reitman's has the strengths of an unbiased primary source. First, he had no particular audience to satisfy, as did the other more sensational writers. Second, he was no romantic, for his narrative does not try to hide the ugly side of tramping. He did, however, have a self-admitted tendency to exaggerate, but exaggeration seems to have come in the way he used numbers and by his emphasis on danger and violence, rather than in outright fabrication. Certainly his character sketches ring true.

3. Reitman, "Following the Monkey," in Reitman papers, 123–24.

4. Ibid., 162–63. Paul T. Ringenbach, in *Tramps and Reformers, 1873–1916: The Discovery of Unemployment in New York* (Westport, Conn.: Greenwood, 1973), comments on the difficulty of blacks, whom he claims were excluded from trampdom (71–72). The "Time Kid" described by Reitman epitomized the loner by choice: he specialized in long-distance trips at high speed, going anywhere far for only the slightest reason.

5. *Washington Post,* 4 August 1893, 4. The notion of tramps wintering in Florida did not go uncriticized. The *Railroad Gazette,* in an article titled "Tramps," reprinted an interview with a tramp from the *Philadelphia Press* (16 January 1880): " 'I thought the tramps went south in the winter?' 'Some of 'em do, of course. But not so many as you think. . . . Southern railroads are awful hard to beat, and walking don't agree with me.' "

6. Ringenbach, 5, points out that cities were wintering spots for tramps in the North.

7. Reitman's fear of the South probably was well justified. Stories of sheriffs rounding up transients and blacks to fill out county chain gangs abound. In 1922 a notorious case suggested the mortal dangers of wintering in Florida. A twenty-two-year-old North Dakota farm boy who had decided to see the country by riding the rails died from a beating given him near Tallahassee, where he had been arrested and leased out as a convict laborer. Only because of massive publicity generated by his angry North Dakota family did the case surface in the national media. See Gudmunder Grimson, "Whipping Boss," *North Dakota History* 31 (April 1964), 128–33.

8. John J. McCook's survey of tramping in 1893 was picked up by many newspapers. The *Washington Bee* (9 September 1893), 4, a black newspaper, cited with no comment much of his reported work, including the erroneous fact that of 1,349 tramps interviewed, only one was a southerner.

9. But see Table 3 for an important qualification of the significance of the South: The dummy variable estimating the southern regional impact is statistically insignificant.

10. See the articles by Cooper, Davis, and Tygiel in this collection for examples of "stay away" pleas, which indicate the problem created when local opportunities attracted too many workers.

11. The Washington records do not allow us to ask more specifically where the lodgers were born, other than by nation. However, J. J. McCook's 1891 tramp survey asked place of birth by state, and one southern city, Louisville, administered his tramp questionnaire. The results: Of 134 legible answers, 73.9 percent of the respondents were born in the United States. Of those born in the United States, 16.2 percent were born in southern states. By any of these measures, the proportion of southern tramps staying with the Louisville police was considerably smaller than those staying in Washington in the same era. This was probably because of Louisville's location in an old and well-traveled transportation network. The small proportion of southerners should warn us that using point of trip origin as a definition of the "southerner" may well exaggerate the number of people who were southern by virtue of birth. (McCook papers, reel 3).

12. See the article in this collection by Weiner for an extended discussion.

13. Monkkonen, *The Dangerous Class: Crime and Poverty in Columbus, Ohio, 1860–1885* (Cambridge: Harvard University Press, 1975), 160.

14. The actual number of northerners to southerners for these occupations are: tinner, 8:1; molder, 9:2; bricklayer, 4:1; butcher, 4:1; soldier, 4:1. See the articles in this book by Tygiel and Cooper for discussions of two other skilled groups, carpenters and cigar makers.

15. "Theory of the Tramps," *Washington Post* (20 November 1892). See also, "Tramps as Epicures," *Washington Post* (6 November 1893).

16. A strange poem, "The Tramp of Shiloh," by Joaquim Miller, appeared with illustrations in *Frank Leslie's Illustrated Newspaper* (Supplement, 3 January 1880). It casually captured the fear surrounding the southern tramp as barnburner. When turned away from a house where he had begged for food, the poem's tramp narrator threatens: "Good-by! I must learn to creep into your barn; / Suck your eggs; hide away; / Sneak around like a hound—leave a match in your hay— / Limp away through the gray!"

John C. Schneider

Tramping Workers,
1890–1920:
A Subcultural View

American tramps in the late nineteenth and early twentieth centuries are comprehensible to historians as an itinerant segment of the labor force, but their generally similar circumstances suggest the possibility of some cultural identity and social organization as well. The idea that they were a "subculture" comes immediately to mind. Most people equate subcultures with "deviant" behavior. Deviants are those who violate widely accepted social norms and are thoroughly stigmatized for so doing. The literature on deviant behavior has tended to focus on the bizarre—the sociology of "nuts, sluts, and perverts." Scholars who have developed explicit theories of subculture take a broader and "softer" perspective. In their view society might even consist entirely of subcultures overlapping each other. The most useful definitions, however, assign to subcultures a measure of self-sufficiency and isolation from a social and cultural mainstream. A synthetic definition emphasizing the most salient characteristics of a subculture will suffice here: members of a subculture share relatively distinct personal traits, engage in relatively unconventional behavior, and associate with one another on a relatively segregated basis.[1]

The evidence lends sufficient support to the idea that tramps were a subculture, but this does not necessarily mean the men formed a homogeneous and cohesive group. There were significant differences among them. The many typologies of transient and unattached men offered by contemporary observers make this clear. A major distinction undoubtedly existed between men who had a special feeling for life on the tramp and those who pursued it less self-consciously. This dichotomy is helpful in understanding how the tramping subculture evolved into the more clearly deviant skid row subculture of more recent times.

Establishing the personal traits of men on the tramp in the late nineteenth and early twentieth centuries is a formidable task, but six different samples from the period 1879–1913 supply at least some information on over 5,000 homeless men. The earliest sample is of arrestees reported without an address in the daily blotters of the Detroit police department over a two-year period from 1879 to 1881.[2] A second sample consists of persons arrested as vagrants by the Omaha police department between 1887 and 1913.[3] The records of police station lodgers in Washington, D.C. used by Monkkonen in his essay are still another set of data from police sources.[4] John J. McCook's well-known survey of 1,349 tramps in 1891 is a different kind of sample, but useful.[5] Lastly, Alice Solenberger collected data on 1,000 homeless men applying at the Chicago Bureau of Charities from 1900 to 1903. She published her findings several years later along with similar data on 200 men taken from the files of the Associated Charities of Minneapolis in 1910.[6]

These samples are not entirely representative of the larger population of tramping workers. The subjects were mostly men truly homeless, truly down and out, or particularly susceptible to arrest. Still, when used with additional scattered evidence on the personal traits of migrant workers and other men of the road, they offer some basis for answering the question of whether or not these men were bound together by characteristics other than just their sex.

The statistics (see Table 1) reveal that homeless men did in fact share a number of characteristics. First of all, the overwhelming majority of them were unmarried and probably never had been married. The voluminous contemporary literature on tramps described a life on the road in which women played only a limited part. Female tramps existed but in small numbers. On occasion a homeless man established something of a "permanent" relationship with a woman, who might even travel with him. By and large, however, the women in the life of transients were prostitutes and bar girls.[7] The full implications of this for sexual behavior were not often broached by observers in the period before World War I. Homosex-

Transient Men,
1879–1913, by Marital Status, Race, Age, Occupation, and Place of Birth

	Detroit Homeless Arrestees (1879–81)	McCook Tramp Survey (1891)	Wash. D.C. Police Lodgers (1891–95)	Chicago Charity Applicants (1900–1903)	Minneapolis Charity Applicants (1910)	Omaha Arrested Vagrants (1887–1913)
Unmarried	82	93[a]	N/A	87[a]	83[a]	N/A
White	95	99	86	96	98	86
Under 20 years	9	4	7	12	9	
20–29	36	39	39	24	33	
30–39	31	31	21	20	20	N/A
40–49	16	17	15	19	14	
50–59	6	6	12	12	14	
Over 59	2	3	5	14	11	
Professional/Proprietor	3	2	4	10	5	4
Clerks/Office	2	1	3	12	5	2
Skilled Manual	24	35	35	23	21	14
Semi-skilled	24	19	15	12	12	17
Unskilled	41	42	42	36	51	56
Other/None	6	1	1	8	6	7
United States	49	56	77	65	45	78
Ireland	23	20	10	6	4	11
England/Scotland	13	9	5	7	8	2
Canada	11	0	1	3	4	0
Germany	2	4	5	9	6	5
Scandanavia	1	4	1	2	19	3
Other	2	7	2	8	15	2

(a) Includes small percentages of divorced and/or widowed.

uality was clearly central to the relationship between hardened tramps and the runaway boys they often adopted to train in the ways of the road. Studies in California suggested that homosexuality was also common in lumber camps, and it was surely not unknown in other settings where homeless men congregated.[8]

Second, the men in the samples were in the prime of life—their twenties, thirties, and forties. Other quantitative and impressionistic sources corroborate this conclusion and actually point to an even greater percentage of men in just their twenties and thirties.[9] Charity applicants seemed to be a somewhat older group. Many were undoubtedly turning to charity because their age made them incapable of or ineligible for various kinds of casual work. Men staying at the Chicago Municipal Lodging House in the early twentieth century were considerably younger than the charity cases Solenberger interviewed in Chicago in the same period.[10] The relative youthfulness of the men indicates that tramping was a way station in life, not a final stop. It was part of the premarriage work strategy of many adult men.

Third, homeless men were overwhelmingly white. Blacks were no more conspicuous among tramps than they were among adult males in the general population, where they totalled just under 10 percent. They were probably most numerous in the South and areas bordering on the South. A third of Kansas City's transients were reputedly blacks. However, blacks were not part of the larger social world of white homeless men. Lodging houses routinely discriminated against them, and in work camps they were given separate bunkhouses. Nels Anderson recalled that as a young migrant laborer in the first decade of the century he worked in a Montana railroad camp with a construction crew that included about a dozen blacks. The white workers would have little to do with them. When cold weather set in, the whites moved on but the blacks stayed behind. "Perhaps they feared to leave and make that long walk to Forsythe," Anderson writes, "passing the all-white camps, feeling strange that far north and knowing the bias in other camps against them."[11]

Fourth, most homeless men were prepared only for manual work, principally of a semiskilled or unskilled nature (although skilled workers frequently tramped, especially when the economy was depressed). The common story of the ruined merchant or the discouraged lawyer escaping to the life of the tie and rail should not be taken as indicative of the typical tramp's background and skills. In some of the better lodging houses and in rooming houses generally one might expect to find a healthy sprinkling of clerks and office workers. These were more stable men, however, who were not likely to drift from city to city, nor to try the fields and timberlands during certain seasons of the year. Writers who posed as tramps gave themselves away when they could not produce the calloused hands of working men for inspection by the police or fellow travelers.[12]

Finally, there is the question of ethnicity, and given the heterogeneous character of the American population in these years this may be the most important question of all. The percentages of foreign-born among the samples of homeless men are substantial—between 22 and 55 percent. Immigrants were known to pursue certain kinds of migrant work. Scandinavians preferred lumber work, Poles construction or lumber work, Finns mining, and Italians railroad section work.[13] Nevertheless, the almost two-thirds percentage of native-born in the sample for Chicago—the most important tramp center in the country—is significant. The percentage of native-born among all adult males in Chicago in 1900 was only 46.5, a figure that would undoubtedly be even lower if only working-class males were included.[14] Moreover, in every sample but one (Minneapolis), practically all of the foreign-born were from the British Isles or Canada. English was their native tongue and they might have more easily assimilated. Anderson noted in his study of Chicago's homeless men that those few from the newer southern and eastern European immigrant groups seemed "out of place."[15] This muted ethnicity may help to explain why so many observers believed that tramping workers were overwhelmingly "American."[16]

Newer immigrants might not have been prominent in the tramp's world because their steadier work habits made them less peripatetic. A common feeling among labor agents in the years just before World War I was that recent immigrants were more likely to stay and finish jobs in the camps to which they were sent. A Duluth agent, for example, testified that on a railroad job "the immigrant will work by the side of a thrashing or harvesting crew and never think of leaving his work to take service with it." "American labor," on the other hand, "is of a roving disposition and can not be depended on to continue until the work is completed. . . . ."[17] If most immigrants took their casual or migrant work more seriously than did others, this might also have meant that their tramping careers were much shorter, only a brief prelude to finding steady work in their new circumstances.

The spectacular increase in unattached men passing through their communities during the late nineteenth century worried many Americans, and their concerns found expression in the popular portrait of the perfidious and unwelcome tramp. Here was a shiftless and indolent character, forever on the road, never working, endlessly begging, and if necessary stealing or committing acts of violence to get what he wanted.

Colorful and primitive though he was, the tramp of the magazine racks was not a prominent figure among transients. Professor McCook at one time believed that tramps would not work even if offered a job, but his own research convinced him otherwise. His survey, for example, revealed that nearly 60 percent of the men claimed to have held a job within the previous month, and over 80 percent within the previous three months. If they were not working it was because there were no jobs available. They might boast of their skill at avoiding work but what they really meant, wrote McCook, was that they had not been tied to a steady job. Others familiar with tramps agreed that these were by and large men who worked for a living and took pride in their work. "There is an instinct of workmanship," the tramp writer William Edge claimed, "in even the most confirmed bum."[18]

Clearly the violent behavior attributed to tramps was also a misrepresentation. Only one of the 173 homeless arrestees in the Detroit sample was charged with a violent crime—simple assault. There is little evidence that tramps routinely "rolled" each other for their harvest wages or abused farm housewives. On the contrary, most seemed almost incapable of violence. Men who chanced upon one another in boxcars, on park benches, or at saloon tables struck up friendly conversations almost instantly and shared job information, stories, perhaps a bottle of whiskey. "I never lived and moved with a better-hearted group of people," the writer

Harry Kemp noted of his own experiences on the road. Edwin Brown, who in the interest of lodging house reform impersonated a tramp in visits to cities all over the country between 1909 and 1912, experienced first-hand some of this good fellowship among transients. In Pueblo, Colorado, he once spent a night in the grimy city jail with a score of other tramps, and as he paced about in the dark of the early morning one of his cellmates said, "Friend, you will find it warmer over there." Brown thought to himself, "I wonder why he called me 'friend?' A spirit of kindness from one man to another, in a place like that! Think of it!" Tramping workers sometimes paid dearly for their friendly and trusting attitudes, however. "Yeggmen" and "vampires of the road"—small bands of wandering toughs and criminals—preyed upon unsuspecting tramps around camp-fires and in boxcars.[19]

Most transients may have been law-abiding workers rather than pan-handlers and villains, but it was nonetheless true that their work habits varied greatly and that few labored at any one job for an extended period of time. Some followed the wheat harvest all the way from Kansas to the Dakotas, but many others did not.[20] Some worked the harvest as part of an annual circuit of outdoor "moving" jobs. These were the men who according to Ben Reitman labored "on a construction gang in Ohio in the spring, in the wheat fields of North Dakota in the fall, in the orange groves of California in the winter and the following summer as . . . stevedore[s] on the Great Lakes." A California citrus grower complained in 1914 that many of his temporary help were shiftless men, part of a large group who "every year go around the circle on the brake beam."[21]

Some of the men routinely took short layoffs between each job, while others worked steadily through the warm months and then "holed up" in urban lodging houses during the winter. Still others never did sustained work at all in summer or winter, in field, forest, or factory, but instead drifted from job to job without seeing any of them through. Railroad camps lost up to a quarter of their workers daily, helping to spawn a saying among employers that there were three crews connected with any un-dertaking, "one coming, one going, one on the job."[22] Employers accused workers of leaving a job as soon as they had enough money for a good drunk.[23] Anderson reported that some of Chicago's homeless men worked at literally dozens of jobs over the course of one winter.[24] Men traveling on the road might work just long enough in town or on a farm to get meals and lodgings for a night or two, perhaps a week. Indeed, they might simply chop some wood or mow a lawn for a "poke out" dinner. "He works for a while in each place," one observer wrote of the tramp, "and then moves on. He rubs elbows with home-living men, and they frequently find him a good worker, but they find him a good goer as well."[25]

Exactly what made men go on the tramp—shifting from place to place and job to job—was the source of endless speculation among observers and the men themselves. It seems safe to say that the principal reasons were volatile labor market conditions and the nature of itinerant work in an expanding nation. Men had to go where the jobs were.[26] Many therefore saw their homelessness as a temporary expedient. "The hobo was no perennial who thought of his go-about existence as going on and on," Anderson wrote in his autobiography. "One day he would settle down." Most did very quickly—less than 5 percent of McCook's tramps admitted to having been on the road a year or more. Ben Reitman believed that even 40 percent of the runaway adolescents tramping aimlessly on the nation's railroads eventually became respectable and stable workingmen. Tramps who wanted to settle down were often frustrated in their attempts. In his *Autobiography of a Super-Tramp* William Davies unwittingly spoke for many migrants when he complained in jest about being laid off from a job "just as I began to feel the inclination for this more respectable life."[27]

One of the most common explanations for tramping workers, however, was that the men were afflicted with wanderlust, an irresistible urge to roam that some believed was a pathological condition. "We can't help ourselves," one veteran of the road told an investigator. Another said that tramping had "got into my blood. I would not hold down a job longer 'n two weeks now if I was made to."[28] Boys and young men were supposedly most susceptible to wanderlust, and to the lure of the railroad especially. "Buffalo Scotty" recounted his entry into trampdom: "Well, when I was fifteen, a railroad was bein' built ten miles north of the farm. I kept teasin' Dad to let me take a day off to see it; but the more I teased, the tighter he froze. At last, one afternoon in August, I was mendin' the fence in the lower cornfield, the wind kept blowin' the engine's whistle over the hills, an' every time them whistles came I felt my own steam risin'. At last I quit work. I just stood and listened. An' about one minute later I was a hobo for life—wid legs cuttin' air!"[29]

For those who wanted to make of tramps a lazy and irresponsible group the wanderlust theory had much to offer, and it was only part of a substantial argument reformers made about the psychological instability of homeless men.[30] The behavior of many tramping workers does indeed suggest that there was more involved than simply labor marketplace conditions. Anderson noted that tramps were easily piqued on the job and routinely walked off on the slightest pretext. Solenberger reported that many of the homeless men she interviewed found it impossible to stay on any job "where they felt themselves driven and under pressure." Tramping may actually have been a way for many men to strike back against the regimen of the industrial workplace. Tramps chided the man who remained chained to one job, according to Anderson. They felt he "ought to leave a job once in a while simply to assert his independence and to learn something else about other jobs." Some men simply enjoyed casual and moving work. They spoke of the exhilaration of laboring in the great outdoors. "I think this nomadic life," wrote a tramp to McCook, "is a healthy life."[31]

One of the most vivid popular images of the tramp had him hidden away for the night in boxcars, alleyways, haylofts and other improper places affording peace and quiet without risk of discovery by the police. Many transients undoubtedly did live this way, particularly in the warm summer months. Thirteen percent of the tramps in McCook's survey said they regularly slept "anywhere they could."[32] Most of the time, however, tramping workers slept in a setting with large numbers of other men like themselves. There were bunkhouses in the railroad and lumber camps, as well as on some of the larger farms, such as those in the "bonanza" wheat country along the Red River in Minnesota and North Dakota. Guaranteed accommodations such as these were a luxury, and more typically the men had to contend with the uncertainties of a day-by-day existence. This brought them to police stations, cheap hotels, lodging houses, and rescue missions.

When transient workers began passing through cities in much larger numbers after about 1870, they often had no choice but to turn to police stations for a place to spend the night. An unintended consequence of the recent development of professional police departments, the lodging of homeless persons became one of the most important services the police provided. Police lodgings in Detroit, for instance, increased ninefold between 1865 and 1880. Ninety-five percent of the lodgers were men. New York's police department was furnishing almost 150,000 lodgings annually by 1890. Police stations were overrun with tramps at night. Until bunks were provided in 1875, lodgers at Detroit's central police station had to sleep on the floor. That was still the case in some Chicago stations at the turn of the century. Police lodgings had become an urban scandal. Only after 1900 did most departments begin to curtail the practice.[33]

The presence of so many highly transient men living outside of private households ultimately led to a small revolution in urban housing between 1880 and 1910: the decline of traditional boarding houses and the proliferation of rooming and lodging houses. Offering short-term accommodations and without dining facilities and the often over-solicitous air of domesticity that boarding houses had, rooming and lodging houses appealed to tramping workers. The rooming houses could be quite respectable and comfortable. The lodging houses were not. For twenty-five cents per night a man got a tiny cubicle covered with wire mesh. For ten cents or less he spent the night crammed with scores of other men into a large room filled with bare wood bunks or thin pieces of canvas strung from posts and beams. New York reportedly had 300 of these "cheap lodging houses" by 1890, and other cities had proportionately as many. By then Jacob Riis and others were exposing the dark, damp, and dirty insides of these places to a curious public.[34]

The concern about cheap overnight lodgings and the general plight of the homeless man led to a variety of efforts to provide tramps with some alternatives. The philanthropist D. O. Mills built two "workingmen's hotels" in New York City during the 1890s and another in 1913. They had clean single rooms, a large library and reading hall, and restrictions on drinking and smoking. Similar hotels opened in Chicago. With their decorous air and nightly rates as high or higher than the better class of lodging houses, the Mills Hotels appealed more to "respectable workingmen" who were prepared to stay for an extended period of time. Hotel managers clearly preferred such men to tramping casuals and looked applicants over carefully before admitting them.[35]

Tramps were more likely to stay in municipal lodging houses. Boston opened its "Wayfarers' Lodge" in 1879 and other eastern cities followed in the 1890s: Washington (1893), Springfield, Massachusetts (1894), Lowell, Massachusetts (1896), New York (1896), and Syracuse (1899). By the time of World War I the tramping worker could expect to find in any large city a "model" lodging house run either by the city or by a charitable organization (perhaps with partial city support). There was almost always a work requirement for the bed and board, usually splitting wood or doing street repair. The municipal lodging houses did yeoman service—Chicago's provided nearly 100,000 lodgings in the first four years after it opened in late 1901. But the men went to these institutions reluctantly. They disliked their regimented and patronizing style, and they were annoyed at having to do the required work, especially in the morning when time could be better spent searching for casual day work on the outside. When they left the municipal lodging house they were often branded with the odor of disinfectant on the clothes they had had to turn in for fumigation the night before.[36]

The tramp who found the police station unreceptive and the lodging houses too expensive or too crowded could turn to the city mission. The first rescue mission for homeless men was the famous Water Street Mission in New York, started in 1872 by a reformed river thief named Jerry McAuley. Although McAuley only offered most men a place to sit for an hour or two, and perhaps a bowl of soup, his mission provided about 5,000 lodgings its first year and more as it expanded. Similar missions opened in Duluth and Chicago in the next few years, and by the 1880s and 1890s they were to be found in many cities. In 1891 The Salvation Army opened the first of its men's shelters in New York; it added 44 more in cities around the country over the next decade. The missions often expected the men to pay for their lodgings (in addition to attending a religious service, of course) but the rate was usually only about ten cents. Mission evangelists clearly had the best interests of homeless men at heart, yet their religious zeal sometimes came across as less than sympathetic to the tramp's social predicament. The superintendent of a St. Paul, Minnesota mission described his charges as "drunken, habit-bound, diseased, filthy, vermin covered, hungry, hopeless, helpless, hell-bound men without home, without God, and without friends." Most tramps tried to avoid the missions.[37]

Tramping workers were not unconventional simply because they were unsettled, lived outside traditional homes, and enjoyed the company of other men. There was a great deal of population mobility in the United States during the nineteenth and early twentieth centuries. Studies of factory labor reported high turnover rates. Tenements, apartment buildings, household boarding—as well as rooming and lodging houses—threatened the traditional urban home. A male ethic dominated society. Men of all walks of life went out to places to be with other men—friends, associates, and those with like interests. Such fraternizing outside of the home was an accepted part of a man's life both before and after marriage. Saloons, clubs, and lodges did not compete with the home, they supplemented it. Even within the home the husband could retire to the "library" or "den," a male retreat now a standard feature of the proper middle-class residence. Tramping workers were unconventional rather because they moved about at such an extraordinary rate, because they lived one night at a time in police stations, cheap lodging houses, and missions, and because they pursued a male-oriented life style as an *alternative* to "normal" home and social life.[38]

The male-oriented life style of tramping workers focused not only on their work—just think of the isolated winter lumber camp—but also on their social interaction, particularly in the city. The tramp came to the city for a variety of reasons. Temporary or seasonal jobs were available there, from good factory work to menial employment in warehouses or on the docks. Migrant laborers found the city a good resting place between jobs, especially during the slack winter months when they might subsist for some time on the stake they brought back from the harvests and construction camps. The railroad, which tramps depended on so heavily for their transportation, brought the men to the city, for that was where rail lines converged and terminated. Stealing rides in "side-door Pullmans" and otherwise appropriating free space on trains was a dangerous mode of travel—fatal accidents reportedly claimed nearly 25,000 railroad trespassers from 1901 to 1905 alone—but a migrant casual had to be a "boxcar madman," as the tramping poet Vachel Lindsay put it, in order to survive.[39] The "jungle" camps where tramps slurped mulligan, told stories, and talked about jobs and police bulls tended to cluster in and around the city near railroad yards and bridges. Finally, it was in the city that men often found out about work available on the farms, along rail lines, and in the lumber camps. While tramps often distrusted the many employment agencies in the city, they found them indispensable in locating jobs in the distant countryside.

The gathering place for transients in the city was a well-defined subarea known in the tramp's argot as "the main stem." The main stem formed around cheap lodging houses. Its development belonged to the larger process of increasing functional and social differentiation in urban land use during the second half of the nineteenth century. There were boardinghouse-saloon districts catering to transient and unattached men in cities before the Civil War, but these were not the larger and more complex subareas that formed in the last quarter of the century. The evolution of the main stem was often rapid. Homeless men completely changed the face of the Minneapolis "Gateway" area between 1880 and 1900. In San Francisco the South of Market district, which still had well-to-do residents in the 1860s, had become a haven for miners, sailors, farm laborers and other transients by 1880, with half the city's lodging houses. A full three-quarters of the buildings in New York's Bowery area at the turn of the century catered to homeless men. Two-thirds of the city's licensed lodging houses could be found there.[40] Main stems were invariably located in downtown areas within easy access of the railroad yards or docks. The first time he set foot in Minneapolis as a young tramping worker, Nels Anderson found "as if by instinct" that city's transient men's neighborhood.[41]

The cities of the Midwest and Far West were best known for their main stems since they harbored proportionately if not absolutely more transients than cities elsewhere. As the major distribution point for the many seasonal jobs in the Great Lakes area and up and down the Mississippi Valley, Chicago was a mecca for migrant workers. In the early twentieth century several hundred thousand seasonal laborers passed in and out of the Illinois city every year. An estimated 60,000 transients wintered there in 1907–8. Minneapolis, Omaha, San Francisco, and Seattle were some of the other cities where the migrant labor population was large, as each was situated on major transportation lines leading to seasonal farm and lumber work centers.[42]

Transient men found on the main stem all the places they needed, not only cheap hotels and lodging houses but also second-hand clothing stores, employment agencies, saloons, inexpensive cafes and restaurants, and brothels. Of these the saloon was surely one of the most important, providing a variety of services besides cheap drinks. It was a haven in the winter. "The saloon keeper," one observer wrote, "is practically the only man who supplies free warmth to the chilled and shivering wanderers on the street."[43] It was a rest stop, a place for tramps fresh from a journey "on the rods" to wash the dirt and grime from their faces. Bartenders would often hold a tramp's winter stake for safe keeping. Employers sometimes visited saloons looking for temporary help. There was also the generous lunch provided by many establishments simply for the price of a schooner of beer. Reminiscing about the Chicago of his youth, Ben Reitman wrote that "a large part of the city's male population who were hungry and broke in the 80s and 90s sustained themselves in great part on free lunch." Anderson noted that in the years before World War I the "barrel house" was a favorite resort of tramps. Here a man could quench his thirst, fill his stomach, find a whore in a back room, and flop for the night.[44] The saloon was, in short, a major social center for homeless men. In the parks and on the street corners they might face inclement weather or a hostile cop on the beat. The lodging houses rarely had lobbies and generally did not allow the men to linger in the daytime. The saloon, however, was always there—warm, friendly, and inviting.

Jungles, boxcars, bunkhouses, and other gathering spots for tramps outside the city were only way stations on the journey that led inevitably to the main stem. "To the homeless men," Anderson wrote, "it is home, for there, no matter how sorry his lot, he can find those who will understand."[45] The main stem facilitated the entry of newcomers into the fraternity of tramping. The interaction among homeless men on the stem was undoubtedly a critical factor in the evolution and embellishment of their distinctive argot, which embodied common feelings among the men while serving as a badge of membership in the group. A tramp setting out for a city he had never seen before knew that when he arrived a familiar environment awaited him. He looked forward to encounters there with other transients. One tramp said he felt better in Chicago than "anywhere else in the world." Homeless men had a lasting appreciation for their patch of urban turf. "If you want to do me a favor/ When I lay down and die," the words of an old tune went, "Plant my bones by the main stem/ So I can hear the trains go by."[46]

There was, to be sure, much about the main stem that was reflected in the urban mainstream. Tramps were not the only ones who used job agencies, enjoyed free saloon lunches, and visited prostitutes. Anderson noted that occasionally workingmen from surrounding neighborhoods would visit Chicago's "hobohemia" for some of the unique excitement it offered.[47] The urban lower classes and transients interacted regularly and there may not have been, for example, any saloons patronized exclusively by homeless men. Even so, the line between the main stem and the rest of the city was clear—spatially and socially. Transients dominated these early skid rows and identified with them. When the men came to the city they came to the main stem. It was a home for the homeless.

Tramps were mostly unmarried white men in the prime of life who worked at manual labor and were either natives of the United States or immigrants from the British Isles or Canada. They traveled about at an exceptionally high rate and eschewed any semblance of family-oriented home life. Most worked regularly but at many jobs during the course of the year. They interacted primarily among themselves, both in the workplace and in urban lodging house districts. They even had their own vernacular and apparently their own "look." William Edge was gratified the first time a tramp took him for a confrère. "My hands, coarse and calloused, and vocabulary and voice passed muster," he wrote. "My clothes were satisfactory; my general attitude, carriage, bearing, stamped me as a bum."[48]

Tramps therefore had all the salient characteristics of a subculture established at the outset of this paper. A less salient characteristic such as shared attitudes or beliefs would be harder to discern since tramps were such an inarticulate group. There is some evidence to suggest, however, that tramps did not all think alike. These differences may not have been enough to invalidate the argument that a subculture existed, but they probably were enough to complicate the sense of "community" among tramps.

Contemporary reformers and investigators often went to great lengths to differentiate among elements in the tramping population. Each of these elaborate classifications was a little bit different from the next one, but they are best summed up in Ben Reitman's familiar typology dividing the men into three groups: "hoboes" who worked and wandered, "tramps" who dreamed and wandered, and "bums" who drank and wandered.[49] There may have been geographic distinctions as well. Nels Anderson claimed that the "weary Willie" type—the tramp described by Josiah Flynt—was mostly an eastern character who would have felt out of place among the robust men who worked their way around the West. One of McCook's correspondents promised to send photographs of some of his tramping brethren between St. Louis and San Francisco so that the professor could see how "the western stiff is quite different from the eastern." The first time Edge arrived in Chicago from the East he was struck by how different the men look and carried themselves. In eastern cities, he wrote, the migrant worker "went dumbly from job to job impelled by the relentless forces of modern capitalism. He was simply a man beaten by the economic system. In Chicago, the hobo seemed to be a hobo by choice. The men were large, strong, conscious of their disinheritance. They seemed not to be the victim of circumstances; they came to Chicago of their own free will, to 'get by' during the winter."[50]

Although these distinctions suggest differences in behavior among transients, the real difference appeared to be in attitude. There were two main groups. Men in the first group went on the road to work. The rest worked to live on the road. One group was best defined by its relationship to the economy and labor market, the other by its social psychology.

The first group was much the larger and comprised the great mass of tramping workers—the men about whom Walter Wyckoff wrote, for example.[51] Few if any of these men had monikers or the self-consciousness of those who did. They had no strong passion for tramping, but they accepted it readily, even gladly, for the work opportunities it brought. Most probably found their way out of tramping in a fairly short time, even if in no hurry to do so.

The second group was made up of the more self-conscious migrant workers as well as Reitman's "tramps" and "bums," including a group that did not wander at all known as the "home guard"—men who lived and worked year-round on the main stem. For men in this second group the road and the stem held a great attraction, and working (sometimes begging) was done in large measure to live the life of boxcars and jungles, lodging houses and missions. This was a motley group, therefore, comprising relatively steady workers in addition to the vagrants found in Flynt's pages. What they had in common was their unabashed preference for homelessness and its rejection of a degree of social responsibility. Some may have lived only on the fringes of the larger subculture of transients, for an animosity existed between steady migrant workers and "professional" vagrants.[52] In fact there were men who resemble today's skid row derelicts. There are remarkable similarities between Flynt's descriptions of certain turn-of-the-century tramps and the picture of homeless men that emerged from the many studies of skid rows in the 1950s and 1960s.[53]

Speculation about these perennial skid row types is beyond the scope of this paper, but in any case such men were only a small minority on the old main stem. That was soon to change, however. The 1920s and 1930s were transitional years for the tramping subculture. Farm mechanization, western population growth, widespread use of the automobile, and the rise of the welfare state were among the factors that reduced and altered the migrant work force. By the 1940s there had been a drastic reduction in the numbers of itinerant workers who were unattached males traveling long distances. Depression transients who had briefly augmented the floating population in the 1930s disappeared as well in the 1940s, and the metamorphosis of the main stem into skid row continued. By the 1950s the perennial derelicts had become the majority. Relying heavily on rescue missions, treated by welfare agencies, and ordered around and continually processed by the criminal justice system, homeless men in the mid-twentieth century appeared pathetic and dispirited in contrast to their main stem predecessors. Skid row stood as but a remnant of the great tramping subculture of America's industrial age.

Notes

1. On deviance, see M. Michael Rosenberg, Robert A. Stebbins, and Allan Turowetz, eds., *The Sociology of Deviance* (New York: St. Martin's Press, 1982); Alexander Liazos, "The Poverty of the Sociology of Deviance: Nuts, Sluts, and Perverts," *Social Problems* 20 (Summer 1972), 103–20. On subculture, see Claude S. Fischer, "Toward a Subcultural Theory of Urbanism," *American Journal of Sociology* 80 (May 1975), 1319–41, and *The Urban Experience* (New York: Harcourt, Brace, Jovanovich, 1976); Michael Clarke, "On the Concept of Sub-Culture," *British Journal of Sociology* 25 (December 1974), 428–41; Charles A. Valentine, *Culture and Poverty* (Chicago: University of Chicago Press, 1968); J. Milton Yinger, "Contraculture and Subculture," *American Sociological Review* 25 (October 1960), 625–35.

2. General Arrest Ledger (1865–1912), Metropolitan Police Department, Detroit City Archives, Burton Historical Collection, Detroit Public Library. The original sample totalled 918 arrestees. Of these 173 had no recorded address. See my *Detroit and the Problem of Order, 1830–1880: A Geography of Crime, Riot, and Policing* (Lincoln: University of Nebraska Press, 1980), 110–12, 158–59.

3. Jail Register (1887–1913), Omaha Police Department, Nebraska State Historical Society. The original sample totalled 1509, but thirty-one women were excluded from this analysis. I have described and interpreted the Omaha data more fully in "Omaha Vagrants and the Character of Western Hobo Labor, 1887–1913," *Nebraska History* 63 (Summer 1982), 255–72.

4. Register of Lodgers, Third Precinct, 1891–95, Metropolitan Police Department, Records of the District of Columbia, National Archives and Records Service, RG 351. The total number of male lodgings recorded in the register was 977, including repeaters at the rate of about 15 percent.

5. McCook published some of the results of his survey in "A Tramp Census and its Revelations," *Forum* 15 (August 1893), 753–66. The completed questionnaires and his own tabulations of them are available on Roll 2 of the microfilm edition of the

McCook Papers, published by the Antiquarian and Landmarks Society of Connecticut (Hartford) in 1977.

6. Alice W. Solenberger, *One Thousand Homeless Men* (New York: Russell Sage, 1911), 20, 135, 306–7.

7. John J. McCook, "Tramps," *Charities Review* 3 (December 1893), 63; "Leaves from the Diary of a Tramp: III," *Independent* 53 (19 December 1901), 3012; and "Leaves from the Diary of a Tramp: VIII," *Independent* 54 (10 April 1902), 874; James Forbes, "The Tramp; or, Caste in the Jungle," *Outlook* 98 (9 August 1911), 874; Nels Anderson, *The Hobo: The Sociology of the Homeless Man* (Chicago: University of Chicago Press, 1923, 1964), 141.

8. Carleton H. Parker, *The Casual Laborer and Other Essays* (New York: Harcourt, Brace & Howe, 1920), 73–74; Anderson, *The Hobo*, 144–49.

9. T. F. Ring, "The Boston Wayfarers' Lodge," *Proceedings of the National Conference of Charities and Correction* (1885), 324; Mariner J. Kent, "The Making of a Tramp," *Independent* 55 (March 1903), 668; Clarence S. Thompson, "Tramping as a Pastime," *Charities and the Commons* 16 (22 September 1906), 619; Orlando F. Lewis, "Concerning Vagrancy: Municipal Lodging Houses," *Survey* 22 (4 September 1909), 755–56; Robert H. Gault, "Pathologic Vagrancy," *Journal of the American Institute of Criminal Law and Crimonology* 5 (September 1914), 321; Tracy W. McGregor, *An Introduction to Twenty Thousand Men* (Detroit: McGregor Institute, 1916), 15–16; *Report and Handbook of the Department of Health of the City of Chicago, 1911–1918* (Chicago: Department of Health, 1919), 1080.

10. *Rept. of Chicago Dept. of Health*, 1080.

11. Nels Anderson, *The American Hobo: An Autobiography* (Leiden, Netherlands: E. J. Brill, 1975), 70–71, 77–78, 94. Also Forbes, "The Tramp; or, Caste in the Jungle," 874–75; Glen H. Mullin, *Adventures of a Scholar Tramp* (New York: Century, 1928), 189–90; Paul T. Ringenbach, *Tramps and Reformers, 1873–1916: The Discovery of Unemployment in New York* (Westport, Conn.: Greenwood, 1973), 71–72.

12. On the increase in skilled tramps during depressions, see Schneider, "Omaha Vagrants," 262–64. On roomers, see Albert B. Wolfe, *The Lodging House Problem in Boston* (Boston: Houghton Mifflin, 1906), 88–92; Franklin K. Fretz, *The Furnished Room Problem in Philadelphia* (Philadelphia: University of Pennsylvania, 1912), 67–68.

13. "Immigrants in Industries," *Senate Documents*, 61st Congress, 2nd Session, 1909–10, Vol. 80: 331, 339–40.

14. U.S. Census Office, *Twelfth Census of the United States: 1900. Population : Part I* (Washington: Government Printing Office, 1901), 954, 968.

15. Anderson, *American Hobo*, 150–51.

16. Josiah Flynt Willard [Josiah Flynt], *Tramping With Tramps: Studies and Sketches*

of Vagabond Life (New York: Century, 1899), 286; U.S. Industrial Commission, *Reports of the Industrial Commission*, 19 vols. (Washington: Government Printing Office, 1900–1902), 11:102; George Creel, "Harvesting the Harvest Hands," *Harper's Weekly* 59 (26 September 1914), 294; C. Luther Fry, "Migratory Workers of Our Industries," *World's Work* 40 (October 1920), 601.

17. "Immigrants in Industries," 339, 341–42; "Final Report and Testimony by the Commission on Industrial Relations," *Senate Documents*, 64th Congress, 1st Session, 1915–16, vol. 24: 5109–10. Also Ernest Poole, "A Clearing-House for Tramps," *Everybody's Magazine* 18 (May 1908), 652.

18. John J. McCook, "The Tramp Problem: What It Is and What to Do with It," *Proceedings of the National Conference of Charities and Correction* (1895), 289; McCook, "Leaves from the Diary of a Tramp: VII," *Independent* 54 (13 March 1902), 620–21; Roll 2, McCook Papers; Ben L. Reitman, "Following the Monkey," undated ms., 196–97, Folder 1, Reitman Papers, Manuscripts Collection, University of Illinois–Chicago Circle Library; Morrison I. Swift, "Tramps as Human Beings," *Outlook* 52 (31 August 1895), 342–43; William Edge, *The Main Stem* (New York: Vanguard, 1927), 112.

19. Harry Kemp, *Tramping on Life: An Autobiographical Narrative* (New York: Boni & Liveright, 1922), 126, 129; Edwin Brown, "Broke," *The Man without the Dime* (Boston: Four Seas, 1920), 28–29, 60; Charles E. Adams, "The Real Hobo: What He Is and How He Lives," *Forum* 33 (June 1902), 442–43; Leon R. Livingston, *The Curse of Tramp Life, By A-No. 1, The King of the Hoboes: A True Story of Actual Tramp Life* (Cambridge Springs, Pa.: A–No. 1 Publishing Co., 1912), 96–99.

20. "The Spectator," *Outlook* 83 (4 August 1906), 787.

21. Reitman, "Following the Monkey," 25; "Final Report and Testimony by the Commission on Industrial Relations," 23:4959.

22. Adams, "The Real Hobo," 443; Parker, *Casual Laborer*, 77–79.

23. "Final Report and Testimony by the Commission on Industrial Relations," 23: 4966; 24:5109–10, 5150.

24. Anderson, *The Hobo*, 117–19.

25. Clarence S. Thompson, "Tramping as a Pastime," *Charities and the Commons* 16 (22 September 1906), 619.

26. See, for example, Don D. Lescohier, *The Labor Market* (New York: Macmillan, 1919).

27. Anderson, *American Hobo*, 2; McCook, "A Tramp Census," 755; Ben L. Reitman, "Wanderlust, The Tramp's Disease," undated ms., 1–2, Folder 10, Reitman Papers; William H. Davies, *The Autobiography of a Super-Tramp* (New York: Knopf, 1917), 45.

28. Roger Bruns, *Knights of the Road: A Hobo History* (New York: Methuen, 1980),

144; Stuart A. Rice, "Vagrancy," *Proceedings of the National Conference of Charities and Correction* (1914), 461–62. For the pathological view, see Reitman, "Wanderlust, The Tramp's Disease."

29. Poole, "Clearing-House for Tramps," 650.

30. The classic in this regard (but also one of the most provocative) is Parker, *Casual Laborer.*

31. Anderson, *The Hobo,* 74; Solenberger, *One Thousand Homeless Men,* 136; John J. McCook, "Leaves from the Diary of a Tramp: VI," *Independent* 54 (6 February 1902), 337.

32. Roll 2, McCook Papers.

33. Schneider, *Detroit and the Problem of Order,* 106; Marcus T. Reynolds, *The Housing of the Poor in American Cities* (repr. of 1893 ed.; New York: Arno Press, 1969), 122; *Detroit Daily Post,* 15 February 1875; "Chicago Police Station Lodgings," *The Charities Review* 10 (May 1900), 97. On the extent and function of police lodgings, see Eric Monkkonen, *Police in Urban America, 1860–1920* (Cambridge: Cambridge University Press, 1981), 86–109.

34. Wolfe, *Lodging House Problem;* Solenberger, *One Thousand Homeless Men,* 2, 314–29; Jacob Riis, *How the Other Half Lives* (repr. ed.; New York: Hill & Wang, 1957), 59–67; "New York Lodging-Houses," *Harper's Weekly* 34 (7 June 1890), 450–51; "A Bed for a Dime," *Omaha Republican,* 23 February 1890, 4; Alvan F. Sanborn, *Moody's Lodging House and Other Tenement Sketches* (Boston: Copeland & Day, 1895).

35. John L. Thomas, "Workingmen's Hotels," *Municipal Affairs* 3 (March 1899), 73–94; William T. Stead, *If Christ Came to Chicago* (Chicago: Laird & Lee, 1894), 162–63; "Decent Lodgings for Poor Men," *Independent* 75 (11 September 1913), 638.

36. Homer Folks, "Report of the Committee on Municipal and County Charities," *Proceedings of the National Conference of Charities and Correction* (1899), 106–83; "Municipal Lodging Houses," *Municipal Journal and Engineer* 9 (December 1900), 148–49; Benjamin C. Marsh, "Methods Employed by American Cities to Eradicate Vagrancy," *Proceedings of the National Conference of Charities and Correction* (1903), 414–15; Alice C. Willard, "Reinstatement of Vagrants Through Municipal Lodging Houses," ibid. 409; Lewis, "Concerning Vagrancy," 749–59; Stuart A. Rice, "The Failure of the Municipal Lodging House," *National Municipal Review* 11 (November 1922), 358–62.

37. Arthur Bonner, *Jerry McAuley and His Mission* (Neptune, New Jersey: Loizeaux Bros., 1967); Keith A. Lovald, "From Hobohemia to Skid Row: The Changing Community of the Homeless Man" (Ph.D. dissertation, University of Minnesota, 1960), 132–33; Norris Magnuson, *Salvation in the Slums: Evangelical*

Social Work, 1865–1920 (Metuchen, New Jersey: Scarecrow Press, 1977), 55–56; *Seventh Annual Report of the Union Gospel Mission* (St. Paul, Minn.: Union Gospel Mission, 1910), 12–13.

38. Stephan Thernstrom and Peter Knights, "Men in Motion: Some Data and Speculations about Urban Population Mobility in Nineteenth-Century America," *Journal of Interdisciplinary History* 1 (Autumn 1970), 7–35; Sumner H. Slichter, *The Turnover of Factory Labor* (New York: D. Appleton, 1919); Charlotte Perkins Gilman, "The Passing of the Home in Great American Cities," *Cosmopolitan* 38 (December 1904), 140–47; G. S. Crawford, "Club Life vs. Home Life," *Arena* 16 (August 1896), 418–31; "In Defence of the Husband's Hour," *Harper's Bazaar* 35 (June 1901), 184–86; Jon M. Kingdale, "The 'Poor Man's Club': Social Functions of the Urban Working-Class Saloon," *American Quarterly* 25 (October 1973), 472–89.

39. Orlando Lewis, "The American Tramp," *Atlantic Monthly* 101 (June 1908), 745; Nicholas V. Lindsay, "Rules of the Road," *The American Magazine* 74 (May 1912), 55.

40. Lovald, "From Hobohemia to Skid Row," 121–22; Alvin Averbach, "San Francisco's South of Market District, 1850–1950: The Emergence of a Skid Row," *California Historical Quarterly* 52 (Fall 1973), 199–202; Ignatz L. Nascher, *The Wretches of Povertyville: A Sociological Study of the Bowery* (Chicago: J. J. Lanzit, 1909), 33; Paul Kennaday, "New York's Hundred Lodging Houses," *Charities and the Commons* 13 (18 February 1905), 486. For nineteenth-century urban spatial differentiation and the first appearance of transient men's subareas, see Schneider, *Detroit and the Problem of Order,* Chapter 2.

41. Anderson, *American Hobo,* 68.

42. Solenberger, *One Thousand Homeless Men,* 7–9, 139, 330; Anderson, *The Hobo,* 104–6.

43. Stead, *If Christ Came to Chicago,* 165.

44. Reitman, "Following the Monkey," 21; Anderson, *The Hobo,* 27.

45. Anderson, *The Hobo,* 4, 11.

46. Bruns, *Knights of the Road,* 142; George Milburn, *The Hobo's Hornbook: A Repertory for a Gutter Jongleur* (New York: Ives Washburn, 1930), 243.

47. Anderson, *The Hobo,* xvi.

48. Edge, *The Main Stem,* 194.

49. Ben L. Reitman, "The American Tramp," undated ms., 3–9, Folder 8, Reitman Papers. For some of the more detailed classifications of homeless men and migrant workers: Flynt, *Tramping with Tramps,* 114–21; E. Lamar Bailey, "Tramps and Hoboes," *Forum* 26 (October 1898), 217–20; Edmund Kelly, *The Elimination of the Tramp* (New York: G. Putnam & Sons, 1908), 9–11, 103–7; Solenberger, *One Thousand Homeless Men,* 9–11; Mary Conyngton, *How to Help: A Manual of Practical Charity*

(New York: Macmillan, 1909), 57–58; McGregor, *Introduction to Twenty Thousand Men*, 4–15; Peter Speck, "The Psychology of Floating Workers," *Annals of the American Academy of Political and Social Science* 69 (Janaury 1919), 74–75; Lescohier, *The Labor Market*, 255–75; Anderson, *The Hobo*, 87–105; Towne Nylander, "The Migratory Population of the United States," *American Journal of Sociology* 30 (September 1924), 130–36.

50. Anderson, *American Hobo*, 69, 128; "Bob" to John J. McCook, 8 February 1902, Folder 0, Roll 11, McCook Papers; Edge, *The Main Stem*, 202.

51. Walter Wyckoff, *The Workers: The East* (New York: Scribners, 1897), and *The Workers: The West* (New York: Scribners, 1898).

52. Leon R. Livingston, *Life and Adventures of A–No. 1, America's Most Celebrated Tramp* (Cambridge Springs, Pa: A–No. 1 Publishing Company, 1910), 33–34; "How to Tell a Hobo from a Mission Stiff," *Survey* 31 (21 March 1914), 781; Anderson, *The Hobo*, 7–8.

53. For an overview of midcentury skid row studies, see Howard M. Bahr, *Skid Row: An Introduction to Disaffiliation* (New York: Oxford University Press, 1973).

Eric H. Monkkonen

Afterword

Social historians, in general, have ignored tramps and tramping. Instead they have opted to analyze the late nineteenth- and early twentieth-century middle-class observers of tramping. There have been several reasons for this. The attitudes of the articulate and powerful are relatively easy to identify and analyze. Virtually all forms of our literary evidence concerning this period have come from this point of view, with the exception of a few valuable accounts by educated participant observers. Tramps themselves have for too long been absent from the historian's picture. As the essays in this book demonstrate, even by conservative population estimates, tramps traveled across an earlier America in massive numbers, and information about them abounds. This information may be analyzed with the full array of methodological techniques at the historian's disposal, ranging from the relatively traditional analysis of newspapers to rarer oral interviews, to quantitative analysis, and to the reexamination of contemporarily published secondary materials. The authors of this book have only had to forgo the examination of the private papers of individual tramps, although it would not be too surprising if someday this also becomes possible. For example, the correspondence between J. J. McCook and Bill Aspinwall, a tramp in the late nineteenth century, can be found in the McCook Collection, and one can hope that similar correspondence may be discovered.[1]

But the larger reason for our ignorance of tramps is not that the sources do not exist, but that tramps simply do not fit our visions of the American past, even the most critical ones. They were poor, mostly single working men (and sometimes women) in constant if sporadic motion.

Their lives contrasted with family-oriented men and women whose geographic mobility was tempered by the (accurate) perception that most financial and cultural rewards accrued to those who finally settled down and persisted. Historians, lacking the conceptual tools to analyze tramps either separately or as a part of the larger culture, have been more blind to their presence than were their nontramping contemporaries.

As the essays in this book demonstrate, this no longer need be the case. For just as historians have begun to analyze the history of slavery, of childhood, of women, of ethnic groups, and of various working-class cultures in the nineteenth century, so we can begin to analyze the world of industrial tramps. To do so it may be necessary to free ourselves from gemeinschaft/gesellschaft dichotomies which have dominated our approaches to thinking about society in the nineteenth and early twentieth centuries. This analytic framework, repeated in a multitude of forms, contrasts the fixed, deep, primary relationships of community with the superficial, contractual relationships of mass society. In the organic gemeinschaft there was a fixed and shared conception of the social order. Although highly inequitable in the distribution of wealth and power, the shared sense of obligation and mutual responsibility tempered the inequality. This intimate, traditional community mirrored the family's ascribed roles, rules, and sense of wholeness. From birth a web of powerful social relationships enmeshed the individual. The proponents of this analytic dichotomy (or, perhaps, continuum) almost always made the distinctions from their location in mass society; thus community was always elsewhere—in earlier times, in small villages, in other nations. The onset of modern urban and industrial life shattered the gemeinschaft, they argued. Replacing it, the new, rationalized, mass society, quintessentially urban in form, gave individuals liberty at the cost of humane mutual caring. Only a few thinkers, notably Max Weber, welcomed this new order.[2] For the organic order of the old, the new substituted function-specific social groupings which permitted the greatest exercise of egoistic individualism. In it people know one another by fragmented, secondary aspects of self— as customer, teacher, employee, police officer, tramp, cousin—but not as a whole person with an individual history intertwined with one's own. In mass society, power no longer carries with it responsibility. Only formal rules bind society together. Alienation becomes the fate of all.

As brilliantly articulated by sociologist Georg Simmel in 1903, it was to be expected that the anonymous life of metropolitan society created a "metropolitan personality."[3] This personality tended, under conditions of mass life, towards anomie and deviance.[4] Simmel's account is logically unassailable unless one remembers that residentially stable urbanites lived in a mutually constraining and supporting web of family, neighborhood, and ethnic subculture. But if we accept Simmel's compelling logic, tramps sprung from this web should have been propelled into the downward spiral of dissaffiliation, anomie, deviance, and criminality. Although this scheme still has great utility and intuitive appeal, it simply is not adequate to the task of analyzing the eddies, whirls, and streams of moving workers in the industrial era.[5]

Yet it was from this analytic position that Progressive era urban reformers often acted (and, one might note, often still act). Government had to respond to the disorganizing consequences of mass life by creating formal organizations to replace the mythic garden of gemeinschaft. But our examination of tramps and tramping in this book makes clear that although residential stability may have been an important desideratum, the life of the moving worker did not destroy in him or her all sense of individual values, of family, or of home. These values may be seen, on a simple scale, in the traditional moniker of the tramp: Peoria Pete, for example. Typically the moniker drops the family name and is instead prefixed with a place name. The place names denoted a home place of large enough size so that others were likely to have heard of it—no hamlets provided place names. The family name had disappeared because outside of one's originating area, kinship no longer provided an important identifier. Thus Peoria Pete retained his individual identity, and he redefined his communal ties for a larger and different audience. His moniker tied him to a home far better than would a family name in his transient world. The moniker and other traditions of tramping did not create for the tramp the web of privileges and obligations of kin ties, small town relationships, or even those of big city neighborhoods. But the use of monikers does suggest that transiency was not in itself a rejection of these ties and bonds.

The essays in this book show how tramps worked to replace their temporarily lost kin, craft, and neighborhood networks. These replacement networks can be seen in the bachelor subculture described by Schneider, in the traditions of women who tramped shown by Weiner, and in the loosely systematized attempts by unions to maintain organization. One should not romanticize the success of their efforts, however. The adoption of a moniker is a far cry from the tedious and difficult daily responsibilities of family and neighborhood life. As some of the examples in Tygiel's and Davis's essays demonstrate, many tramps did indeed tramp to escape such responsibility. But these individual escapees did not betoken a massive abdication of traditional values.

If anything, recent research in the social history of slaves, of women, and of various working-class cultures implies that tramps too maintained the cultural values of their origins. Cut off from the modest avenues to power of the residentially permanent, tramps probably espoused the values which denied to them the potential power offered by organization. Only the IWW could even begin to get any organizational leverage on tramps.[6] Ironically, then, most tramps shared the values of the more privileged, residentially stable people who feared them.

At the same time that tramping reinforced traditional, mainstream social values, it worked towards creating a homogeneous culture. The amalgam of ethnic and regional backgrounds found in the lists of tramps examined by the authors of this book indicates that in the tramp experience may be found the one place where the melting pot really melted. Our evidence for this comes from the lack of any suggestion of significant ethnic cohesion in tramping. At most, one might have found two or three young immigrants traveling together. Significantly, most monikers were regional and urban rather than ethnic. There is no evidence that any one ethnic group dominated any particular form of tramping. Schneider, in a different article, has shown how the stream of tramps flowing through Omaha became less ethnically mixed and dominated by the native-born only as industrial tramping began to wane in the early twentieth century.[7] Ethnic diversity, then, characterized the mass industrial phase of tramping.

Thus, in this group of traveling workers we have a case where the economic system created an economic class in a classic Marxian sense. But this class's self-consciousness embraced "American" values by transcending ethnic and regional loyalties. In Peoria, Pete would have been forced to maintain his ethnic and family identity: on the road, he became American.

Prior to 1920, residential stability was a necessary, if not sufficient, element of power.[8] In general, the person or family who managed to stay in one locale reaped power and its benefits unavailable to those who moved. Only stability in a declining or decaying region would have been of little benefit. The power available to the residentially stable came in the broadest sense, from economic advantage to social prestige to political influence to the ability to pass on gains to future generations. In one sense, much of the power came to the residentially stable through their particularly high access to information. They knew where jobs were to be found, money was to be borrowed, investments were to be made, schools to be attended, and friendships to be formed. The richer information access of the stable worked in reverse too; they knew more and were better known. Those with jobs and credit to offer preferred known to unknown persons. The rapid population growth of the country and its great size meant that, by default, a premium had to be put on personal acquaintanceship, on names and faces. The credit reporting agency of Dun and Bradstreet made its business that of reporting on local reputation.[9] In a "nation of strangers," rewards went to the familiar. Of course, short-range residential moves within the scope of a person's power arena did not eliminate the power gains. Thus, an elite member with a regional power access might comfortably make moves across the region while a working-class person of some neighborhood power and prestige might only make comfortable moves of a shorter distance.[10]

Major literary figures of the nineteenth century reflected the problematic nature of growing anonymity, particularly that of the wanderer. From Melville's "Bartleby the Scrivener" to Ishmael in *Moby Dick* to his *Confidence Man* and to Twain's *Mysterious Stranger,* the stranger represented at best alienation and despair and at worst evil incarnate.[11] Criminal courts too expressed concern about the consequences of growing anonymity, as they increasingly prosecuted thefts based on duplicitous or false personal information. False forms of identification, fraudulent credit bills, and deception by strangers may not have increased in reality, but court vigilance certainly did.[12] That anonymity actually caused either increased criminality or the personal ills of alienation seems doubtful, for the empirical evidence suggests that many indexes of disorder decreased or, at least, did not increase with increasing social scale.[13] If anything, transients and strangers probably behaved more cautiously and conservatively simply because in stressful situations people revert to old ways of behavior rather than innovating or deviating.

But from the perspective of the relatively privileged, more permanent population, the appearance of strangers triggered expectations and fears of deviance, social disorder, instability, and the unexpected. Historian Paul Boyer has delineated some of the responses of urban elites to the anonymity of growing cities, their reactions constituting what criminologist Paul Rock has called a "moral panic."[14] Urban elites tried to counter anonymity by replicating institutional features of small town life in the city, the YMCA, for instance, trying to create a personal, associational counterbalance to the city. But the only effective way to restore face-to-face relationships was through social units of actual small scale, where residents persisted over years, truly building bonds dependent on personal knowledge.

As the acquisitive entrepreneur epitomized the expansion of late nineteenth-century industry, so the tramp epitomized its working people. The tramp created the fluid, adaptable, moderately skilled, and strong workforce on which the expanding and changing industrial world absolutely depended. The captains of industry were not alone in needing workforces which could expand or shrink on demand. Tramping workers made residential stability and occupational security possible for those working-class families vulnerable to fluctuating labor force demands. Their departure from town during an unemployment crisis made it possible for nuclear families to stay put. As they traveled, the tramps picked up job skills and information they used to enhance the labor pool elsewhere. Thus the mobility of tramps enabled family stability and helped foster a more unified work culture. Many tramps, no doubt, expected to be rewarded in the future when they, in turn, could stay in one place and have a family life.

Certainly the most imaginative analysis of the second half of the nineteenth century in the United States was enunciated by Frederick Jackson Turner in what has become known as the "frontier thesis." One of the social functions of the frontier he posited to have been a "safety valve" feature, which allowed urban social pressures to be vented like excess steam in a boiler. The operative mechanism of the frontier's safety valve had been open land, where the urban poor could take up farming. This, we now know, had never been even a remote possibility. If anything, rides to be stolen from railroads stood as a far more real safety valve. But it must have been a comfort for the more secure and stable residents of the United States in the 1870s and 1880s to expect that the growing numbers of anonymous urban poor could have removed to the frontier if necessary.

At about the same time in the 1890s that the Bureau of the Census declared the frontier to be officially closed, Progressive urban reformers began to look at the problems of the urban poor, including the transient poor, the tramps. During the decade of the 1890s reformers for the first time realized that the tramps were victims of unemployment, not simply lazy degenerates who refused to become farmers or seek work. Historian Paul Ringenbach argues that during this decade urban elites "discovered" unemployment.[15] His position is confirmed by the work of tramp reformer and college professor J. J. McCook, who in his early research could not admit that the causes for tramping were anything other than individual defects in tramps. Ultimately the reactions and perceptions of the residentially stable concerning tramps, whether cynical or sympathetic, had little significant impact on tramps or tramping. Individual attitudes and actions simply could not affect the larger economic and industrial structure or the regional, sectoral, and cyclical shifts which created the tramping work force.

Unlike the frontier posited by Turner, the tramping frontier was essentially urban, industrial, and attuned to nature only for its potential for extractive industry. And tramps, unlike the archetypal independent frontiersman, were dependent wage laborers. Their major means of asserting independence was the railroad, symbol of the late nineteenth century's far-flung and faceless corporate enterprises. Victims of the growing pains of the urban industrial complex which has shaped modern America, tramps, and the few agencies which assisted them, paid the social costs incurred by economic change and expansion. Others reaped the benefits. Of course, the primary beneficiaries were the owners of the economic enterprises which could with great confidence hire workers for irregular periods of time. If they passed their savings on to consumers, then the consumers also benefited. Only one thing is clear: tramps did not benefit.

Historian of the family Tamara Haraven has shown how families mediated between New England factories and their employees.[16] The family and its extended kin ties recruited new employees, matched factory needs and individual skills, and provided the various welfare cushions needed to sustain a steady and healthy labor force. As the contributors to this book show, the institution of tramping provided one means to cushion the shock of unemployment or underemployment for families—they could send adult males out on the road. We have speculated that this may have been simply one aspect of the typical family life course for working-class families. Young men tramped until they could return home or settle in a new place and begin forming families, depending on others to tramp once their family responsibilities made it more difficult for them to tramp. But there was a second possible outcome to tramping: that those men who tramped never formed families, that the hardship of life cutting ice, shoveling snow, and working summer construction attenuated their life expectancy as well as the prospects of family formation. As Weiner's essay implies, few marriage matches occurred on the road.

Let us speculate for a moment that those men and women who became tramps for life chose this form of existence over the fixed residential family and that the institution of tramping represented a socially useful if unpleasant alternative. Certainly this is one of the mixed messages which emerges from the literature. The decline of massive industrial tramping in the early twentieth century decreased the more or less legitimate opportunity it offered for escape from family and fixedness. At the same time, the decline in the total number of tramps meant that more and more, tramping became the domain of misfits and deviants. And thus working-class people who in the late nineteenth century might have been able to reasonably choose a way of life outside of the nuclear family could no longer, in the twentieth century, do so other than by becoming one with the misfits. Jack London's tramping experiences should be viewed from this perspective, for he represented a minority of tramps on the deviant side, clearly differing from most of his companions when he travelled halfway across the country with Coxey's Army. For London the life of a tramp embodied freedom, adventure, and, most important, a living challenge to the mainstream cultural values. By the mid-twentieth century London would have found far fewer companions, though he would have loved the world delineated in Jack Kerouac's *On the Road*. But we must remember that such interesting and articulate people made up a small proportion of the mass tramping of the late nineteenth and early twentieth centuries.

The articles on tramping presented in this book enrich current scholarly research on working-class culture in the way that residential mobility studies have enriched urban history. By implication, mobility studies have raised several important questions. Is it valid to posit an ethnic, class, or local culture, the study of which by virtue of the methodology alone is limited to one place, when we know that the individuals comprising the population of the place change? Residential mobility studies, from those conducted by James C. Malin in the thirties to the more recent ones summarized by Robert Barrows, all show that over a decade only about 40 to 60 percent of a populace remained in any one city or county.[17] Our tramping articles here examine an even more volatile population, workers who cannot be said to have lived anywhere. For these people local cultural ties ranging from political involvement to ethnic organization were almost completely impossible.[18] Their thin cultural world was at its most supportive when they were members of unions which recognized their needs as travelers. Far more commonly their culture was manifested as the "main stem" bachelor subculture described in Schneider's essay. The cheap lodging houses, bars and restaurants of the main stem were a far cry from the workingmen's bars on which most students of working-class culture focus.[19] Tramps, perforce the most explicitly defined American working class, were cut off by their very transiency from most opportunities for class action. And no wonder that their strongest organizational hope, the IWW, met with violent repression.

The social fact of residential mobility has forced historians to re-emphasize the importance of the nuclear family. In addition it has caused us to look at subregional, regional, and national systems of urban circulation rather than at one place as the locale for individual life and action. On the other hand the social fact of mass industrial tramping emphasizes that the local working-class cultures which labor historians study are but one part of a more complex picture. By virtue of their residential fixity they may well represent the most privileged members of the working class.[20] In certain ways, both residential mobility and the individual mobility of tramps remind us of the importance of formal social organizations, be they labor unions or churches or political clubs or county poorhouses or the uniformed police. These formal organizations often provided sign posts and shaping agencies for the swiftly moving stream of humanity. The shape of the culture of ordinary people often depended on these and the many other formal organizations because the folkways and mores depending on a more stable population base simply never had a place to form.

Turner emphasized the importance of the frontier to show the anti-organizational features of American life. One wonders that if he had known of the continued impermanence of the population he might have emphasized instead the importance of formal organizations for shifting populations.[21] The contributors to this book all see themselves as writing "history from the bottom up," an approach which highlights and analyzes the contributions of ordinary people to history.[22] As with Turner's approach, this perspective places high value on individuals and tends to devalue the study of elites. Yet the logical outcome of our research is a refocusing on the history of formal organizations. Of course, the context and questions asked by the organizational history are quite altered compared to an elite-centered history. For now we would wish to place organizations in the social milieu created by an impermanent society, and new and quite different questions would be asked of this history.[23] How did organizations deal with impermanence of membership? What were the larger consequences for organizational structures? Did power always accrue to the permanent? If so, did the mobile constitute a disenfranchised class, as suggested by Thernstrom and Knights?[24] Did the mobile shape existing organizations to deal with their own particular problems? In all of this, literacy assumes a crucial role, as newspapers often proved to be the bulletin boards of the various substrata of society. Geographers have shown us how to use newspapers to map communication fields in the United States. Could not historians use newspapers to map cultural and class regions and the circulation consequences of residential mobility and tramping? Several of the articles in this book show that the more we look, the more articulate the "inarticulate" appear to have been. While messages in the labor press inquiring of the location of travelers may not make a direct statement of values, they certainly show one function of the labor press in tying together the complex world of workers.

Mobility, then, whether of whole households or of individual tramps, poses a major challenge to social historians. It may be a challenge which goes unanswered. Certainly the difficult fact of residential mobility has lurked behind various studies in social history for almost a half century without provoking any significant historical questions. So too tramping has never been a big secret, yet we have failed to incorporate it into any larger framework of United States history. Although somewhat different phenomena, both tramping and residential mobility seem almost to be answers looking for questions. The research reported in this book, we hope, has begun to provide some of the appropriate questions.

Notes

1. For the McCook-Aspinwall correspondence see John J. McCook *The Social Reform Papers of John J. McCook* (Hartford: The Antiquarian and Landmarks Society of Connecticut, 1977). For an entertaining, anecdotal book which reproduces some of the livelier material, including photographs, from the McCook Collection, see Roger A. Bruns, *Knights of the Road: A Hobo History* (New York: Methuen, 1980).
2. Max Weber, *The City* (New York: Free Press, 1958).
3. Georg Simmel, "The Metropolis and Mental Life," in Donald N. Levine, ed., *Georg Simmel: On Individuality and Social Forms* (Chicago: University of Chicago Press, 1971), 324–39.
4. For a clear diagram of this tendency to deviance, see Brian J. L. Berry, *Comparative Urbanization: Divergent Paths in the Twentieth Century* (New York: St. Martin's Press, 1981), 16.
5. Thomas Bender, *Community and Social Change in America* (New Brunswick,

N.J.: Rutgers University Press, 1978); Raymond Williams, *The Country and the City* (New York: Oxford University Press, 1973).

6. Melvin Dubovsky, *We Shall Be All: A History of the Industrial Workers of the World* (Chicago: Quadrangle, 1969).

7. John C. Schneider, "Omaha Vagrants and the Character of Western Hobo Labor," *Nebraska History* 63 (Summer 1982), 255–72.

8. Richard S. Alcorn, "Leadership and Stability in Mid-Nineteenth Century America: A Case Study of an Illinois Town," *Journal of American History* 61 (December 1974), 685–702.

9. For an exemplary use of credit reports see Michael Katz, *The People of Hamilton, Canada West* (Cambridge: Harvard University Press, 1975), 176–208.

10. See, for instance, Colin G. Pooley, "Residential Mobility in the Victorian City," *Transactions, Institute of British Geographers*, New Series, 4 (1979), 258–77.

11. See, for instance, Louise K. Barnett, "Bartleby as Alienated Worker," *Studies in Short Fiction* 11 (Fall 1974), 379–85.

12. For a discussion of theft by trick, see Monkkonen, *The Dangerous Class: Crime and Poverty in Columbus, Ohio, 1860–1885* (Cambridge: Harvard University Press, 1975), 28, 92–100, 171–72.

13. Monkkonen, "A Disorderly People? Urban Order in Nineteenth and Twentieth Century America," *Journal of American History* 68 (December 1981), 539–59; Roger Lane, *Violent Death in the City: Suicide, Accident, and Murder in Nineteenth-Century Philadelphia* (Cambridge: Harvard University Press, 1979).

14. Paul Boyer, *Urban Masses and Moral Order in America* (Cambridge: Harvard University Press, 1978); Stanley Cohen, *Folk Devils and Moral Panics* (London: Paladin, 1973).

15. Paul T. Ringenbach, *Tramps and Reformers, 1873–1896: The Discovery of Unemployment in New York* (Westport, Conn.: Greenwood, 1973).

16. Tamara Haraven and Randolph Langenbach, *Amoskeag: Life and Work in an American Factory-City* (New York: Pantheon, 1978).

17. Stephan Thernstrom, *The Other Bostonians: Poverty and Progress in the American Metropolis, 1880–1970* (Cambridge: Harvard University Press, 1973), Ch. 10; Robert G. Barrows, "Hurryin' Hoosiers and the American 'Pattern': Geographic Mobility in Indianapolis and North America," *Social Science History* 5 (Spring 1981), 197–222. For an excellent analysis which summarizes county level data for New York in the mid-nineteenth century and tries to reestimate persistence rates based on new evidence, see Donald H. Parkerson, "How Mobile Were Nineteenth-Century Americans?" *Historical Methods* 15 (Summer 1982), 99–110.

18. For a rich description of working-class life in a more stable community, see

Daniel J. Walkowitz, *Worker City, Company Town: Iron and Cotton-Worker Protest in Troy and Cohoes, New York, 1855–84* (Urbana: University of Illinois Press, 1978).

19. Jon M. Kingsdale, "The 'Poor Man's Club': Social Functions of the Urban Working-Class Saloon," *American Quarterly* 25 (October 1973), 472–89; Peter De Lottinville, "Joe Beef of Montreal: Working-Class Culture and the Tavern, 1869–1889," *Labour/Le Travailler* 8–9 (Autumn/Spring, 1981/1982), 9–40.

20. Robert E. Park's essay of 1925, "The Mind of the Hobo," in Park, Ernest W. Burgess, and Roderick D. McKenzie, *The City* (Chicago: University of Chicago Press, 1925), 156–61, discusses the disability imposed by transiency and draws the Simmelian conclusion that wanderlust is like drug addiction.

21. Frederick Jackson Turner, "The High School and the City," unpublished manuscript (14 June 1895), Huntington Library, Turner Collection.

22. Barton J. Bernstein, *Towards a New Past: Dissenting Essays in American History* (New York: Random House, 1968).

23. Walter S. Glazer, "Participation and Power: Voluntary Organizations and the Functional Organization of Cincinnati in 1840," *Historical Methods* 5 (September 1972), 151–68; Robert F. Berkhofer, Jr., "The Organizational Interpretation of American History: A New Synthesis," *Prospects* 4 (1979), 611–30.

24. Stephan Thernstrom and Peter R. Knights, "Men in Motion: some Data and Speculations on Urban Population Turnover in Nineteenth Century America," *Journal of Interdisciplinary History* 1 (Autumn 1970), 7–35.

Patricia Ferguson Clement is an assistant professor of history at Pennsylvania State University. She is the author of *Welfare and Poverty in the Nineteenth-Century City* (1984).

Patricia Cooper is a Drexel Fellow, Drexel University. Her publications include *From Hand Craft to Mass Production: Men, Women, and Work Culture in American Cigar Factories, 1900–1919* (1984).

Michael Davis is an editor of the *New Left Review* in London. His book *The Pope's Battalions* (1984) deals with political Catholicism and the workers' movement.

Douglas Lamar Jones holds a J.D. degree from Harvard Law School. His publications include *Village and Seaport: Migration and Society in Eighteenth-Century Massachusetts* (1981) and *Law in Colonial Massachusetts* (1984).

Eric H. Monkkonen is a professor of history at the University of California, Los Angeles, and author of *The Dangerous Class: Crime and Poverty in Columbus, Ohio, 1860–85* (1975) and *Police in Urban America, 1860–1920* (1981).

John C. Schneider is an associate professor of history at the University of Nebraska–Lincoln. His publications include *Detroit and the Problem of Order, 1830–1880: A Geography of Crime, Riot, and Policing* (1980).

Jules Tygiel is an associate professor of history at San Francisco State University and author of *Baseball's Great Experiment: Jackie Robinson and His Legacy* (1983).

Lynn Weiner is a faculty associate in the Department of History at Northwestern University and an instructor at Roosevelt University. Her books include *Working Girl, Working Wife, Working Mother: Change in the Female Labor Force in the United States, 1820–1980* (1984).

Index